THE
SONG
OF THE APE

THE
SONG
OF THE APE

Understanding the Languages
of Chimpanzees

A N D R E W   R .   H A L L O R A N

St. Martin's Press
New York

Title page drawing of Little Mama courtesy of Ashleigh Kandrac.

www.stmartins.com

Design by Kathryn Parise

LIBRARY OF CONGRESS CATALOGING-IN-PUBLICATION DATA

Halloran, Andrew R.
    The song of the ape : understanding the languages of chimpanzees / Andrew R. Halloran.—1st ed.
        p. cm.
    Includes bibliographical references.
    ISBN 978-0-312-56311-0 (hardcover)
    ISBN 978-1-4299-3327-8 (ebook)
  1. Chimpanzees—Behavior.   2. Chimpanzees—Behavior—Case studies.   3. Chimpanzees—Psychology.   4. Animal communication.   5. Animal sounds.   6. Halloran, Andrew R.   7. Primatologists—Biography.   8. Zoo keepers—Biography.   I. Title.
    QL737.P96H358 2012
    599.885—dc23
                                        2011041344

First Edition: March 2012

10   9   8   7   6   5   4   3   2   1

IN MEMORIAM

J. Robin King

(1947–2010)

Who taught me that the mysterious island

is the one under my boots.

CONTENTS

ACKNOWLEDGMENTS

I am extremely indebted to my wonderfully talented editor, Daniela Rapp. Her talent, guidance, and assistance have made this process an exceptional experience.

It goes without saying that I owe an enormous amount of gratitude to Lion Country Safari and everyone involved with creating and maintaining this wonderful place. From the extremely dedicated staff to the happy and healthy animals, there is no other place like it on earth.

Terry Wolf has been indispensable to this project. His accounts of the early years of the park have long fascinated me. He was kind enough to recount everything as I began this project and to take time to read everything that I wrote.

The people that worked with me on the chimpanzee islands during these years showed remarkable patience with everything I was doing. I'd like to point out that it was Michele Schwartz Matias who first notified me that Higgy was on the boat.

Throughout this entire period, I worked with Kelly Greer Froio, whose care and affection for these particular chimpanzees was an inspiration for this project.

Steve Ross and the research staff at the Lincoln Park Zoo's Lawrence E. Fischer Center for the Study and Conservation of Apes were tremendously helpful in serving as local collaborators and facilitating the Chicago portion of my research. Also at the Lincoln Park Zoo, everyone at the Regenstein Center for African Apes was crucial to this project. Without the help of both Dominick Travis and Jill Moyse, I may never have recorded any decent samples of Hank's group.

I thank Ashleigh Kandrac for her wonderful artwork.

My research assistant Christina T. Cloutier sat in the mud for hours recording chimp vocalizations. She also spent a very tedious evening categorizing vocal spectrograms. I am extremely grateful to her for being part of this project from the beginning.

I would like to thank Andrew J. Marshall for providing me with the initial recordings of the Lion Country Safari chimps from 1995.

I would like to acknowledge the continued guidance of Douglas C. Broadfield with this project and beyond.

I thank Susan Love Brown for convincing me to write this book in the first place.

The direction given by Prisca Augustyn at the beginning of this project was instrumental to its success.

My family is the best one could ask for. Lina and Gavin have been there throughout everything, serving as sounding boards, offering suggestions, and showing remarkable patience for this and other projects. Everything is better when they are around.

Finally, none of this would have ever occurred without my agent, Jesseca Salky, who was able to look through my chaotic jumbles and understand exactly what it was I was trying to do with this book.

Infinite truth has infinite expression.

—*The Srimad Bhagavatam*

Book XI, Chapter XV

ANTHEM

Exsules

I wasn't quite sure of anything—except, that is, for the pounding pain in my head. I was also slightly aware of the fact that I was wavering in and out of consciousness beneath the swamp water. When I swam to the surface and opened my eyes, the horrifying reality of my situation appeared all around me. I was floating in the middle of a canal. From the land behind me, I could hear shouts of obscenities. Floating in front of me was a rowboat. Inside the rowboat were five adult chimpanzees. One of the five, a particularly angry female, was swinging a long deck brush at my head and screaming. I quickly surmised that I had been knocked unconscious by a previous blow and, luckily this time, ducked out of the way.

So, why was I floating in a canal? Why was someone shouting obscenities behind me? Why were five chimpanzees in a rowboat, who were they, and how did they get there? The answers to these questions would put me on a quest to understand how chimpanzees communicate with each other. This quest would lead me to the discovery that the grunts, chirps, pants, and hoots that I was constantly hearing were actually a complex system of learned calls with dialect, meaning, and syntax—the language of chimpanzees.

I was a zookeeper working at a drive-through animal park in south Florida. This park was a five-hundred-acre preserve where the animals roamed in relative freedom. Guests could drive around the park and watch the animals from the safety of their cars. I took care of thirty-five chimpanzees. Chimpanzees possess both extreme strength and extreme intelligence, a combination that made them the most dangerous and unpredictable species at the park. For this reason, they couldn't roam around the guests like the other animals. Instead, they were separated by a water barrier. They lived out on a series of adjacent islands within the preserve. Guests had to view the chimpanzees from across a murky nine-meter canal.

The thirty-five chimpanzees were divided into four groups. Each group lived on a separate island. Each day, each group would move to a different island via a system of drawbridges that connected the islands to each other. Once on their new island, the chimps would find the food that had been scattered by the zookeepers and gather hay and branches to make their nests to sleep in. Acting as they would in the wild, the groups would be extremely territorial about whichever island they were inhabiting on any given day. They would patrol the edges of the island and shout at the other groups. Within the group, they would exhibit the highly complex political systems seen with chimps in the wild. In each group, there was an alpha male, a female hierarchy, alliances, disputes, reconciliations, and social roles. The way these chimpanzees lived in semicaptivity provided a glimpse of how these animals actually live in the wild. There was very little human interaction and the guests were far away from the animals. Mother chimpanzees were raising their own infants and alpha males managed their own groups.

Each group had its own unique attributes. There was a group of retired laboratory chimpanzees who, after twenty-five years, were still reeling from the effects of their past. Victims of their years of solitary confinement, they acted unnaturally and aberrantly, rarely socializing and gesturing wildly to themselves. There was also a group with an ineffective alpha male which resulted in constantly shifting alliances, violent confrontations, and an uneven distribution of food.

There was an extremely laid-back group that, with the exception of daily bickering between a brother and sister, never had any real confrontations. Finally, there was the largest group at the park. This group of seventeen chimpanzees had ages ranging from a one-year-old to a sixty-eight-year-old. There were four nursing mothers, several juveniles, and a few adolescents. The chimps came from all different backgrounds: one retired circus chimp, two ex-pets, one raised in a zoo nursery window display, and several born right there on the islands. Among the group, there was an ambitious uprising male, a deranged female, a neurologically impaired male, and the alpha male who had managed the group for decades. The group, which had been named after him, became the focus of my exploration into the language of chimpanzee. The group was known as Higgy's group, and Higgy, himself, was its two-hundred-pound leader.

In order to tend to the chimpanzees, I would maneuver around the canal on a rowboat. I would go to an empty island, clean it, set it up with food and branches, and open the drawbridge to let the chimps cross over. Because the chimps were so unpredictable and dangerous, I would never be on the same island with them. In fact, I propelled my boat with a long gondola pole. This served two purposes: it gave me more control than an oar, and it allowed me to push away from any chimp island that the wind or waves would blow me into.

On this particular day, I had pulled my boat up onto the shore of the mainland so that I could clean a building which we used to hold chimps who needed veterinary care. The building was directly across from the island that Higgy's group was presently occupying. I walked inside without realizing that I had failed to secure my boat properly. About fifteen minutes after I had started cleaning, I heard my coworker yelling something from outside. Surmising that she was probably angry at me for something trivial, I threw down my hose and walked outside to see what was going on. When I got there, she was screaming and pointing toward Higgy's island. It seemed that my careless failure to secure the rowboat had resulted in it blowing directly over to the chimpanzees. Now, five chimpanzees were sitting in the boat. Higgy was in the back, holding the gondola pole and calmly pushing the boat out into the water.

Seeing which chimps were in the boat with Higgy left little doubt in my mind as to what was occurring. There had been something of a civil war going on within the group. An adolescent male named Hank began to challenge Higgy for power. At first, it had just been he and his mother, Cindy, going up against the rest of the group. In time, however, Hank had put together an alliance of females that all supported him. His alliance had become so strong that Cindy was kicked out of her own son's alliance and had to go back to Higgy. There were months of violent altercations and wounded chimpanzees culminating in a sense that Higgy had generally lost his influence over the group. So on this day, Higgy had chosen to leave the group with his four remaining loyalists. The exiled chimpanzees on the boat with Higgy were the neurologically impaired male named Elgin; an unpredictable and vicious female named Gin; Hank's oversized mother, Cindy; and a very small sixty-eight-year-old female named Little Mama.

Sitting in front of Higgy, to his right, was Elgin. Elgin sat facing forward, with his right arm resting on the side of the boat. He was silent and calm and was, as always, dutifully following Higgy in whatever the alpha male was doing. When he was an infant, he had suffered from encephalitis, causing swelling in his brain. This left him epileptic, shaky, and slow. The only reason he was able to survive with other chimps was because Higgy took such good care of him. Higgy defended him against any aggression and always made sure that he ate. In return, Elgin was fiercely loyal to him.

At the front of the boat was Gin, who had been raised as a pet in an orange grove in central Florida. She had been isolated from any other chimpanzee before arriving at the animal park as an adult. The isolation had left her unpredictable and deranged. For some reason, though, she connected with Higgy. The two formed such a strong bond that her power and influence in the group was second only to his. Her association with Higgy had made her much more socially functional than her savage demeanor would have predicted, even mothering several offspring.

In front of Higgy, to his left, was the mammoth female chimpanzee who had mothered Hank. Cindy had arrived at the park as a socially awkward ex-pet. She had largely been rejected by every chimpanzee she had come into contact with except for Higgy. The bond she had with the alpha male seemed profound so it came as a surprise to everyone that she seemed to engineer and support Higgy's overthrow with her son. The strategy she had launched had backfired, ending with her being ousted after her usefulness to the alliance had expired. Higgy, unable to afford turning anyone away from his side, quickly accepted her back.

Also on the left side of the boat, in front of Cindy, was the small, unassuming, elderly female named Little Mama. Her quiet demeanor and low social rank hid her profound importance to the group. At sixty-eight years old, her years and experiences were double those of the chimps nearest to her age. She had been wild caught as a juvenile in Africa, transported to the United States, had performed in a circus for three decades, and was finally brought to the animal park to become part of its first chimpanzee group. She largely stayed away from group politics. However, she was staunchly loyal to Higgy and, like Elgin, would follow him anywhere he chose to go.

Higgy propelled the boat forward with the pole. When he was a short distance away from the island, he looked back. On top of a shelter, in the middle of the island, stood Hank with his core alliance. Hank was a massive male with an intimidating stare. The hair on his shoulders was standing straight up and he rocked back and forth as he watched Higgy on the boat. Apparently seeing that Higgy was now looking at him, he called out a series of hoots, then a loud scream. Higgy responded with a few calm grunts and turned his head away. The others in the boat paid no attention to Hank at all. At this, Hank gave another call, this time accompanying it by stomping loudly on the shelter. All five in the boat glanced back to Hank for a few moments, then went back to facing forward. The boat was getting closer to the mainland.

As I stood there trying to figure out what to do, the immediate danger of having the chimpanzees reach the shore was racing through my head. The water was the only barrier protecting myself, my co-worker, and all of the guests driving through the park from the chimpanzees. The five on the boat were about to breach that barrier. Without thinking, I jumped into the canal and swam toward the boat. My initial thought was that I was going to just push the boat back to the island. This, however, proved to be a poor plan. When I reached the boat, Gin grabbed my deck brush and began hitting me over the head with it, screaming at me with each blow.

While recovering in the water, I noticed that one end of the rope that we used to tie up the boat was floating beside me. The other end was attached to the back of the boat. The rope was extremely long because we also used it as a safety feature (when one of us had to be near the chimps, the other person could be on the shore holding the rope and could pull the boat back very quickly). I quickly thought of a new plan. I grabbed the end of the rope and swam it over to my co-worker. I tried to communicate my plan, but my coworker was still shouting obscenities. Finally she stopped long enough for me to shout some instructions, throw her the rope, and ask for the fire extinguisher that was hanging in the building. She ran in, retrieved it, and threw it back to me. I swam back over to the boat, holding the fire extinguisher above my head. When I got near the boat, I sprayed the extinguisher into the air with a quick burst. This frightened the chimps back enough that I was able to reach the side of the boat and push it toward the island. Luckily, I caught Higgy off guard and he wasn't pushing against me with the pole. The boat went streaming back to the island. I followed the boat, sprayed the extinguisher in the air, and shoved it again. This time the boat went all the way back to the island. I sprayed the extinguisher again; this time I didn't let up. The extended spray of the extinguisher in the air startled the chimps and they all jumped off the boat. I yelled to my coworker, who pulled the rope as hard as she could. I clung onto the boat with one hand and let it drag me back to the shore. I crawled up to the shore, took a look back at the island, and collapsed. As I lay in the mud, Higgy and his alliance retreated to one side of the island. Hank and his group stayed on top of the shelter.

The incident had a profound effect on me. I kept thinking of how planned and orchestrated the escape seemed to be. I began to wonder how this orchestration was communicated. In order for such a plan to occur with that many individuals involved there had to be an extremely complex form of communication going on. Certainly information more intricate than just the present situation was being transmitted. The five chimps in Higgy's alliance somehow knew to get on that boat with Higgy at the instant the situation presented itself. The chimps aligned with Hank knew *not* to get on the boat. They also knew not to interfere with the escape. The initial boarding of the boat occurred within a matter of moments and it happened in relative silence (as neither I nor my coworker heard anything).

I became obsessed with what had happened and the implications it held. I was preoccupied with the notion that, perhaps, chimpanzees communicated on a deeper and more complex level than I had ever imagined. Perhaps chimpanzees had their own language; a language which, unlike other forms of animal communication, was learned, differed from population to population, had definitions, had a structure, and conveyed information that didn't necessarily relate to a present time or place. For years, I had detested the pseudoscientific studies where people attempted to teach apes to understand and use human language in labs. Apes using sign language seemed to me to be nothing more than a circus trick masquerading as science. The thought that, while people were attempting to teach human language to chimpanzees, they had their own language all along was alluring. I began to immerse myself in studying everything I could about chimpanzee communication. I was fascinated by the theory that different chimpanzee calls had definitive structures associated with them. I was even more amazed by the idea that chimpanzees appear to learn and pass down their calls. I began to look for ways to observe these things in the chimpanzees I worked with. How could one scientifically determine if chimpanzee calls were, indeed, a language?

I arrived at the animal park one morning, a few weeks later, to find that Gin had bitten off most of Hank's left cheek. It was soon determined that the civil war was not going to end anytime soon and that the presence of Hank and his alliance was putting all of the group in jeopardy. A decision was made to send Hank and six other chimpanzees to another facility, dividing Higgy's group in two. All at once, the opportunity to compare this divided group had presented itself. I began devising a plan where I could study, through observation, sound analysis, and statistics, the phenomenon of chimpanzee communication. I could begin by determining the different calls that Higgy's group was using. I could learn what they sounded like, what made them unique, who used them, and what they were used for. I could then look at Hank's group to see if these calls were still being used, if they were changing, or if new calls were being added. In this, I could begin to see for myself if there was meaning behind the calls, if the calls evolved, and if chimpanzees had dialects. If successful, I would be able to understand how chimps communicate, how that communication system functions, and determine if there truly was a language of chimpanzees.

However, before any of this could be accomplished, I needed to understand how Higgy's group came to be, where their calls had come from, and how each individual's history combined to form the group lexicon. The following is a written account of that understanding. It is the story of five chimpanzees, their histories, their calls, and the meaning of these calls. It is an account of what happened to this group and why it has overwhelming implications for us all. It is an exploration of the scientific study of language and chimpanzees.

1

Little Mama

I had heard of Little Mama before I actually met her. Stories of the elderly little chimpanzee were frequent among those who worked with primates. She was, after all, one of the oldest chimpanzees in captivity. Still, nothing prepared me for the thrill of actually seeing her for the first time. Sitting in the middle of a large group of chimpanzees with a piece of burlap draped over her head and shoulders, Little Mama was unmistakable.

On my first day on the job at the animal park, I was given a pair of binoculars and a photo book of every chimpanzee with instructions to "learn who they are." As I sat in the mud, I stared at Little Mama with fascination. I had no idea about where she had come from or her importance to the social fabric of this group of chimpanzees. What I was also unaware of was how every chimpanzee call I was hearing had been brought over by Little Mama from Africa over sixty years before. Little

Mama would become the cornerstone of my own understanding of how chimpanzees communicate.

However, our exploration into the language of chimpanzees must begin decades before Little Mama's birth. It must begin in the laboratories. Twenty years before her birth, scientists began a quest to discover the ability of apes to learn and understand human language. It was a quest that spanned a century and continues today, without success. It was a quest that attempted to transform the wild chimpanzee into a cultured, language-using human. It was a quest that existed in vain while, all along, in the forests of Africa, something far more amazing existed: a story of a little chimpanzee, born in the wild, who was about to be thrown into our world.

1916
Philadelphia, Pennsylvania

In a dimly lit hall on a spring evening, Dr. William Furness addressed the crowd gathered at the American Philosophical Society. Indeed, it must not have been the talk he had wanted to give. I can imagine the dour faces of his academic peers as he lectured. I can also imagine their skeptical looks centered on the subject matter of what the psychologist was saying. Dr. Furness was speaking about his attempts to teach two orangutans and two chimpanzees to speak.*

As he spoke about his firm belief that, if apes were taught correctly, they would be able to carry on a complete conversation with a human (in any language they were taught), he must have sensed the hostility in the room. Despite trying to focus on the successes of vari-

---

* A transcript of Dr. Furness's lecture can be found in *Proceedings of the American Philosophical Society* vol. 55, no. 3 (1916).

ous cognitive tasks the apes were able to do, he must have known that he would eventually have to admit that the last six years, and the swan song of his scientific career, was a complete and utter failure.

The notion that apes had the capacity for language had led Dr. Furness to travel to south Borneo and capture two wild orangutan infants. Later he purchased two juvenile chimpanzees from an exotic animal dealer in Liverpool, England. He did so believing that he would be able to phonetically train these apes to speak. He reasoned that since cognitive tests had shown these apes to be capable of extremely complex actions, language must be within their reach. Once he taught these animals how to speak, he surmised, he would be the first scientist to finally bridge the gap between humans and the rest of the animal kingdom. Visions of interviewing the apes for scientific publication drove his daily training sessions.

Unfortunately, it had not worked out the way he had expected. In six months of daily sessions with one of the orangutans he had his greatest success. The orangutan was able to clearly articulate the word "papa." Not only this, but the psychologist was able to get her to associate the word "papa" with himself. When hearing the word, she would cling to him and repeat it. He was attempting to teach her to say "cup" and vocalize a *th* sound when the baby orangutan unexpectedly died.

In relating these results to his audience, he attempted to focus on the positive. Even though her speech was limited, he assured them, "she *understood* almost everything." This did little to sway his listeners.

What of the chimpanzees?

"On the whole," lectured Dr. Furness, "I should say that the orang holds out more promise as a conversationalist than does a chimpanzee."

Only one of the chimpanzees, it seemed, had survived the captive environment of Furness's home. The surviving chimpanzee, named

Mimi, spent her days in lessons learning how to say the word "cup."
However, despite the psychologist's attempts to form her mouth in
the appropriate way with his fingers and a spoon, she was never able
to say it. After five years of training, she was able to say one word,
though poorly. Mimi was able to say the word "mama."

As he toiled on through the rest of his lecture, Dr. Furness must
have realized that he wasn't winning over his crowd. Finally, he ad-
mitted that his language experiment had been a failure. He ended by
quoting an English clergyman who claimed to sleep well knowing that
man held dominion over the animals through language.*

After citing the quotation, Furness looked up and stated: "I regret
that I am forced to admit, after my several years [in] observation of
the anthropoid apes, that I can produce no evidence that might dis-
turb the tranquil sleep of the reverend gentleman."

Furness's lecture was published as "Observation on the mentality of
chimpanzees and orangutans." Though, for the most part, dismissed,
one significant primatologist took note. His name was Robert Yerkes.
Perhaps, he thought, Furness had just used the wrong training methods.†
At this point, Dr. Yerkes began to formulate his own study; a study that
would dominate the primatologist's attention for decades to come.

What was escaping both Dr. Furness and Dr. Yerkes was that, at
that very moment, the sounds of chimpanzees communicating were
echoing though the forests of Africa. Within these echoes were bits of
information far more complex than the words "papa," "mama," or

---

* The clergyman was Rev. Sydney Smith, who stated: "I have sometimes, perhaps, felt a
little uneasy at Exeter 'Change from contrasting the monkeys with the 'prentice boys who are
teasing them; but a few pages of Locke, or a few lines of Milton, have always restored me to
tranquility."
† Yerkes wrote in 1925: "Perhaps the chief reason for the ape's failure to develop speech
is the absence of a tendency to imitate sounds." However, he was about to undertake a project
which would rely on such imitation; a project which, as we will see, will also fail.

"cup." What was being transmitted was the ever-present drama of the world of the apes: births, deaths, warfare, intimidation, alliances, happiness, sadness, hopes, fears, and plans for survival. Twenty years later, a chimpanzee would be born in these forests which would bring this communication to the human ear.

1936
Jong River, Sierra Leone

In a dark, tropical forest, the cries of a newborn chimpanzee broke the still of the night. The sound alerted all of the chimpanzees in the group to the nest where the young mother had just given birth. As births are always a cause for excitement in a chimpanzee group, everyone awoke to see the new infant. Together they climbed the large tree where the mother had made a nest of branches and twigs. Upon arrival, they found the mother cleaning her female offspring by the light of the moon.*

The group, numbering over forty members, could not all fit in the tree. Some clung to the trunk and branches of the tree while others surrounded the bottom. Some were able to fit in the nest with the new mother and infant. Those in the nest gave hoots to the chimps in the branches. The chimps in the branches gave calls which the chimps at the bottom of the tree responded to with other calls. From a distance, another chimpanzee call was heard. This one started with low hoots and erupted into a loud scream. Immediately recognizing the call, the chimpanzees on the ground moved away from the tree.

---

* The events recounted here are based on observations of chimpanzee births. There, of course, were no eyewitnesses to Little Mama's birth so, obviously, I have absolutely no idea of the details. I write this conjecture to relate a picture of a functioning chimpanzee group in the wild.

Running toward the tree was the leader of the group, the alpha male. At full speed the male raced up the tree, knocking over any chimpanzee in his way. When he reached the nest, the alpha male sat beside the new mother and gave a loud call into the air. The surrounding chimpanzees reclaimed their spots.*

The new mother appeared not to notice the presence of the other chimpanzees. She was very busy cleaning her new infant. As she held her, she gave low grunts to her baby. The infant nuzzled her mother and began to nurse. At this point, a three-year-old chimpanzee, out of curiosity, got very close to the infant. The new mother gave an abrupt yelp. This sufficiently frightened the small chimp to a safe distance. Seeing how frightened the juvenile was, the new mother held out her hand. The three-year-old touched her fingers and they both hooted together. Peace was restored. Comfortably nursing, the new infant failed to react to the whole exchange.

While the new mother cradled her infant, the alpha male began to groom her. As he groomed her, he gave comforting calls. Having witnessed the newest member of their group, the rest of the chimpanzees dispersed to their own nests.

As the night continued, the tired mother fell asleep with her infant attached to her breast. The alpha male fell asleep beside them.

An infant chimpanzee is completely helpless at birth. This newborn chimpanzee will rely on her mother for everything. From protection to learning traits on how to survive in the environment, the newborn chimpanzee is dependent on both her mother and her group. Over the next few years of this newborn's infancy and juvenile period, she will

---

* I have always been amazed by the sheer power of the vocalization of an alpha male chimpanzee. All of the other chimps immediately recognize it and, for certain calls, will scatter and hide as soon as they hear it. After the object of his vocalization has been identified (and summarily dealt with), everyone calmly resumes their old position.

learn what to eat, how to obtain food, how to behave with other chimpanzees, and other survival techniques. She will learn all of this from her group—as these traits are unique to her group. In a few short years, she will become an expert on everything that her group collectively knows. Through this, she will learn the most important trait central to a chimpanzee's survival: she will learn to fluently transmit information to any member of her group. She will learn to communicate.

Four thousand nautical miles away, another chimpanzee birth was occurring. Only at this birth, no group was present to teach the newborn how to survive. No alpha male came to investigate. No chimpanzee calls echoed through the night. Instead, the newborn was on a concrete floor surrounded by masked lab technicians watching in silence.

Pushing the technicians aside, another masked individual appeared in the room. This senior technician grabbed the mother and told the others to carefully put the infant in a separate cage. While the newborn cried, the technicians did as they were told. One of them produced a sterile baby bottle. Pushing it into the newborn's mouth silenced the cries.*

At this point the senior technician removed his mask and smiled. This newborn chimpanzee, he thought, would show the world that a chimpanzee can talk. This newborn's name was Gua and would be the subject of the much publicized "Gua project."

Two newborn chimpanzees, separated by half the globe, arrived in two very different worlds. Both would attempt to do what chimpanzees are naturally inclined to do: both would attempt to communicate with the world they were given.

---

* The details of Gua's particular birth remain a mystery. The events written here are those common to many captive chimpanzee births. I have used such births to construct this imagined account.

1936
Orange Park, Florida

Robert Yerkes arrived at his primate laboratory early in the morning to begin what he thought would accomplish what Furness could not. Yerkes, fascinated by the prospect of an ape being enculturated by humans and learning to talk, had overseen the birth of the newborn chimpanzee named "Gua." He enlisted the help of a husband-and-wife team of psychologists, Winthrop and Luella Kellogg. The Kelloggs had a baby boy, Donald. Dr. Yerkes reasoned that if he could place an infant chimpanzee with an infant child, they would be raised the same way. This would lead to an enculturation process whereby the ape would pick up the same traits as the human child, including language. The end result would be a talking, human-acting chimpanzee.*

The Kelloggs jumped at the chance to be a part of this project. They gladly accepted Gua, who was now seven and a half months old, into their home. Gua would be raised as Donald's sister. At first, the experiment produced some remarkable results. Gua ate with a spoon and fork on a high chair beside Donald. Both Gua and Donald were able to recognize spoken words and commands. Although she preferred to crawl, Gua actually learned to walk upright before Donald.

Donald and Gua became very much like siblings. They would play together and learn from each other. Because of Gua's influence, Donald would bite people out of both play and aggression. Also, because of Gua's influence, Donald would walk around on his knuckles even after he learned to walk upright. Gua taught Donald how to spy on

---

* For documented records of the Gua project, see E. Hearst and J. H. Capshew, *Psychology at Indiana University: A Centennial Review and Compendium* (1988).

people underneath doors. Donald would also produce a series of grunts which he would use back and forth with Gua.

Gua used the same forms of contact as Donald. When she was put to bed, she would reach out for a human-style hug. She would give kisses. She appeared to mimic facial expressions to show various emotional states. As much as she appeared to view Donald as a sibling, she viewed Winthrop and Luella as parents.

The differences between the two also produced some interesting results. Though both were able to recognize visitors, Donald would clearly recognize people by their faces while Gua would have to smell the visitor before she recognized them. The other difference, of course, was speech. Despite Yerkes's dream of having a talking ape, Gua could say nothing.

After a while, out of frustration, the Kelloggs attempted to train Gua to speak in much the same manner as Dr. Furness. Luella Kellogg would try to form Gua's lips in order to make her say "papa." Nothing worked and Gua was never able to talk. At this point, the Kelloggs appeared to lose interest in the Gua project.

Winthrop Kellogg began corresponding with Dr. Yerkes concerning Gua's progress. He had become frustrated with the speed of Gua's learning. He also expressed his concerns that Gua could, one day, become violent and hurt Donald. At the same time, Luella became deeply concerned about the fact that Donald was acting more chimplike than Gua was acting humanlike. Donald continued to grunt like a chimp and was behind other children in his speech development. He was also more attached to Gua than other human children. In addition to this, Donald was still biting people.

Finally, the Kelloggs had reached their limit. They returned Gua to Dr. Yerkes. Gua was placed in a cage and became the subject of behavioral experimentation by Ada Yerkes, Robert's wife. In a very short time span, Gua's life had gone from being a child reared in a human home, complete with a two-parent family, a sibling, a house, clothing, and a bed, to being a caged laboratory primate. Months later Gua contracted pneumonia and died.

The Gua project had been an abject failure. Gua had not learned to talk. Gua was a chimpanzee attempting to communicate like a chimpanzee in a human world. Her counterpart in Sierra Leone, however, was communicating just fine.

1938
Jong River, Sierra Leone

The clearing of the forest echoed with the sounds of chimpanzees. Grunts interspersed with loud yelps reverberated through the trees. Occasionally the sound of a chimpanzee performing a massive dominance display would silence the other chimpanzees. In addition to the vocalizations, the sounds of branches shaking, branches breaking, and the ground being slapped combined with the calls to create a symphony of chimpanzee communication. With each sound, a new piece of information was being transmitted.

The young chimpanzee was now two years old. She had been napping on her mother's back when she awoke and looked around. Dusk had fallen and the group was getting situated for the night. She and her mother climbed up the branches in the middle canopy of trees surrounding the clearing.*

---

* Once again, these accounts are pure conjecture. However, a great deal is known and documented on the specifics of the chimpanzee capture and pet trade practices in West Africa. I have based this early account of Little Mama's history on events typical of a juvenile chimpanzee captured for sale in the United States, and my imagination. The events depicted in the following pages are there to paint a picture of live animal capture. Everything from the injuries, fear, and group behavior (though they are my own conjecture of Little Mama's particular history) occur with startling regularity in documented cases of primate captures. Live captures of chimpanzees and other primates throughout the world continue

Like all chimpanzees, the group was nomadic. Every morning they would get up, travel away from where they had slept the night before, forage for food, and settle on a new spot. A major portion of their nightly routine was setting up camp, in a sense. They would do this by finding just the right spot in the trees to build a nest. Nest building is something that is unique for each chimpanzee. Some build enormous nests with branches, twigs, and any piece of loose debris they happen to find throughout the day. Others merely smash a bunch of branches together and sleep on top of them. The young female and her mother were of the former variety.

The two of them spent the evening building their nest. The young female picked up her mother's technique. Nest building, like all learned traits, gets passed down through the generations. The mother's technique was learned from her mother. She would pass the same technique with perhaps a few of her own alterations to her offspring. Slowly, down through the generations, the style may change a bit, but the initial seed of this technique would remain.

As darkness filled the clearing, the chimpanzees sounded the day's last vocalizations. The alpha male called out several times, surveying his group as they called back to him. When the two-year-old's mother called out to the alpha male, the juvenile followed her lead and also called. The alpha male responded. In very little time, the entire group fell asleep. The forest that, a few moments before, had been filled with the sounds of chimpanzees was silent and still.

Throughout the night there would occasionally be chimp sounds. An infant would wake up and cry. The mother would hold her young

---

to this day. For a very complete account of both the ecology of chimpanzees in West Africa as well as the live animal capture occurring there, I recommend the book *West African Chimpanzees,* compiled and edited by Rebecca Kormos, Christophe Boesch, Mohamed I. Bakarr, and Thomas M. Butynski.

close and the crying would cease. Like humans, the chimps used a combination of both vocalizations they had learned from their group and vocalizations that were genetic calls. For example, a chimpanzee might use a particular call that he learned from his group and is specific to his group. However, a chimpanzee will also produce genetic yelps that they don't have to learn (much like a human crying). One such genetically programmed call is the alarm call—a sound which a chimp produces to warn others in their group of danger.

The sound of such an alarm call woke the two-year-old chimp from her sleep. She sat up in the nest to the sounds of frantic alarm calls in the distance. Before she could make a sound, she was scooped up by her mother. Clinging onto her mother's back, the two of them climbed higher up the trees. The two of them peered down into the clearing. They watched as the alpha male climbed down into the lower canopy and began to violently shake branches in a massive display.

Appearing in the clearing were five men. One of the men carried a large burlap sack. The rest had rifles slung around their shoulders and flashlights in their hands. The men whispered to each other as they stared at the alpha male's display in the lower canopy. Finally they turned away from the male's display and began to shine their flashlights into the upper canopy.

The young female clutched the back of her mother without making a sound. As the light from one of the flashlights came closer, she let out a whimper. The light hit her eyes, making her squint. Fear caused her to scream out loud. Her mother stood up in the branches of the canopy to make a threatening display. She screamed at the men below and hurled branches at them. One of the men aimed his rifle at the screaming mother. He pulled the trigger. The mother fell from the canopy with her young child still clinging to her back.

The fall broke the leg of the young female. She looked around to see her mother's bloody and immobile body under her. The alpha male quickly rushed down to her defense. When he leapt toward one of the men, he was quickly shot. He, like the young chimp's mother, lay completely still. A group of older females had also descended to the ground. They began to charge at the men. They, too, were shot. The young female, in pain, continued to scream as loudly as she could. The man with the burlap bag pried her off of her dead mother's back and dropped her into the sack. As it was tied, she saw the remains of her group for the last time.*

Inside the sack, the young female heard the alarm calls of her group growing more and more distant. The pain of her leg continued to grow more intense until, finally, the pain along with the stress caused her to lose consciousness.

When she awoke, she found herself lying on the burlap bag in a large metal cage inside the hut of an animal broker in Sierra Leone. The animal broker, having realized that she had a broken leg, was preparing a splint. He drew out a sedative dart and loaded it into his dart gun. He pointed it at the young female and fired. The chimp screamed and within a few moments was unconscious once again.

The next time she awoke she was in another cage, with a splint around her leg and still laying on the burlap sack. This cage was aboard the cargo hold of a large boat bound for New York City. The young female, alone and frightened, looked around for her mother. Not finding her, she desperately clung to her burlap sack for comfort.

Several times a day, a man came through the cargo hold with a large bucket of water. When he poured the water under her cage to rinse it clean, the water splashed her. She learned to climb, with the splint on

---

* Live primate capture has a horrendous ecological impact, indeed. To get one chimpanzee, it is often necessary to kill several who are attempting to defend their group mate. This is not limited to chimpanzees. The pet trade is even more active in Central and South America, mainly with capuchin and squirrel monkeys.

her leg, to the top of the cage when he came around. Sometimes he would throw the water down so hard it would still splash her. To avoid this, she would wrap the burlap sack around her shoulders and head to shield herself from the water.

Once a day the man would push slices of fruit through the bars of her cage and give her a fresh bottle of water. The cargo hold was hot and loud with the sounds of all the other animals on board. Again, the burlap around her head provided an adequate shield for her—this time against the noise of the cargo hold.

Weeks later, the ship pulled into port in the United States. The American animal dealer waited at the docks, eager to see what this shipment had brought him. When the ship docked, he lit a cigar, climbed aboard, and went down into the cargo hold. There, he went about surveying all of his new animals. When he approached the cage of the young female chimpanzee, he began to laugh. The chimp was looking at him with the burlap sack wrapped around her head like a shawl. He remarked that the chimpanzee looked just like his mother and decided that they should call her "Little Mama." With that, Little Mama's life in the United States of America had begun.*

1939
Bloomington, Indiana

Winthrop Kellogg had just completed his new canine observation center. Since the Gua debacle, he had continued to study comparative animal behavior—although not with apes. He now preferred to work

---

* To this day, Little Mama holds a burlap sack around her shoulders and head. When I first began working with these chimps, Little Mama was always the easiest to identify because of her "shawl."

with such animals as water snakes and dogs in the safe confines of the university laboratory.* He was, by all accounts, done with apes. His correspondence with Robert Yerkes had become increasingly nasty. Yerkes, it seemed, had not at all liked that Kellogg published a book detailing the Gua failure. In fact, he was so angry about it that he had all accounts of the study stricken from the records of the Orange Park station to imply official disapproval of Kellogg's research.

Winthrop Kellogg, one would imagine, felt betrayed. He had, after all, offered his family up as test subjects. Seeing the effect the project had on his family, especially his son, Kellogg vowed that, for the rest of his career at Indiana University, he would conduct all of his research in a lab.

Yerkes was still convinced that ape language was possible. Upon looking at Kellogg's notes and seeing that Gua had seemed to comprehend vocal commands, he reasoned that the failure had been not because of improper training or methodological issues but because a chimpanzee was not biologically structured for speech. Larynx placement was too high on a chimp for proper vowel formation. Also, brain areas for speech motor function had not been found in chimps. The proper methodology would have been to teach the ape to communicate gesturally. The proper way, thought Yerkes, would have been to teach Gua sign language.†

So began a primatological obsession with training chimpanzees to use sign language. Decades would follow without success whereby laboratory chimpanzees would be taught signs they would never truly understand. While this was going on, a little chimpanzee had arrived in America, bringing with her only the language she had learned from the group she had been born into.

---

* In fact, his paper on training water snakes to use a maze is the first recorded study of learning in snakes (see Kellogg and Pomeroy, 1936).

† Yerkes had actually been mulling over training apes to use sign language even before the Gua project. As he criticized Furness's project, he speculated that the answer may be in getting an ape "to use their fingers, somewhat as does the deaf and dumb person."

1940
Hershey, Pennsylvania

The ex-Olympic ice-skater waited eagerly for the truck to arrive, carrying her new protégé, a young chimpanzee. Her touring company, an ice-skating circus, had purchased the chimpanzee from an animal dealer with the intention of training her to skate and perform with the show.

The truck arrived with the promised crate in the back. The ice-skater ran over to the crate to meet the chimp. She opened the crate to see Little Mama, once again with a burlap sack around her head. She smiled at the chimp and took her to her trailer. Little Mama had found her home for the next thirty years.

Over the next period of time, Little Mama learned the art of ice-skating. As she trained, she became more comfortable in her surroundings. She even attempted to communicate with her trainer. Unfortunately, the trainer merely heard a series of screeches and had no idea that there may have been a greater meaning involved in what Little Mama was attempting to communicate. Still, the chimp and her trainer found methods of communication which did not rely on the vocal. They developed a series of gestures that, while not as complex and useful as Little Mama's vocalizations, filled the need of communication.

Training Little Mama to ice-skate took a lot of patience. Even getting past the unfamiliarity with clothing and shoes, there was still ice to contend with. Little Mama had, obviously, never seen ice before. Though frightened, her temperament was good and she was eventually able to be part of the show.

In a tented show in Minnesota during the mid-1940s, Little Mama made her debut with the ice-skating show. Backstage, her trainer dressed her in a clown outfit, complete with a pointed hat, polka-dotted shirt, face paint, and a red rubber nose glued to her face. Her feet were crammed into ice-skates, which caused the bone that she had once broken to ache.

When she was introduced, the crowd cheered at the chimp on ice skates. Gliding across the ice, Little Mama was silent.

The crowd was captivated by the little chimp in front of them. Her antics amazed them. They laughed at her makeup and gasped at her skating. None of them had any idea about where she had come from or what she would be doing right now if she had been left in the wild. To them, she existed only as a trained circus animal. Silently, sliding around ice on skates, wearing clown makeup, and being called "Little Mama," the young female chimpanzee was as far removed from the banks of the Jong River as she could be.*

1968
Loxahatchee, Florida

A recently opened wild animal park in south Florida had only one species of animal: lions. In fact, the park was a fenced-in area of five hundred acres of swampland with lions roaming free. Tourists could pay to drive through the area and have the lions jump on their car. The park was looking to expand its animal collection and confine the lions to a smaller section of the preserve. Therefore, they began to add such animals as hippos, elephants, and zebras. All of these animals could be successfully kept in a cage-free manner in the preserve and still have

---

* In these ice-skating shows, the "amazing ice-skating chimpanzee" (who was usually billed as an adult male) was actually several different juvenile female chimpanzees. Different females would travel to different locations and star as the billed ice-skating chimp. Because of this, it is difficult to pinpoint exactly where Little Mama had performed. The events I've just recounted come from an amalgamation of reports of many different ice-skating chimpanzee performances (any number of which may have been Little Mama).

visitors view them from the safety of their cars. It would, in effect, be just like going on safari. What they were missing though, were apes. The problem was, of course, how apes could be displayed without a cage or some sort of barrier. The park then devised a very clever way of doing this. Knowing that chimpanzees lacked the ability to swim, the park simply dug out a large pond around a large island that guests could drive by.* Now they could put a large group of chimps on the island and guests could watch these animals without a cage, acting as they would in the wild. They began their search for chimpanzees.

Chimps, in fact, are quite overpopulated in captivity. Chimpanzees used in laboratories and entertainment generally outlive their usefulness after their adolescent years.† They become too big and too dangerous for either industry. Therefore, they either end up being euthanized or living out the rest of their lives in a cage.

In 1968, Little Mama had found herself in such a cage. She had actually had an extremely long career in entertainment. She had not been retired because of aggression or outgrowing her usefulness. Little Mama was stuck in an animal dealer's cage because her circus had shut down.

By 1960, the popularity of circuses had begun to wane. The exponential rise in popularity of movies, television, and popular music led to an exponential decline in the popularity of circuses and other traveling variety shows. Along with this, a greater awareness of how animals were being kept in captivity was forcing circuses to adopt more expensive animal care. Smaller attractions, such as the one Little Mama belonged to, were being forced to close.

---

* It was originally thought that the chimpanzees would have a natural fear of water. Not so! In fact, the chimps frequently utilize the water in their displays, splash other chimps, and dig around for turtles in the water. On really hot days, they will bathe in the water up to their necks.
† In fact, almost all of the chimpanzees that are in films and television are juvenile chimpanzees. This may account for how surprised many are to find out that adult chimpanzees can weight up to 200 lbs.

By the end of 1967, Little Mama had donned her pair of ice-skates for the last time. Now a relatively elder chimp at thirty-two, there were few places for her to go. Nearly thirty years after her arrival to the United States, Little Mama was once again packed into a crate and sent to an animal broker.

Since her arrival at the ice-skating show, Little Mama had remained silent. Occasionally she would hoot in delight at a treat or yelp if she got hurt; however, she had not vocalized in any sort of communicative way in thirty years. As she was packed into her crate this time, there were no screams or hoots. Little Mama just looked on, clutching a burlap sack, as the crate was nailed shut.

The broker who housed Little Mama learned of the animal park in south Florida and quickly contacted them regarding the gentle ice-skating chimp he had in his care. It was agreed that she would be sent to the park to be part of their first chimpanzee exhibit. She would be the matriarch of a social group. For the first time since being stuffed in a burlap sack in the clearing beside the Jong River, Little Mama would be interacting with other chimpanzees.

In late 1968, Little Mama's crate was in a rowboat, headed for her new swamp island home. The zookeepers lifted the crate and placed it in the center of the island with several other crates. When the door swung open, Little Mama placed her burlap sack around her shoulders and calmly walked outside. She looked around to see, for the first time since her very early childhood, other chimpanzees approaching her. These chimps were not much older than she had been when she left Africa. They appeared to be just as frightened as she was. She held out her hand to them and repeated the same low grunts her mother had used to calm her down that day at the Jong River. As if they had known her their entire lives, the young chimps came running to her. When she embraced them, she began to vocalize more to them. The vocalizations that came out of her carried with them the whispers of all the chimpanzees at the Jong River. There were, within her own voice, the voices of the alpha male, her juvenile friends, members of her group, and her mother. Little Mama had carried with her, all of these years, a vocal lexicon that had been passed to her from her group. She, alone, had kept it alive. She, alone, would pass it to her new group. This would be the foundation of every vocalization ever made by a chimpanzee at the park; the seeds of which I would discover when I analyzed them four decades later and happened across the language chimpanzees were using without our help. This lexicon would stand as a monument to the miracle being overlooked in the name of pseudoscience and circus acts.

In late 1968, in one corner of the world, a chimpanzee was being trained to use sign language. In another corner, a chimpanzee was being taught to do math problems. In yet another part of the world, a chimpanzee was being trained to perform a circus act. In Loxahatchee, Florida, Little Mama was passing on a learned lexicon of chimpanzee calls.

Twelve hundred miles away from Loxahatchee, a psychiatrist named Dr. Donald Kellogg, son of Winthrop and Luella Kellogg, brother of Gua, was found dead. The cause of death was a self-inflicted gunshot wound.

When the existence of mind in the mutes is recognized, the qualities it manifests become the subject of investigation.

—LEWIS HENRY MORGAN

2
Cindy

The way one chimpanzee calls to another chimpanzee is a complete account of that individual's history. It is a subconscious record of every encounter, every interaction, and every experience in the life of that chimpanzee. Likewise, the way a human speaks to another human is an unabridged and candid glimpse into every moment of a person's life. The language we use, the inflections we add, our rate of speech, our voice's pitch, and our individual idiosyncrasies show our origins, our interactions, our times of stress, our times of peace, our times of happiness, our times of sadness, our times being nurtured, and our times being isolated. Our voices strip us of our pretexts and leave us naked to the world.

Of all the features that affect how a chimpanzee calls or how a human speaks, the most profound is isolation. Isolation is a deadly nemesis to a social primate. The following accounts explore how isolation can affect, or even destroy, a social primate. These are reports of how any period of isolation will bear its imprint into every action, every relation, and every vocalization a primate utters. These are stories of those who create isolation and the victims who are left with the scars. These are stories of the evolutionary drive to break down the closed door of a life alone and communicate with the world. These are stories of the evolutionary drive to speak.

1969
Arcadia, California

The door swung open to reveal a large barrel-chested man in a rage. The little girl screamed when she saw him. This enraged the man even further and he began to growl like a dog. The twelve-year-old girl, strapped to a child's potty chair, covered her face and head with her arms. Still growling, the man removed his belt and began to beat the little girl. Because the girl was beaten anytime she made a sound, she knew that the beatings would not stop until she stopped crying. The girl was finally able to stifle her cries by forcing her mouth to stay closed and breathing through her nose. Silence restored, the man ceased the beatings and calmly put his belt back on. Leaving the room, he slammed the door shut. The little girl, afraid to make a sound, stared at the floor in front of her potty chair and continued to breathe heavily though her nose.

The twelve-year-old girl had been completely isolated almost since her birth. Her father had decided, for an unknown reason, that the newborn baby was mentally handicapped (he was wrong). Unwilling to face the world with such a child, he locked her away in her bedroom. At night, she was kept in a caged bed. Her mother, also seemingly a victim of the abusive patriarch, was not allowed by the father to have any contact with her daughter other than to give her food or move her from the cage to the potty chair. No one had ever spoken to her. All twelve years of her life had been spent in this fashion.*

The girl had never learned to talk. In fact, it is safe to assume, she had been almost completely isolated from language. Her parents never spoke around her. The only sound she heard from her father was the bizarre growling sound he would make while beating her. She had never been read a story, heard a radio, or listened to a conversation. She had no concept of words or symbols. The thoughts and memories swimming around in the little girl's head were not attached to words and were, therefore, extremely hard for her to conceptualize or understand.

For about the first six years of life, a child's brain is more like a sponge than a computer. The world around them is absorbed rather than learned. For example, when a child is exposed to a language before the age of six, the language is picked up rather quickly without anyone needing to teach grammatical rules, syntax, or many definitions. The same is true with other behavioral traits. Children acquire the ability to walk by watching their parents walk and absorbing the style in which they move. This isolated girl, for example, had only brief exposure to her parents walking and thus would never truly acquire its mechanics. As with walking, children acquire the ability to vocalize sounds by exposure (in this case listening to the sounds around them); hence, a child has the same speech mannerisms as his or her parents. This period in a person's life history is known as the "critical period" and is key to the survival of any species which relies on learned behavioral traits.

As the girl continued to stifle her cries and stare at the floor, she was surrounded by all she had ever been exposed to. The walls of her room,

---

* For her protection, the little girl's name was never revealed to the public. When accounts of her abuse reached the media, she was known only by her pseudonym, "Genie."

the straps of her chair, and the cage around her bed had blocked her from ever acquiring anything from another individual and left her wasting away in her critical period. She had been left alone in a silent world.

This critical period is essential to language ability in humans. A human is born with an innate sense of grammar and can piece arbitrary language symbols (words) together in order to make a sentence. The brain is hardwired to understand language phenomena such as tensing, possessives, and other elements of syntax which give words their true meaning. Once the baby acquires the words of a language, she innately understands how those words can fit together.

The human brain is structured to understand grammar in a fixed number of ways. Since the meanings of words are dictated by their placement and usage in the greater context of a sentence, an utterance without grammar is little more than a series of unconnected definitions which cannot properly be comprehended by the human mind. Different languages utilize different grammatical combinations, all of which the human brain is hardwired to understand. This is the structure of the mind. This structure is how the human species understands and relates to the world around it.

When a baby acquires his first language, he acquires both the arbitrary symbol system of words and the grammatical combination which those words can fit together. Before language, the baby's brain is like a series of switch boxes with each box representing two mutually exclusive functions of grammar. During the time that the baby is exposed to a language, each switch box is either pushed up or down depending on the language. Once all of the switch boxes have been fired one way or the other, the baby has the grammatical combination which he will use to relate to the world through the language he has acquired. He understands the usage of language.

This series of switch boxes is the genetically hardwired grammatical ability that humans possess. Each choice on each box is an equally valid grammatical rule. What is acquired is which direction each box will fire. The baby acquires this with the acquisition of definitions.

If the baby acquires another language before the critical period is over, he can switch the boxes back and forth to accommodate the new language. However, if the child only learns one language during the critical period, the baby's switches are fixed to that one combination. Learning a second language after the critical period is extremely difficult because one must continue to translate the new language's grammar into the grammar of their first language for it to make any sense. Once the critical period ceases, the switches are burned in place and become the sole way a human can relate to the world through grammar.*

The twelve-year-old little girl had barely been exposed to *any* language. Therefore, her switch boxes had never been fired in any direction. She had passed the age of her critical period, which had left her completely unable to relate to the world in any sort of symbolic fashion. The human brain is predisposed to understanding the world with symbols. The girl had no ability to do that. The world, to her, could make little to no sense at all.

The mother of the little girl was hardly allowed to see her. After these beatings the mother would go in to check on the girl. When the door opened slightly, the connection of looking at her mother's eyes was the most socialization the girl had ever known. Seeing her mother's eyes would have immediately calmed the girl and given her a sense of peace.†

---

* This overly simplistic explanation of X-bar theory (as it's known in linguistics) doesn't do this extremely complex concept justice. The theory was originally proposed by Noam Chomsky and has been a foundation for studies on universal grammar in humans. For an in-depth exploration of X-bar syntax, Ray Jakendoff's 1977 classic, *X-bar Syntax: A Study of Phrase Structure,* cannot be beat.

† Mother-to-child face-to-face interactions play an extremely important role in development and socialization. Developmental psychologists have studied such interactions (see Cohn and Tronick, 1988).

Humans, like all primates, rely on socialization for survival. This goes back to the earliest stages of primate natural history. As the primate order evolved, vision became more acute based on the eyes getting closer together, achieving a high degree of depth perception. This afforded the new order of animals the ability to hunt for small insects and live a life in the trees.* However, what it cost was peripheral vision, making the animals much more vulnerable to predation. As a result, primates developed complex social groups and communication systems. For example, if a predator was lurking behind a monkey, a member of the monkey's social group could sound an alarm call which would alert the individual to the predator. Primate social groups became a hedge against losing their peripheral vision. Socialization in primates is essential.†

Due to socialization, the primate order relies on learned behavioral traits in addition to genetic traits. Primates, in general, spend a longer period of time in maternal care and learn how to survive in their ecosystem by absorbing the information from their social groups. Primates without these learned behavioral adaptations do not survive.

Because human language is so critical to how the species socializes and passes down behaviors, a human without language will never be able to function. Not only does language allow for the ability to learn essential behaviors, it also allows the species to relate to the world in the complex cognitive way the human species understands its sur-

---

* This is known as the "visual predation theory" (see Cartmill, 1974).

† Much is always made of primate alarm calls as a form of altruism. When primates give such a call, they naturally call attention and expose themselves to the potential predator while allowing their group to flee. In order for you to survive as a primate without your peripheral vision, you must have a social group with altruistic group members who will warn you of danger. These warnings take the form of a communication system. The more complex these systems get, the more adept at survival a species can become. Altruism in primates, I believe, is the evolutionary springboard of increasing complexity of primate communication systems.

roundings. Without being able to attach symbols to thoughts, humans are unable to understand the world. The human brain is structured to need these symbols.

As the little girl sat in her room alone, finally able to swallow her cries, she was unable to understand much of what had transpired. She had no word or concept for the father that had burst into the room. She had no word or concept for his rage as he beat her. She had no word or concept for the comfort of her mother's eyes. She had no words or concepts for the four walls of her room or her potty chair. She had no words or concepts for herself. Like a monkey in a laboratory or a pet chimpanzee in a cage, she had been deprived of the socialization required of her species.*

While this little girl sat strapped to her potty chair, an infant chimpanzee was sitting in a cage in another part of the country. This chimp was being loaded onto a truck to be sold as a pet. She had been wild caught as an infant and, like this little girl, had been isolated from much, if any, contact or socialization.

1970
Okeechobee, Florida

Labored breathing and the clanking of metal were the only sounds coming through the darkness. The air was still and extremely hot. Occasionally a small cry or a loud screeching would resonate. Since nothing would return these sounds, they wouldn't last long. Finally, from beyond the darkness, came the sound of a door being unlocked.

---

* Genie's abusive childhood has been well documented. The episode I have constructed here is culled together from such accounts. The most complete text of her condition is Russ Rymer's book, *Genie: A Scientific Tragedy*.

The door to the trailer slid open to reveal a large crowd amused at what they saw. Inside the trailer were baby primates of all kinds, each in its own metal cage. Most cages contained, in addition to the animal, a blanket, a baby bottle with milk, and a cut-up banana. Each baby primate was holding onto a stuffed version of its species, representing the mother it had been taken away from.

These animals were being sold as pets. They had been caught in the wild, shipped to the United States, and bought by an exotic pet dealer. The pet dealer had loaded them into his truck where he displayed them from town to town. This is typical of a traveling exotic pet show. Animals are kept in a large trailer where they can be quickly exhibited to a crowd. Though they sometimes bill themselves as "educational," these pet shows are nothing of the sort. Their main goal is to sell exotic animals to people as pets.

In these shows, the exotic pet dealer will address the crowd in front of him. He may say something like, "These darling animals will become part of your family." He might even follow it up with, "You can train them to clean up after themselves, put on clothes, and eat with a fork and spoon." To add to the educational portion of the show, he'll say something like, "Scientists have even proven that you can train the chimpanzees to talk!"

The crowd will be enamored at the information they are getting from the dealer. The thought of owning such an intelligent animal as a pet will be enough for some of them to begin looking through their wallets. They will examine the chimpanzees inside their cages in the trailer. What they will probably see is that the chimps will be pressing their faces against the cage to feel the breeze that exists outside the trailer. The open trailer door will have provided a temporary relief from the stale air and the darkness.

While they gasp for air, the chimpanzees will notice the crowd in front of them. They will see a diverse group of people with all sorts of different reasons for wanting a pet primate. Most will want a pet that they can use to impress their friends. Some may be truck drivers looking for traveling companions. Others may be fathers with their sons. Some might be roadside zoo owners looking for new animals to fill empty exhibits. Occasionally there will be a different type of pet seeker in the crowd—the kind that wants a pet to raise as a child. To these type of pet seekers, the idea of a chimpanzee as a surrogate child is usually irresistible.

After giving some brief "facts" about the animals, the dealer will run through his primate inventory. In addition to the chimpanzees, he may have capuchin monkeys from Nicaragua, rhesus macaques from Sri Lanka, and gibbons from Indonesia. None, however, will get the same reaction as the chimpanzees.

The dealer will feed off the crowd's enthusiasm for these apes. He'll respond to it by giving his chimps a backstory. "The chimpanzees are newborn babies. They were caught a few weeks ago in different parts of the deepest jungles of Africa. I just picked them up from the boat yesterday. They are so young that they will look to you as their parent."

Immediately, this will pique the interest of the pet seekers, especially those looking for a surrogate child. At this point, someone will inevitably ask if the chimpanzees have names.

He'll quickly make up names on the spot. The names he creates will be amusing.

"Did you say that one's name is 'Gin'? Like the drink?" someone will interrupt.

"Yes, indeed." The dealer will smile.

"Hell, I'll take it!" the buyer will say, pulling out his wallet.

Another buyer will quickly point to another chimpanzee and ask about her. They will have an exchange where the dealer will make up another name and assure the buyer of how healthy she is.

At this point, the potential buyer will confer with the friend he brought along. He'll tell his friend that he feels a "real connection" with the infant chimpanzee.* His friend will tell him that it's probably "meant to be." They'll both look over at the chimp who will still be attempting to get to the cooler breeze outside. By this time, however, she'll be pressing her entire body against the bars of the cage.

"It's obvious that she knows I want her. Look how she's already trying to come to me!" the buyer will say.

With that, the chimpanzee will be purchased and sold to live out the indefinite future in a human household.

Such was the scene when a four-month-old chimpanzee named Cindy was purchased in 1970. Cindy had been caught by poachers in central Africa when she was very young. She had been put on a boat and shipped to the United States with other exotic animals to be sold as a pet. Infant chimpanzees usually do not survive the boat ride from Africa. Like a newborn human, it is very difficult for an infant chimpanzee to survive without maternal care. She needed to be bottle fed every few hours, and the care provided on the boat was less than adequate. Still, Cindy had survived and was healthy enough when the animal dealer purchased her on the dock.

When Cindy's cage was put into the back of her owner's car, she would have peered out from the bars in silence. She would have clutched her stuffed chimpanzee and explored her new world. She would have had no memories of where she had come from or who her group had been. She would lead a life isolated from all other chimpanzees. She would be nurtured by a human world.†

---

* These "spiritual connections" with animals have resulted in the injuries and deaths of many zookeepers and pet owners.

† This begs the question of whether a critical period is uniquely human. Tetsuro Matsuzawa has done some incredible studies on this and has found that, in the case of acquiring tool technology and use, chimpanzees clearly show evidence of a critical period. He has observed the critical period ending at about age five in chimpanzees.

While Cindy was beginning her life in captivity she shared an unknown bond with the isolated little girl in California. Both had been isolated, both had been separated from their natural way of life, and now both of their lives were about to change dramatically.

1970
Temple City, California

As the little girl and her mother sat in front of the social worker, everything became clear. The social worker stared at them in horror as the mother recounted the last thirteen years. When the pair had walked into the welfare office, the social workers had naturally assumed that the small girl was an autistic six-year-old child. They arrived at this conclusion by her complete silence and lack of responsiveness to any sort of question or gesture.

The two had come in for money. The mother had tried to convince the welfare office that the little girl was blind. The social worker could clearly tell that this was not the case. However, there was something not quite right about the girl. First of all, the way she walked was strange. She walked in this sort of bunny style, walking on her toes and stretching her hands in front of her for balance. There was also the way she seemed frightened of everything around her. The social worker began interrogating the pair. Finally, after much questioning, the mother explained her story.

The little girl was thirteen. She had been isolated from all human contact for her entire life. She was without social behaviors or language. The girl and her mother had fled from the abusive father but needed money. The mother had decided to tell the welfare office that the girl was blind so that they could receive benefits.

The story quickly made news all over the world. Stories of the isolated child intrigued both the general public and the scientific community of psychologists and linguists. She was given the name "Genie" and sent to live at the Children's Hospital of Los Angeles. There she became the focus of several scientific studies. The most profound, however, was one that attempted to look at a critical period in humans. Linguists were keenly interested to see if Genie would ever be able to acquire language since she had clearly passed the critical period and had never been exposed to language in her childhood. So, for this reason, the main focus of the experimentation was to see if Genie could be taught to talk.

1971
West Palm Beach, Florida

Cindy sat on top of a blanket wearing a dress. Perched on her nose was a pair of reading glasses. In her lap was a book. Cindy examined the book and looked closely at each picture before turning the page.* As she posed in this position, her owner snapped a picture.

Cindy's first year as a pet had consisted of being raised as a human child. She ate three meals a day, had a bedtime, and played with toys. She received an enormous amount of attention and care from her owner. He played with her, talked to her, and taught her tricks. Cindy was trained to do certain gestures if she wanted things. For example, if she wanted food, she would tap the top of her head. If she wanted a drink, she would fold her bottom lip out.

There is a Robert Yerkes type of notion that many pet owners

---

* For the duration of Cindy's life she enjoyed looking at magazines and books. Anytime her group was given magazines or books to play with, the other chimpanzees would quickly rip them up and throw them around. Cindy would sit quietly and study each page, *then* rip it up and throw it around.

hold. They believe that the more time a pet spends interacting with humans, the more humanlike that pet will become. This idea is even more prevalent among those that own (or take care of) chimpanzees. It is, however, not the case. The reason for this certainly isn't that human behavior is too complex for another species to master. On the contrary, each species has an innate set of complex behaviors that are uniquely suited to allow that species to survive its own particular ecology. In primates, these innate behaviors become unlocked when socializing with others of their species. This allows for these innate behaviors to become modified by an individual's social group which creates an extremely fine-tuned set of behaviors specific to both the natural history of the species and the unique ecology of each group.

A problem arises when a primate is never socialized with another of her species and is socialized with a different species instead. Such is the case with a pet chimpanzee who is acquired at an early age. Though the chimpanzee is being socialized, the socialization is only occurring with humans and not chimpanzees. Since humans do not carry the same innate behaviors carried by a chimpanzee, those behaviors are never unlocked in a pet. Therefore, the pet chimpanzee can only pick up on behaviors that are common to both humans and chimpanzees and as a result can never live up to her full behavioral potential. Sure, she may be able to pick up on small behaviors. She may be able to be taught to use a fork and spoon. She may be able to be taught to comb her hair. She may even be able to be taught gestures or hand signs. However, she will never be able to act like a chimpanzee unless she is socialized with a chimpanzee.

I would guess that Cindy's photo session was a frustrating affair. I would imagine that after long bouts of attempting to situate Cindy in just the right pose with the reading glasses, dress, and book, she would finally sit still long enough to take an out-of-focus and off-centered picture. Before her owner could take another picture, I can see Cindy taking the glasses off her nose and pulling them apart.* I can also speculate that she would have ripped the book apart and torn her nice dress. Would she have done this because she was barbarically less complex than a human? No. In fact, she would have behaved this way because her innate chimpanzee behaviors would not have gelled with the innate human behaviors that her owner would have wanted her to exhibit.

The nature of a primate species is like the door to a safe. In order to get the combination to that safe, a primate must socialize with other primates of that species. Socializing with a different species gives the wrong combination and the door is never unlocked. There is a very limited amount of time in a primate's life during which the door can be opened. If the primate is not socialized by a certain period, the door to that safe is welded shut—doomed to stay closed forever. In 1971, Cindy was almost two years old. Her time was beginning to run out.

1971
Stanford, California

While Cindy was failing at becoming human in Florida, across the country there were claims of a chimpanzee who had managed to communicate using human language. The ghost of Robert Yerkes loomed over the lecture hall as Allan and Beatrice Gardner spoke about their successes in training a female chimpanzee named Washoe to use sign language. Yerkes, who had died in 1959, may have been surprised to

---

* Because of this photo, I used to give my sunglasses to Cindy to see if she'd put them on. It took about seven pairs of sunglasses for me to realize that Cindy would *always* pull them apart.

see his assertion that chimpanzees could "perhaps be taught to use their fingers like a deaf and dumb person" come to fruition in the stories of Washoe. His contention had been modified by the Gardners' own contention that "animals are capable of telling us about themselves if one knows the proper way to ask them."*

Over the past decade, the interest in training an ape to speak had grown. Despite the failures of the Gua project and other attempts to teach language to apes, the subject was still hotly debated. In 1968, the linguist Noam Chomsky had published an immensely popular book called *Language and Mind*. In it, he described language as being uniquely human. This sparked several attempts to disprove Chomsky and this notion. Such was the case with the Gardners.

This evening, at Stanford University, the Gardners began their lecture with Chomsky's conviction that language was solely in the domain of the human species. They then proceeded to dismantle this idea as they spoke about how they had fixed all of the issues with previous language-trained ape projects and had come out with an actual talking ape, albeit a silent one. Like the previous attempts, they had begun with an ape in its infancy, assuming a critical period similar to humans. Unlike the previous attempts, they had not bothered trying to teach the chimpanzee to vocalize. Instead, they had taught her sign language.

After Gua, Robert Yerkes had decided that, because apes lacked the vocal apparatus to produce the same voiced sounds as humans, attempts to teach apes to talk would be doomed to failure. Yerkes had been keenly interested in training a chimpanzee to use sign language but died before he could begin such a project. Fortunately for Yerkes's dream, Allan and Beatrice Gardner also held this interest and "Project

---

* This lecture that was given by the Gardners at Stanford University has been recounted by Francine "Penny" Patterson, the trainer of Koko the gorilla, in her book *The Education of Koko*.

Washoe" began in earnest in 1967, when the Gardners acquired the infant chimpanzee. The intent was to resurrect the notion of a language-trained ape out of the ashes of the Gua disaster. This time, however, the chimpanzee's physical vocal limitations would not be an issue. The chimpanzee would be taught to use her fingers.

In order to encourage Washoe to participate in sign language, the Gardners employed a method whereby anytime Washoe would gesture anything close to an ASL sign, she would be rewarded and her hands would be shaped to make the correct sign. As time went on, Washoe's signs had to be more precise to receive the reward.

Washoe, claimed the Gardners, had learned 132 signs. More importantly, they asserted, Washoe could use these signs in a grammatical fashion. In fact, they claimed, Washoe outperformed children at the same stage in language acquisition in grammatical competency. It was this claim that the Gardners brandished about as their biggest triumph. And, if such was the case, indeed it was.

It had been well established that some animals could attach arbitrary symbols to information. Apes, monkeys, other mammals, and some birds had clearly been shown to be able to understand symbols in some fashion. Animal training relies on arbitrary cues to let the animal know what behavior to exhibit. A whistle blowing may mean one behavior to a trained animal while a hand clap may mean another behavior. Some trained dolphins cue in to hand gestures. These are all symbolic and arbitrary, just like words in human language. However, words by themselves are not language. What *is* language is the ability to take these words, or other symbols, piece them together in a certain sequence, and have that sequence give the word its true meaning. Words, by themselves, do not attain their intended meaning until they are used in a sentence. Consider the sentence: "The miraculous glass shiner prevented the man, outside the window, from seeing the stain on the wall." Words such as "miracle," "shine," "stain," and "wall" are given their meanings by both the order of the sentence and the affixes that are attached to the words. "Window" becomes an entity separating the "man" from the other actions in the sentence. Changing the order and the affixes would give the words (and sentence) a different set of meanings. Doing so could create the sentence: "The shiny stained glass, on the window, prevented the man from seeing the miracle outside the walls." The use of a word gives that word its meaning. This phenomenon is grammar and it is the key feature in language. Without the ability to understand this, one has the ability to learn symbols but not a language.

So if, as the Gardners were claiming that evening at Stanford University, Washoe had learned not only the individual sign language symbols but also how to use them in a sentence, the ramifications would be profound. The Gardners were quick to point to their major piece of evidence of Washoe's grammatical competency. That was her ability to respond to "*wh*" questions such as "what color?" "where baby?" and "who stupid?" To answer a "*wh*" question, one must understand a grammatical order; the word that comes after the "*wh*" word is questioned. The Gardners showed films of Washoe answering such questions with the correct order of signs.

The Gardners' audience was amazed at what they had seen. Truly, the gap between human and nonhuman communication had been bridged. There was finally a talking ape. Yerkes's dream had been fulfilled. The future for this type of study seemed limitless.

In the audience sat a young graduate student in psychology named Francine "Penny" Patterson. She was immediately taken by the Gardners' talk and wanted to continue the research in her own way. While she listened to the lecture and watched the films of Washoe, she decided that she too would teach an ape sign language. This would be the focus of her graduate work. The next day she let her advisor know of her plan, enrolled in a course in American Sign Language, and began a search for her own Washoe. Eventually the trek would lead her to the San Francisco Zoo, where there was a baby gorilla named Koko whose health was deteriorating.* Patterson would be able to persuade the zoo to allow the gorilla to be trained by her in order for her to pursue her "language studies." By July of 1972, "Project Koko" would begin.

All of this seemed like a far-off dream as Patterson watched the lecture. More than anything, she wanted to be able to talk to an ape. The Gardners provided her with an avenue to make that happen.

Another scientist also watched the films of Washoe. His reaction was considerably less enthusiastic than Patterson's. What Herbert Terrace saw in these films was not a chimpanzee who had acquired a language, but rather a chimpanzee who had learned the arbitrary definition of words and was being cued by his trainers to give responses in the appropriate order. Terrace watched the films in slow motion over and over again. Washoe, to him, did not appear to bridge the gap between human and nonhuman communication. Washoe was a trained chimpanzee performing a sequence of events in order to get a reward.†

Terrace, like the Gardners, had wanted desperately to disprove Chomsky's notion. Also, like the Gardners, Terrace had felt that a chimpanzee would truly be able to acquire language. He was just dissatisfied with the "proof" that the Gardners had supplied. Terrace set out to do his own language-training experiment which would go further than Project Washoe. It would either give credence to the Gardners claims or destroy the myth. He would also acquire a chimpanzee.

---

* Koko had, reportedly, been almost at the point of death when she was pulled from her mother. After she was nursed back to health, she was put in the nursery window of the San Francisco Zoo. Patterson had tried before, unsuccessfully, to train Koko when she was with her mother. Now that she had been pulled, the zoo relented.

† I don't mean to imply that Herbert Terrace was at the lecture at Stanford. He may have been, I don't know. However, Washoe's abilities were well known at that point. Terrace had acquired the film clips which would later be used in a *Nova* series film entitled *The First Signs of Washoe.*

He would train the chimpanzee exactly as the Gardners had done, except he would use much more rigorous experiments in determining the success or failure of the project. He would make sure to take away what he saw as any visual cues given to the chimpanzee by the trainer. Like Francine Patterson, he would set out to find an ape to train.

In September of 1971, the morning after the Gardners' lecture at Stanford, the notion of training an ape to talk was rife with possibilities. Two apes were about to come into the world which would deepen the divide over language in a nonhuman species. A gorilla at the San Francisco Zoo was pregnant. She was soon to give birth to a sign language–using gorilla who would become a media sensation. In another part of the country, at a laboratory in Oklahoma, a female chimpanzee was a year and a half away from becoming pregnant with another ape who would become another language-trained celebrity. This ape, however, would destroy the notion of such studies and forever cast a shadow over any future research of the sort.

1973
West Palm Beach, Florida

A pet chimpanzee is a difficult responsibility. The pet owner is taking an animal, which is not a human but is as intelligent as a human, and putting her into a human world. Add to this that a chimpanzee is exponentially stronger and considerably more aggressive than a human. By 1973, Cindy had apparently begun to wear out her welcome with her owner.

Little is known as to what eventually caused Cindy's owner to begin thinking about options for her expulsion from his life. I, however, have an idea. Being as familiar with Cindy's behavior as I am, I can imagine certain scenarios which would cause even the most patient person to rethink having Cindy as a permanent member of his home.

I imagine that the man woke up one afternoon and realized he had unexpectedly fallen asleep. A sinking feeling would have come over him as he realized that he had dozed off with Cindy out of her cage. He would frantically look around to find that Cindy was no longer beside him. *This is just great,* the man would think as he stood up and looked for any signs of her. The first thing he'd notice would be the sounds of running water coming from every faucet in the house. Sure enough, as he approached the bathroom, he would find the faucet and shower head flowing with water. He would also find toothpaste all over the bathroom wall. Shaving cream would be everywhere, with the can on the floor. The water from the toilet would be all splashed out of the bowl and the toilet paper would be strewed around. He would follow a toothpaste footprint out of the bathroom, across the bedroom carpet, across the living room floor, and into the kitchen. In the kitchen he would, again, find running water. This time it would be pouring from the sink. Unfortunately, the stopper would be covering the drain and the water would be cascading all over the floor. He would then find the refrigerator door open. The refrigerator would be completely rummaged through with nothing left untouched. Inside the refrigerator would be a gallon of milk, turned over, with milk on the lower shelves and floor. On another shelf would be salami slices clumped together which would have apparently been chewed and spit back out. Covering the floor in front of the refrigerator would be broken eggs, glass from an orange juice bottle, and a mix of milk, orange juice, and raw eggs.

"Cindy!" the man would yell to no avail. She would be nowhere in sight and not responding.

Moving from the refrigerator, the man would look at the open cupboard door. Sugar and flour would be spilled everywhere. There would be a torn-up wrapper which would have once held the sandwich bread (which, apparently, had been eaten). Another set of footprints, this time made up of egg and sugar, would point toward the door to the garage. The man would follow these footprints to find the door slightly opened with a pile of vomit in front of it. Opening the door, he would find Cindy sitting on the floor of the garage. She would have oil covering her new dress. She would be holding a hammer which she'd be pounding into the cement floor, sending shards of cement flying with each hit. She would appear to be having a wonderful time.

The man would have seen enough. When he scooped Cindy up, she would then let out a scream and sink her canine into his wrist. The pain would cause the man to drop the chimpanzee and yell. Cindy would run, as fast as she could, back into the house. The man would run after her and find Cindy sitting in her cage with the door shut.

As the man washed his bite wound in the sink, it would dawn on him that Cindy would never be the little girl he desired her to be. Everything he had tried had failed. Cindy was not behaving the way that he had trained her to act. The dreams he once had were giving way to the harsh reality that Cindy was not a little human child but a wild chimpanzee.

Taking bandages from the medicine cabinet, the man would worry about how he could continue to house the little chimpanzee. As he bandaged up his hand, he would return to her cage to find her resting comfortably. For all of his failures, one thing Cindy would have done was to become attached to the man as a parent. Cindy would run to him when she was hurt, reach out to him when she was frightened, and need attention from him when she was lonely. He, in fact, had a dependent child. It just wasn't the child he wanted.

The man would then grab a bag of potato chips out of the pantry that had somehow escaped Cindy's reach. Snacking and pacing would help to calm his nerves. When he came back to Cindy's cage, he would see her sitting up and tapping her head. She would want the potato chips.

"No way!" the man would sneer.

Cindy would continue to tap her head, harder and harder each time. The man would continue to ignore her. Suddenly he would hear a strange sound coming from Cindy's cage. He would stop and look at her. Cindy would be holding out her hand, pressing her lips together, and making a raspberry sound.

"Cindy!" he would exclaim. "You're talking!"

Cindy would continue to make the sound. At this, the man would reach into the chip bag and pull out a potato chip. Cindy would reach out her hand and make the sound again. The man would give her the chip. Cindy would eat the chip and then repeat the sound. The man would give her another chip.

From this point forward, Cindy would realize that any time she wanted something, she just needed to vocalize to get it.

My speculation becomes not without merit and fairly important to the lexicon I would study. You see, the raspberry sound Cindy was making was very real and would stay with her throughout her lifetime. I don't know where she picked it up or when she started using it. However, it is a vocalization that was entirely unique to Cindy and she was using it by the time she arrived at the animal park. It would be this raspberry sound and what would happen with it that would initially show me that every group of chimpanzees has its own evolving dialect.

1973
New York, New York

On the film clip, Washoe was signing "baby in my drink." She was referring to a baby doll inserted into her cup. The two psychologists watched the clip over and over again. Such a sentence would truly be a remarkable achievement in grammar for a chimpanzee to use. Not only was Washoe using and understanding a possessive word ("my"), but she was also using a prepositional phrase which denoted a location ("in my drink"). To be able to use this sentence, Washoe must possess a grammatical ability. However, Herbert Terrace and his partner, Laura-Ann Petitto, were not impressed.

At the point that Terrace was ready to begin his own language training project with a chimpanzee, he had already published ground-breaking studies on animal training with pigeons. He was expertly familiar with ways in which to direct an animal to produce a desired behavior. In watching the films of Washoe signing to Beatrice Gardner and her team, Terrace saw the same methods occurring.

As Terrace and Petitto watched the film clip, it was clear to both of them, without a doubt, that what Washoe was doing was not using grammar. She was not, as the Gardners had claimed, divining different meanings from different arrangements of signs. In fact, all she had done was to learn to symbolically label actions and things. All of her supposed grammatical ability was the product of shaping and cueing by her trainers. Her achievement of signing "baby in my drink" was the result of cues given to her by trainers. The evidence was on the film.*

Washoe's trainer, in asking for her to sign about the baby doll in the cup, was pointing before most of the signs Washoe was making. So the trainer was, in fact, giving Washoe the correct order in a step-by-step fashion. The trainer first pointed to the baby doll. Washoe signed "baby." The trainer then pointed in the cup. Washoe then signed "in." So all Terrace and Petitto were seeing was a chimpanzee who was correctly identifying labels which were being pointed out by the trainer. No actual grammatical ability was being displayed.

Another major problem they saw in the film was that Washoe was making far more errors than correct responses. The trainers were

---

* Petitto had to painstakingly make frame-by-frame sketches of Washoe for use in their future publications. The sketches became necessary after the Gardners threatened legal action against Terrace and his team over the use of their film clips.

ignoring all incorrect responses. So Washoe was actually just throwing out signs in any random order and would, occasionally, get the correct order. None of this was satisfying to either psychologist.

If Terrace was to actually disprove Chomsky's notion of language being entirely unique to humans, he had to provide a more scientific approach to teaching an ape to use sign language. The Gardners' study seemed to be nothing more than an exercise in training—not an ape using language. Terrace knew he had to avoid such mistakes in order to convince skeptics of an ape's ability. He set about assembling a team of psychologists to begin his project.

In November, Herbert Terrace acquired a two-week-old male chimpanzee. The chimpanzee was caged up and brought to Terrace's New York City apartment. In order to pay homage to the man he was attempting to disprove, Terrace named the chimpanzee Nim Chimpsky.

While Nim was at the beginning of his life in a human home, Cindy was at the end of hers. While Nim was being transported into Terrace's apartment, Cindy was being transported into the nursery pen of the animal park. While Nim was about to begin his lessons on how to communicate like a human, Cindy was about to finally learn how to communicate like a chimpanzee.

1973
Loxahatchee, Florida

Cindy's owner had finally given up on raising her. Luckily, officials at the animal park had agreed to have Cindy come live in the nursery with other juvenile chimpanzees. No one knew how she would react to seeing others of her species for the first time since her early infancy.

Cindy sat, without her clothes on, alone in the nursery window pen. She appeared out of place sitting in this pen. She didn't seem like a chimpanzee. She didn't sound like a chimpanzee, she didn't move like a chimpanzee, and she certainly didn't act like a chimpanzee. There was straw all around her and a plastic ball. The window to the outside world was covered so she couldn't see outside. She was unaware of her surroundings and attempted to call to her owner. First she folded out her bottom lip and tapped her head. When her owner didn't come she made the raspberry sound. Again, she failed to get a response. Cindy sat back down and looked around.

Painted on the wall of the pen was a large tree with vines hanging from it. Cindy had never seen anything like it. At the base of one of the walls, there was a sliding door that was shut. From behind the door Cindy could hear scratching. She went closer to the door to examine it. When she approached it, she heard loud screeching. After the screeching, something hit the door making a horrendously loud sound.

Slowly, the door began to open. As the door was pulled open all the way, four juvenile chimpanzees ran into Cindy's pen. There were three males named Michael, Romeo, and Bashful. In addition to the three males was one juvenile female named Clumsy. Cindy screamed. She ran to the wall, tapping on her head and making the raspberry sound. Bashful followed after her and grabbed her arm. At first he grabbed her softly. Then he squeezed her. As he squeezed her, he began to violently swing her arm back and forth As he did this he started jumping up and down and making an awful racket. Cindy screamed again. Finally he let her go. Cindy ran to the corner of the pen and buried herself in straw. Clumsy ran over to her and uncovered her. She shoved her hand in Cindy's mouth. Not knowing what to do, Cindy bit down on it as hard as she could.* This

* A chimpanzee putting her hand into another chimpanzee's mouth appears to have different connotations depending on the group. I have witnessed some chimpanzees use this as a reassuring gesture, while in other chimpanzees the gesture seems to be purely dominant and aggressive.

caused all four of the chimpanzees to start screaming. They tackled Cindy and began biting her. Clumsy bit Cindy's face in a rage. Within seconds, blood was covering the straw of the nursery pen. At that, a large door opened revealing a man with a hose.

He raised the hose, pointed it at the melee of chimps and began spraying them. The four chimps separated. Clumsy jumped up and down screaming. The man continued to spray until they all went back into the other room. The sliding door and the large door both slammed shut and Cindy was alone again.

Lying on the straw, Cindy panted silently. She was wet, bleeding, and in great pain. She stared at the painted tree on the wall. The large door again swung open. This time another man wearing a mask appeared. He pinned her down and shoved a needle into her side. At this, she screamed. In an instant, everything went black.

Cindy awoke in the nursery pen, covered in white bandages. The straw was clean and dry and she was alone. For two more days, Cindy stayed alone in the nursery pen. Three times a day, the large door would open and someone would put food in her pen. The food consisted of strange biscuits soaked in juice and cut-up fruit. Sometimes she would get raisins or peanuts. From the other side of the sliding door, she could hear the other chimpanzees. They would screech and bang on the door. Cindy would respond by making her raspberry sound. Every day, she watched for her owner but he never came.

One morning, after she ate, she heard the sliding door slowly opening again. She screamed and ran to the corner. The four juvenile chimpanzees entered the pen and surrounded her again. This time, none of them grabbed her. They touched her arm and examined her bandages. When Clumsy approached Cindy, Cindy cried out in fear. Clumsy put her face up to one of her bandages and pulled it off with her teeth, looking at her stitched-up wound. She made a soft vocalization to her. Cindy made the raspberry sound back to her. Clumsy imitated Cindy.

Cindy then imitated Clumsy's soft vocalization. This time, the sliding door remained open. For the first time since she was in Africa as an infant, Cindy communicated with another chimpanzee.*

Cindy had been introduced to other chimpanzees before she was at the end of her critical period. She would still be able, at this point, to acquire the natural behaviors of her species and her natural way of communicating. This was in direct contrast to Genie, who, at this point, had gone through extensive training but was unable to acquire standard human behaviors and grammatical language.

1974
Los Angeles, California

"I was going to be the next Annie Sullivan!" bellowed Jean Butler, Genie's teacher at the children's hospital.† She was referring, of course, to the legendary teacher of Helen Keller who taught the deaf and blind child to communicate with the outside world.

She was speaking to the group of psychologists and linguists who were frustrated at the lack of progress Genie was making. Their quest to determine if a human child could learn a language after her critical period had begun to reach conclusions that no one wanted to reach. Genie was not learning language.

Since Genie had been moved to the children's hospital, she had been studied extensively. In addition to this, she had teachers such as

---

* Cindy, at this point, would have been nearing the end of her critical period (as would have, probably, the other chimps in the nursery with her). It would have been amazing to go back and see how many of the behaviors Cindy picked up from living in a human home were transmitted to her new nursery mates and acquired.

† Jean Butler's quote that she was going to be the next Annie Sullivan is related in the Nova documentary, *Secrets of the Wild Child.*

Jean Butler, who were attempting to teach her both language and speech. Jean had taken a special interest in the girl and had, for a year, been her foster mother. She attempted to adopt Genie but was denied when others feared that she was using Genie to further her career and didn't have the child's best interest at heart. Since then, her constant questioning of Genie's role as a laboratory subject had been a thorn in the side of the team studying Genie's progress.

Though Genie was able to learn labels and definitions of words, she seemed to be unable to reliably use grammar. She had actually acquired two grammatical sentences from her parents which she could reliably utter. Those were "Stop it" and "No more." In addition to this, Genie had never learned to properly walk. She still had the peculiar bunny-style walk that she had first displayed.

After she was taken to the children's hospital in Los Angeles, Genie's parents had been arrested. Before he could stand trial, Genie's father shot himself. Her mother stood trial for felony neglect. However, she was acquitted on the grounds that she, too, had been a victim of abuse.

As Genie sat through another teaching session, it became apparent to some of the scientists that she would never be able to function as a normal human being. The critical period was an insurmountable wall in the life history of a human.

1975
New York, New York

Herbert Terrace's project with Nim was proving to be problematic. After twenty-two months of constant language training, Nim had failed to learn anything but labels. The Gardners had claimed that, at this point in Washoe's training, she had a vocabulary of thirty-four signs which she was combining to make grammatical sentences. Nim was doing nothing of the sort. By taking out the cueing going on in the Gardners' films and subjecting Nim to more rigorous experimentation, Nim was falling far short of the claims made about Washoe.

It had begun promisingly enough. By the end of the fourth month, Nim had learned his first sign. At the twenty-two-month mark, Nim had acquired a sufficient enough number of signs that he should have been establishing grammatical patterns. However, in looking for any sort of rule-governed combination of signs, Terrace noticed that Nim appeared to arrange signs in a completely random order. Nim would chose appropriate signs for any given situation. However, the signs he would choose would be given no relationship to each other. Nim simply would treat every sign as its own individual statement instead of as a group of signs that were working together to create one meaning.

Though still early in the study, this realization was beginning to deal a crushing blow to the hopes of an ape learning sign language. Terrace himself was beginning to doubt his own hypothesis that an ape could learn a human language. What the results were beginning to show was that, without cueing an ape in the correct order of symbols, the ape had no ability to grammatically piece symbols together. Noam Chomsky had been correct. The way humans understand and use language is not a way another species can understand and use language.

As Project Nim continued, Herbert Terrace began to formulate what would become some of the most profound work of his career.* What Nim Chimpsky was about to show the world was that these sign language–trained apes amounted to nothing much more than a circus trick.

---

* Indeed, Terrace's scientific approach to language training apes earned him the respect of the scientific community. According to Nicholas Wade's 1980 paper in *Science,* linguist Thomas Sebeok is quoted as saying, "In my opinion, the alleged language experiments with apes divide into three groups: one, outright fraud; two, self-deception; three, those conducted by Terrace. The largest class by far is the middle one."

As both Nim and Genie were proving to be untrainable in language, Cindy had been easily learning to communicate and socialize with other chimpanzees. Cindy, unlike Nim and Genie, was picking up and passing on behaviors with others of her species.

1975
Loxahatchee, Florida

The park was closing for the evening. The last few guests were gathered around the nursery window watching a rotund six-year-old female chimpanzee cradling a two-year-old male chimpanzee in her lap. Cindy looked out of the window at the spectators who were all smiling. She looked down at the little chimp in her lap who was sound asleep. A keeper turned off the lights to the nursery and the guests left Cindy and her friend alone in the dark.

Cindy gave a low grunting sound to the little chimp. He woke up and grunted back to her. When Cindy stood up, he slid off her lap. This caused a louder hoot. Cindy extended her arms and made her raspberry sound. The little chimp ran into Cindy's arms and climbed on her back. Cindy walked to the corner of the pen and started making a nest.

Since arriving at the nursery, Cindy had failed to create a real social bond with any of the other chimpanzees. Her relationship with Clumsy was volatile at best. Occasionally she would play with the males, but for the most part, she had kept to herself. She had, however, picked up on their mannerisms and was finally acting like a chimpanzee. She moved like a chimpanzee, interacted like a chimpanzee, and displayed chimpanzee behaviors, such as making nests. She had also picked up on their calls. Though the vocalizations she was picking up from these juveniles were very basic, she was vocalizing like a chimpanzee and able to communicate with others. This allowed her to communicate with the newest member of the nursery group: a two-year-old male who had been brought to the nursery a year and a half after Cindy had arrived. The young male had been the first chimpanzee Cindy had ever truly bonded with.

He had come from another animal park in California, where he had been rejected by his mother. He formed an immediate bond with Cindy, who became like a surrogate mother to him. She was constantly grooming him, playing with him, and embracing him. The connection between them was the first either one had ever had with another chimpanzee. The little chimpanzee had arrived in Florida with a name that none of the keepers knew the origins of. His name was Higgy.

As night fell, Cindy huddled in her nest with Higgy. The two of them grunted to each other. Across the country, near where Higgy had come from, Genie was sitting at the children's hospital attempting to speak to one of the psychologists. Her words were basic and without grammar. Three thousand miles away from the children's hospital, Herbert Terrace was putting Nim to bed. Nim had spent another day utilizing the signs he had learned but without order or any true meaning. Cindy, Genie, and Nim were all mute misfits in a nature withheld from them. Yet, all three of them were naturally driven to interact with the world around them. None of them had the understanding of why they didn't fit in with the rest of their species. None of them had the ability to contemplate how their worlds *should* have been. However, the world is never what *should* be. The world merely *is*. Each individual is given a set of parameters, given to us by circumstance, and, like a carpenter who receives a set amount of materials, each individual is forced to create his or her own world out of what is given. Each moment adds to one's circumstances. Each circumstance alters the way one must face the world. These moments, these circumstances, are forever etched in the behaviors of each individual.

They color the way we understand, the way we act, and the way we speak. Each individual's role on this earth is to utilize those parameters in order to perceive and relate to the environment around them. This is the struggle of existence and the key to survival, behavior, and communication.

One month later, the National Institutes of Health pulled its funding from the Genie project. Left with only negative data and no money, Genie's team suspended its work indefinitely. Genie was sent back to live with her mother. One year later, Genie's mother decided that caring for Genie was too much for her. Genie would spend the rest of her life in foster care without a team of scientists, without a family, and without language.

The knight of faith . . . in the loneliness of the universe never hears any human voice but walks alone with his frightful responsibility.
—Søren Kierkegaard

3

Higgy

The following is an account of the first years that the alpha male
chimpanzee, Higgy, spent at the animal park. In and of itself,
there isn't much to Higgy's story in these first years. He was captive
born in California in 1973. He was hand raised by humans. He was
sent off to the animal park when he was one year of age. He was placed
in the nursery pen of the park where he met Cindy, who became the
first chimpanzee he would socialize with. He spent most of his juvenile
life in this nursery pen. This basic story of a captive chimpanzee, however, had an undercurrent which would dictate and dominate the lives
of a group of chimpanzees. The story of Higgy's group begins here.

As Higgy lived playfully in his nursery pen, the world he would
inherit was being created around him. The following isn't so much
the story of Higgy, himself, as it is the story of what he would become
and what he would lead. It is the story of the creation of a group and

the formation of a chimpanzee communication system out of the individual histories of a group that was beginning to come together.

Much later, when I first encountered Higgy, I found him to be an intimidating figure. He was, first off, enormous (weighing in at almost two hundred pounds). He walked around his island with a strut. The other chimpanzees in his group would clear his path. As the alpha male of his group, he was clearly in charge. When any of his group members were hurt, upset, or scared, they would run to Higgy. Any fights that would start on his island could be halted immediately by one of his vocalizations. He was so intimidating, in fact, that I felt like he was in charge of me.*

He also had, as an alpha male, an extremely protective and patriarchal quality about him. He protected the weak of his group and punished aggression. He always positioned himself, it seemed, so that all of his group was in his sight. He played with the juveniles and groomed the nursing mothers. He was, in every respect, the perfect alpha male.

An alpha male chimpanzee's life is a stressful one. In addition to the duties of protecting his group members, he must also maintain his power. He accomplishes this with displays of power and by politically engaging with his group members, especially the females. The females of a chimpanzee group have the power in deciding who is in charge. They form alliances behind a particular male and that male gains status based on this alliance. If the alliance is powerful enough, he can gain enough status to overthrow the sitting alpha male's alliance. Thus, an alpha male must constantly maintain his coalition with the females of the group. In addition, he must constantly make a show to both the females and the males that he is still powerful enough to

---

* The look Higgy would give you, as one of my coworkers once put it, was as if he was staring straight into your soul. He never let me forget who was in charge. If he ever followed one of my commands it was at his discretion, not mine.

hold his position. He does this by creating awesome displays of power. These displays may include wild, ritualized movements, branch shaking, loud vocalizations, and any other visual, vocal, or tactile means of intimidation and spectacle. These displays have the ability to solidify an alliance, intimidate potential opponents, and secure a male's position within the group. However, if another male performs a stronger display, the alpha's power may begin to wane.

Displays are an extremely important feature in wild chimpanzee communication. Because the social hierarchy is so important to the survival of a group of chimpanzees, these displays have evolved to an extreme complexity. To us, these displays look violent and extraordinary. To a chimpanzee, the display is an identifying characteristic of an individual. Males and females will display to cement their place within the hierarchy. While far from being the only feature that determines an individual's status, display is the feature that advertises and confirms that status. To a chimpanzee, a display communicates an enormous amount of information.*

In all of the following accounts, everything that occurs is based on the perception of an individual and how that perception is transmitted to another. Communication, itself, is based on perception. It is what enables us to make sense out of the information surrounding us. Information, by itself, is incomprehensible. It takes the cognitive process of perception to understand the information, relate to the information, and survive around the information. In all of the following accounts, actions occur based on an individual's perception of information and how that perception is transmitted from one individual to the next. The problem, of course, is that when two individuals have different perceptions of the same information, the results can be disastrous. Perception

---

* By all accounts, Higgy was extremely adept at displays at an early age. He would later pass this ability on to his offspring, eventually to his detriment.

evolves with a species and helps that species survive the ecology unique to it. Without perception, everything is dark.

1975
Loxahatchee, Florida

The sun had begun to rise over the canal. As the light spread out over the sky, it illuminated the road surrounding the canal. The road, at that time of the morning, was empty and silent. In a few hours it would be littered with the station wagons and leisure vans of tourists who had come to see the animals at the park. As the sun climbed further, the canal became baked in the morning light. Popping their heads out of the water were hippos.* The sun had now disconnected itself from the horizon and was illuminating the entire area, including the large horseshoe-shaped island in the middle of the canal. On this island were a few cement culverts and a few large hills. Sitting on top of one of the hills were ten chimpanzees, all facing the western edge of the animal preserve. In the center of the group, with the rising sun at her back, was the oldest chimpanzee with a burlap sack around her head, Little Mama.

Little Mama, like the others, was staring off into the direction of a low rumbling sound. The cause of the sound was not clear. What was clear to the chimpanzees, however, was that something was out of the ordinary.

Like all cognitive organisms, Little Mama and her group-mates were in a constant state of perceiving the information that surrounded them. The information Little Mama was perceiving was changing with each moment. In fact, the information of concern went from being

---

* Some years later, the park had wisely decided that hippos were a rather dangerous addition to the preserve. They were, at first, moved away from the chimpanzees. Finally they were sent away from the park completely.

purely auditory to visual as the rumbling sound gave way to the appearance of a line of yellow machines. There were a large crane, two bulldozers, and several pickup trucks.

I imagine, at this point, that when the construction equipment had approached the shore of the canal, a construction worker would have jumped out of one of the trucks and looked over at the chimpanzee island (anytime there was a job to do around the chimp islands, the workers doing the job would be fascinated by the chimps). The man, like Little Mama, would also be perceiving information. The information he would perceive was that there were ten chimpanzees very close to where he had to work. This was going to make his job difficult and potentially dangerous.

The construction worker and Little Mama were both understanding the information around them through the irremovable filter of perception; each perceiving information in a manner unique to their species. Perception is the way our brains are genetically hardwired to combine bits of information and transform them into an idea. These ideas form the basis of what we perceive as reality. Our understanding of the world around us is the product of how our brains have encoded the information we have come into contact with.*

By information, I don't just mean a set of facts about an entity or idea. Information is not only all matter, actions, sensations, and notions but also the sum total of everything about all matter, actions, sensations, and notions. It is everything about what they are, what they have been, what they will become, where they are, and when they are. Our human brain has evolved to be able to fuse bits of

---

* The best description I know of information, in its physical sense, comes from the great physicist Leonard Susskind. His book *The Black Hole War* gives the following definition of information: "the data that distinguish one state of affairs from another." He goes on to detail what happens when information goes through a black hole.

information together into relatable concepts. This evolution has occurred based on the needs of our species over the course of our
natural history. Because of this, perceptions are specific to a particular species. Chimpanzees see the world in a chimpanzee way. Humans see the world in a human way. Hippos see the world in a hippo
way.

Both Little Mama and the construction worker perceived the
information of each other's presence. Both perceived the information in a way that their brains could understand. Both were utilizing
the knowledge of the information around them to plan their next
moves.

The construction worker's next move probably would have been to
vocalize. "Aye Aye Aye Aaaayeeeeeeee," he would have cried in his
best "monkey" voice.

Little Mama's next move would have been to ignore the man and
concentrate on the large yellow crane which had parked itself in the
middle of the large field beside the island.

Anytime I have ever witnessed construction occurring beside the
chimp islands, I've watched as the chimps studied the equipment and
the workers. It would always make me wonder what was going on inside their heads. Did they know what the equipment was? Were they
trying to figure out what was going to be built? Were they excited to
see a new creation?

On that day a group of zookeepers in a zebra-striped truck appeared in the section behind the construction workers. Taking care of
the chimpanzees was a dangerous job. During these years, in order to
feed the chimps, a keeper had to row a tiny boat across the canal to the
island. On the way, the hippos would attempt to capsize the boat to get
the food and attack the keeper. If the keeper was lucky enough to make
it to the island, he had to dump food on one end of the horseshoe then
paddle over to the other side to quickly clean before the chimps could

make it around the island. This usually took several tries before any cleaning was accomplished.*

The keepers had come out to distract the chimps away from what was about to occur beside them. They got into the rowboat, which had been docked on the shore of the canal. One of the keepers rowed over to the other side of the horseshoe with a large bag of doughnuts. Dumping the doughnuts on the ground, he called to the chimpanzees. The air was quickly filled with chimpanzees happily chirping about the appearance of doughnuts. They ran over to the other side of the island and, for a brief moment, forgot about the yellow equipment beside them.

Little Mama, however, probably stayed perched on the hill looking out. Having been at the animal park for almost seven years, she would have begun to notice recent changes to her world. The biggest change was that, one year before, a new group of chimpanzees had moved to another island on the other side of the road. This group of chimpanzees was constantly being observed by a group of people taking notes and studying their actions.

The new group had been taken from a few different National Institutes of Health laboratories. They had been used, for the most part, in hepatitis research and they were being studied to see if chimpanzees who had spent their entire lives in the solitary confines of a biomedical laboratory could ever be introduced to the outside and live with other chimpanzees.† So far the project had been fraught with problems. One of the lab chimps had been eaten by one of the hippos. Another had been so affected by his time alone in a dark cage that he was afraid of everything. One of the females had a habit of

---

* To add to their misery, the tiny rowboat had a massive hole in it. It was a race against time to get to the island before you fell victim to either a sinking ship or a hippo.

†The study was done as part of the great Linda Koebner's graduate work. Linda would go on to found Chimp Haven, a sanctuary for ex-lab chimps. The study was described in her book, *From Cage to Freedom.*

wading across the water and escaping every night. One of the males came down with a very violent illness (which he eventually recovered from).

Only the females of this group had ever really been socialized with other chimpanzees before. In laboratories females are frequently used for breeding while males remain purely test subjects. The two surviving females were in social control of the group. The males spent their days engaged in all sorts of aberrant behaviors such as rocking back and forth and overgrooming themselves.

Little Mama had taken to watching this group with interest. Each chimpanzee was a new addition to her world. She would call to them to no avail. However, she was content to sit and watch. This morning, as she watched the work trucks, the laboratory group was screaming and jumping up and down. This caused some stir among Little Mama's group, who looked up from their doughnuts, hooted a bit, and then continued to eat.

The crane moved closer to Little Mama's island and plopped its arm into the canal relatively close to the shore. Though it was probably not close enough for any of the chimps to actually jump on it, Little Mama took notice. She vocalized loudly to the other chimpanzees. The chimps, hearing her call, immediately realized the situation with the crane, dropped their doughnuts, and ran over toward the crane arm. Little Mama had successfully communicated the information she had perceived.

Animals that depend on socialization for survival, such as primates, rely on information being transmitted between individuals. This is, of course, communication. When Little Mama was watching the crane, she was perceiving an array of information: the crane, the distance of the crane to the island, the desires of her group-mates to jump on the crane, and the fact that her group-mates were not paying attention. She encoded all of this information into a transmittable signal (a vocalization) and transmitted it through the air where it was picked up by the other chimpanzees.*

Unfortunately for the chimps, the vocalization also alerted the zookeepers and the construction staff. After some quick shouting, the crane quickly moved its arm away. At that point all of the keepers got into the rowboat. One of them held a fire extinguisher (the sound and cloud would frighten the chimps back), one held a net, and one held a dart gun. They rowed over to the island and yelled at the chimps to move back. When the chimps moved, the keepers got out of their boat and stood in front of the crane.

Guarding the crane, one of the keepers shouted at the construction workers to get started and to hurry. Their hands were trembling on their fire extinguisher and nets, and the keepers kept their eyes glued on the group of chimpanzees. Each time a chimp would get up, one keeper would shout and another would raise the gun.†

Little Mama was too interested in the movement of the machines to join in the standoff with the keepers. She watched as the crane dug into the ground by the canal. She watched as the canal water flowed

---

* A communication event takes the following form: first information is perceived by the brain into an understandable concept. This concept is known as a "sign." Next, the sign is encoded into a transmittable signal. A signal can take an auditory form such as a vocalization or, in the case of humans, a word. A signal can also be a gesture. Chimpanzees, like humans and other apes, have evolved through their facial musculature an enormous array of facial gestures which can all carry a sign. A signal can also be tactile, such as grooming, a hug, or anything else involving contact. Finally, a signal can be chemical. A chemical signal can involve scent marking or any other chemical transmission that can be smelled or tasted. Once the sign is encoded into a signal, a channel must be chosen. Such a channel can be a tree brach for a scent marking, the atmosphere for an auditory call, a visual sightline for a gesture, etc. Once the signal is put into this channel, the receiver picks it up and decodes the signal back into its original sign. The understanding of a sign, the ability to turn a sign into a certain signal, and the choice of channel are all specific to a particular species. Hence the fallacy of attempting to communicate with a nonhuman species by using a human communication system.

† The events of the construction of this island have kindly been recounted to me by wildlife director Terry Wolf.

into the areas the crane would dig. She watched as the crane continued to do this in a large circle. A new chimpanzee island was being created beside Little Mama's island. More chimpanzees were to come out to the section. Little Mama's social world of chimpanzees was about to grow exponentially. The section was about to get a lot louder.

Across the park, Higgy sat in his nursery pen playing with Cindy. Cindy was tackling and tickling him. Higgy was laughing. The other four chimpanzees sat and watched the two of them play. Higgy got up and walked over to the other chimpanzees and put his hand on the head of one of the males. The chimp hooted at Higgy. Higgy hooted back. Higgy, at his very young age, had become a bit of a leader in the nursery pen. His status had helped Cindy's relationship with the other chimps.

Higgy's world was very small. It consisted of three walls, a large window, and five chimpanzees. He had no concept of the other chimpanzees on the island, the construction going on beside their island, or that they were building his future kingdom—a kingdom where he would command a group, raise juveniles, pass along behaviors, and pass along a lexicon.

At the same time, something was being observed in the mountains of Africa which would give science its first taste of how a chimpanzee, like Higgy, could transmit and pass down learned behaviors. It would be a discovery which would highlight the notion that what chimpanzees were doing on their own was far more fascinating than what we could train them to do.

1975
Mahale Mountains, Tanzania

The two young primatologists stood very still as they watched what was transpiring in front of them. One of them whispered notes into his cassette recorder. The other clicked away at her camera to document the event. Both knew the implications of what they had been witnessing over the last two weeks.

In front of them, two chimpanzees from a group known to them as the Kajabala group had come to greet each other. A female, identified as Chausiku, approached another female, identified as Wakasila. When they approached each other, they simultaneously raised their arms over their heads and clasped each other's wrists. They began to mutually groom the underside of the other's arm. This led to a full grooming session.

This was the fourteenth occurrence of this social custom that the two of them had seen in the Kajabala group. The reason that it was so noteworthy was that this type of greeting had never been witnessed in another chimpanzee group. In fact, other groups in western Tanzania, who had been studied for two decades prior, had never been seen doing such a ritual. Due to the fact that this had been witnessed so many times in such a short period of time, the two primatologists had concluded that they were witnessing a learned pattern of behavior unique to a particular social group. Such learned behaviors are the seeds of culture.*

Furthermore, what they were witnessing was a communication event. Grooming fulfills a role in transmitting information from one individual to another. It carries a message such as "we are aligned," "the situation is calm," "I am not feeling aggressive toward you," etc. By grooming each other in a way unique to one particular social group, these chimpanzees were showing that they had learned a method of communication from their group and that this method was being passed down.

The transmission of information through a learned mechanism is

---

* The two primatologists were William McGrew and Caroline Tutin. The study was groundbreaking and still continues to influence new studies. McGrew would go on to study evidence of cultural traits in chimpanzees as a "cultural primatologist." His sometimes controversial studies are always fascinating to read. His book *The Cultured Chimpanzee: Reflections on Cultural Primatology* is a classic of field primatology.

the basis for symbolic communication. These chimpanzees were attaching a learned label (grasping wrists) to information that they were attempting to transmit (the information that this particular type of grooming represented). This learned label is, in fact, a symbol for this information. Chausiku and Wakasila were communicating with a symbol. This wasn't occurring in a laboratory or under the training of a researcher. This was occurring in the wild without any human interference. This was occurring to fulfill an ecological role for a group of chimpanzees, not to impress a group of scientists.*

1976
Loxahatchee, Florida

There were now four islands in the preserve of the animal park. There was the large horseshoe-shaped island that Little Mama and her group inhabited. Then there was the new island which had been constructed beside Little Mama's. This island contained new chimpanzees that had been brought to the park. Also there was the island across the road from Little Mama's. This island contained the ex-laboratory chimpanzees. Finally, there was an abandoned island far removed from the other three islands. This island was across from zebras and rhinos and was out of sight from the other chimpanzees. It was about to be filled.

The zookeepers had finished preparing all five animal carriers. Together, they carried each carrier to the backs of three different trucks. After all five were loaded, the keepers went into the hospital

---

* As we watch chimpanzees routinely fail at symbolic communication in the laboratory, it's important to remember that what occurs in a laboratory is not indicative of what occurs in the wild. The natural behavior of chimpanzees lends itself to symbolic understanding in a much more compelling way than watching a chimpanzee attach labels onto symbols in a lab.

and discussed the logistics of what was about to happen. The keepers would get the five chimpanzees in one pen and shut the door. The vet would then go in and one by one shoot each chimpanzee with a dart. After all five chimpanzees were down, the keepers would drag them out of the pen and close each of them in their respective animal carriers. Once this was accomplished, they would decide on how to proceed. The keepers and the vet walked over to the nursery.

Inside the nursery, in one pen sat Cindy, Higgy, and a new two-year-old juvenile named Peter. In the other pen sat Clumsy, Michael, Romeo, and Bashful.

In order to get Cindy with the others, a keeper called to her and held out a $100,000 Bar in the other pen. Seeing a candy bar, Cindy leapt to her feet and ran over to the other pen. Higgy began to follow her, but as soon as Cindy was completely in the other pen the other keeper slammed the other door shut. Higgy and Peter were stranded on the other side.

Cindy screamed and ran at the sliding door. She hit the door as hard as she could but it wouldn't open. On the other side of the door, Higgy rocked back and forth angrily. He started hooting at the door loudly.

As Cindy cowered in the corner, the large door opened. In the doorway stood the vet with the dart gun. He aimed the dart gun at Clumsy and pulled the trigger. The dart hit Clumsy in the side. She screamed. The door closed. A few seconds later the door opened again. This time the vet pointed the gun at one of the males and shot, hitting him. The door closed again. When the door opened the next time, Cindy lunged at the vet. The vet yelled and the door closed quickly. Cindy went back to the sliding door and tried to open it again. In a few moments, the large door reopened. Cindy turned to lunge at the vet again. Before she could, a net was placed over her and one of the keepers grabbed both her arms and squeezed. The vet jabbed a needle in one arm. Within seconds, Cindy lost consciousness.

Cindy awoke to find herself in an open cage. Outside the cage was grass and sunlight. She slowly sat up and looked outside. In the distance were trees. She crawled out of the cage. Looking around revealed that she was on an island surrounded by water. There were four other cages besides her own. She ran over to each cage and inspected them. Inside the cages she found the three males from the nursery and Clumsy, all of them sleeping. She hooted at each one of them before searching around for Higgy. Across the water, she saw the vet and three zoo-keepers. In an effort to get to them, she stepped in the water. The feeling of the water on her foot was strange and unsettling. She quickly jumped back onto the island. A feeling of intense grogginess came over her and she began to stumble. She crawled back into her cage and passed out.

She woke up to the sounds of the other chimps screaming and hooting. She looked outside of her cage to see one of the males running back and forth clapping and screaming. Clumsy was screaming at the male and holding out her hand to him. When Cindy walked out of the cage, Clumsy immediately walked over to her and slapped her on the back of the head. Cindy let out a yelp and ran to the other side of the island.

Looking out over the water, Cindy saw that the zookeepers were still watching them. Cindy ran out into the water and held out her hand to them. As she held out her hand, she made her raspberry sound. Without warning, Clumsy ran up behind her and pushed her completely into the water. Cindy sank to the bottom like a stone. She tried to jump up to get her head out of the water, but was unable to. She went to the bottom of the shore and began pulling herself along the weeds to the shallow area. She stood up and ran back onto the shore. She made her way to the middle of the island and sat down among the screaming group of chimpanzees.

Cindy and the other juveniles had been moved to the isolated island deep in the animal preserve. The reason for the move was that the five of them were getting far too large to be held by a nursery pen. Also, with the addition of Peter to the nursery, the pen was too small to hold all of them. Initially they were going to be placed on the new island beside Little Mama. Instead, the park had acquired more adult chimpanzees and it was thought best to place the adults near each other and the juveniles by themselves. Thus, the juveniles ended up on this island beside rhinos and zebras in another section of the preserve.

While this was occurring on the outside islands, Higgy was sitting in the nursery pen with Peter.* Occasionally he would walk around and search for Cindy. Everywhere Higgy walked, Peter followed like a shadow. Higgy would constantly stop and gazed out the window. Cindy was nowhere in sight.

1978
San Francisco, California

The finishing touches on the documentary film *Koko: A Talking Gorilla* had been completed. In the film, Dr. Francine Patterson claimed Koko had a vocabulary of over three hundred signs, well eclipsing the supposed achievements of Washoe. The film, complete with scenes of Koko being tickled and laughing, would quickly endear the world to Koko and make celebrities of both the gorilla and her trainer.

Washoe was also featured in the film; however, in light of Patterson's claimed successes with Koko, the chimpanzee seemed old news throughout the film. Both animals captured the imagination of the viewing public. The film would go on to be an enormously popular documentary.

---

* When I first encountered Peter, I was told that he "knew and used" American Sign Language. I was disappointed to find that all Peter did was smack himself in the face when he wanted a treat. The keepers had taken this to mean that he was signing "eat."

Between the film and the celebrity of the two language-trained apes, the question of whether an ape could learn a human language seemed solved. The claims of Koko and Washoe had both shown the public that apes were able to speak just like humans.*

What the world didn't know is that at the same time Herbert Terrace was finishing up the revisions on his paper detailing Project Nim. This paper, entitled "Can an Ape Create a Sentence?," would forever cast a shadow over both projects. It was only a matter of time before both the scientific community and the public at large would abandon the antics of Project Koko and Project Washoe.

The public's interest in chimpanzees, however, had not waned. In fact, chimpanzee exhibits were some of the most popular in zoos. This was especially true at the animal park in Florida, where Higgy had become a star in his own right.

1979
Loxahatchee, Florida

Higgy's nursery had become the most popular attraction at the animal park. Even at his young age of six, Higgy was an intimidating figure. His hair stood up, he started walking with his trademark swagger, and he seemed in control of his surroundings. He would perform awesome displays in the nursery pens to the amazement of the viewing public. Though his friend, Peter, would attempt displays, his never seemed to garner the adulation of Higgy's.

As the crowd watched Higgy and Peter attempting to outdo each other with their displays, three zookeepers, in a hurry, pushed past

---

* There are few things more depressing than watching *Koko: A Talking Gorilla*. I encourage everyone to watch the film and draw their own conclusions.

the crowd. They rushed into the area behind the nursery pens to retrieve nets and a cage. Alerted that the cage and net may be for him, Higgy stopped his display and watched. He stayed on guard as the keepers rushed out of the nursery toward their trucks. Assured that the danger was not his own, Higgy returned to his display.

The keepers jumped in their trucks and raced out to the preserve. They drove past the new island and the new group. They drove past the laboratory chimp group. They drove past Little Mama's group. Moments later they arrived at their destination, the isolated chimp island.

Surveying the island, they saw what had been reported by one of the guests. Cindy was sitting in the middle of the island with the infant she had given birth to a week earlier. She was trying to hold the infant on her back, but to no avail. The infant kept sliding off.

A week ago, the baby had been a surprise to the zookeepers. Due to Cindy's extremely large size, no one had realized that she was pregnant. When a keeper had come out to feed the chimps, she noticed that Cindy was carrying a newborn infant on her chest. The father, though unknown, was most likely Romeo (he and Cindy had bonded since being moved to the island). The baby never seemed quite right to the zookeepers. She was never really gripping Cindy and seemed weak.

Throughout the week, the keepers monitored the newborn's progress. She seemed to progressively get worse. The other chimpanzees were also trying to take the baby from Cindy. Clumsy, in particular, had been keenly interested in Cindy's baby. At one point, Clumsy had tried to grab the infant. This led to a horrendous fight between Cindy and Clumsy, with Cindy carrying the baby in one arm as she fought.

On this morning, the keepers had seen the baby with Cindy while they were feeding the chimps. She was not looking good, but seemingly no worse than she had looked on the other days. As the keepers were in a different section, they got a report from a guest who had driven by Cindy's island. The report was that Cindy was holding up a dead baby chimp.

The zookeepers attempted to perceive the situation at hand. Four chimpanzees were at one side of the island, paying little attention to Cindy and her baby. Cindy was in the middle, examining her infant. As Cindy picked the baby back up, the zookeepers looked at them through binoculars. Clearly, the baby was dead. Somehow the keepers needed to retrieve the baby from Cindy. They loaded up the rowboat with the nets, cage, and fire extinguisher.

As the zookeepers rowed over to the island, Cindy understood what they were about to do. Grabbing her dead infant by the foot, she began climbing to the highest part of the island's shelter. As she climbed, she screamed at the keepers with a violent guttural cry. On top of the shelter, Cindy, once again, tried to get the baby to grasp onto her back. The baby fell from Cindy's back, off the shelter, and onto the ground below.

The keepers, who were on the island at this point, grabbed the baby, ran back to the boat, and pushed off the island. As the boat left the island, Cindy ran toward them. Running into the water, she screamed as she chased the keepers. They made it to the other end of the canal as Cindy stood, wailing, in waist-deep water.

1980
San Francisco, California

The letter, written by Francine Patterson to the *New York Review of Books,* had been sealed and sent. The letter was in response to positive reviews of the books *Speaking of Apes,* by Thomas Sebeok and Donna Jean Umiker-Sebeok, and *Nim,* by Herbert Terrace. Both books called into question Patterson's Project Koko and questioned the scientific validity of language-trained apes in general. Both books were becoming immensely popular.

The letter was not only an angry reaction to the skepticism leveled by Sebeok and the evidence against language-trained apes coming from Terrace, it was also motivated by the *New York Review of Books* giving both books a positive review. The letter was far from a point-by-point defense of Project Koko. Rather, it was a defensive tirade. It was filled with lines such as "I could not believe my eyes reading this" and references to Thomas Sebeok (one of the most prominent linguists of the time and founder of the semiotic approach to the study of animal communication)* as "ignorant" and was a rambling series of restated claims about Koko's abilities.

Patterson's defensive missive came at the heels of the wave started by Terrace's accounts of Project Nim. When Terrace published his study in 1979, it, in effect, exposed ape language-training projects as unscientific tricks that showed nothing of an ape's capacity for language. In the study he shows Nim, with rigorous controls and guards against cueing, able to learn symbols and labels but unable to piece these symbols together in any sort of grammatical fashion. His work was peer reviewed and was well reviewed by the scientific community.

The damage to the scientific validity of the studies had already been done. The popularity of these projects was waning. It would take a new gimmick for the world to embrace Koko again. Four years later, Koko would produce that gimmick when she would "ask" for a pet cat and get one. Once again, Koko would be on the screen.†

---

* Thomas Sebeok had coined the term "zoosemiotics" which is an objective approach to how animals (including humans) perceive signs and transmit them as signals. Knowing how unique the perception of signs is to each species, he naturally spotted the fallacies of attempting to teach a nonhuman primate to use a human system of signs.

†And how! Koko and her cat, "All Ball," would be featured in *National Geographic,* as the subject of a film called *Koko's Kitten,* and as the subject of at least one children's book. Little is known how any of this increased our understanding of an ape's capacity for human language.

1981
Loxahatchee, Florida

Higgy sat up and hooted to Peter. Once again, zookeepers were rushing into the nursery. Peter ran over to Higgy and sat alert. The keepers grabbed several nets and two cages. Higgy was still. The keepers finished gathering what they needed and rushed out of the nursery. Higgy looked at Peter and tackled him. Peter laughed.

The keepers rushed in their trucks out into the preserve. Once again, they raced past the lab chimps, raced past Little Mama, and raced past the new island to arrive at Cindy's island. This time, when they got out of the truck, they saw Cindy's latest offspring, a two-week-old infant, in the clutches of Clumsy.

Clumsy was sitting high above the shelter, holding Cindy's baby by one arm and dangling her high above the ground. Cindy was screaming and holding out her hand to Clumsy. The four males were racing around the island, hooting and jumping up and down. Every time Cindy attempted to climb up the shelter to get to Clumsy, one of the males would run up and tackle her.

The keepers pulled out binoculars and examined the situation. The baby was okay. She looked frightened but she was alive and clinging onto Clumsy's arm. The keepers knew that they had to retrieve the baby from Clumsy. They didn't, however, know how they were going to do this.

As they discussed the situation, a loud cry came from the infant. Cindy responded to the call and raced up the shelter. One of the males grabbed her. Cindy fought back. The two chimps tumbled down the island. They continued to bite at each other as they fell into the water. At this, the keepers rushed to their boat, dart guns in hand. The two chimpanzees crawled out of the water. Cindy, covered in blood and limping, was clearly injured.

The keepers loaded the cages and equipment into the boat and rowed over to the island. As they got closer, Cindy pulled herself completely out of the water. She crawled up the banks of the shore and one of the keepers fired a dart into her side. She was left to lose consciousness at the edge of the island.

Without Cindy getting in the way, the zookeepers' job was a bit easier. They rushed out onto the island holding their dart guns and nets. Clumsy screamed violently and shook the infant around by her arm. One keeper aimed a dart gun at the group of males, who were now staying at the far end of the island. Another keeper stood with a net below Clumsy and the infant, in case the infant was dropped. The third zookeeper aimed the dart gun at Clumsy.

Clumsy screamed and threw the infant high up in the air. The keeper with the net got under the baby and caught her in the net. The infant was quickly put into one of the cages. Cindy, who was now unconscious, was lifted and brought to the other cage. Both animals were going to be removed from the island until they could figure out what to do. The cages were loaded on the the boat and rowed ashore.*

The incident which had just taken place showed a far greater degree of complexity in communication than anything that had been shown (or even claimed) by Koko or Washoe. The kidnapping of Cindy's baby had been coordinated between the males and Clumsy. Each time Cindy would attempt to retrieve her infant, a male would stop her. That type of coordination takes extremely complex communication to achieve. We are left to wonder how Cindy's infant was abducted in the first place (since it was not recorded or witnessed). We can assume that since removing an infant from a mother chimpanzee

---

* Clumsy would later prove to be a murderous chimpanzee. She would give birth to a female named Two-Nine. The two of them would team up and abduct baby chimpanzees and kill them.

is a difficult task without help, the same type of coordinated attack took place. Finally there was the communicative yelp of the infant to Cindy. Cindy responded to the yelp with enough force to actually get partially up the shelter before she was pulled down by the male. The communication of information allowed for this behavioral event to take place and is a glimpse of how chimpanzees use communication to behave together and survive their surroundings.

Cindy and her infant spent the next few days recovering in the veterinary hospital. During this time, it was determined that Cindy would not be returned to her old group. She was clearly not getting along with them. For her safety, as well as the safety of the infant, it was decided that Cindy and her baby would go live out on the new island with the most recently formed group of chimpanzees at the park.

Four days after the incident with Clumsy, Cindy was moved to the new island. Her initial mixing with the new chimpanzees was difficult. There were the necessary fights followed by grooming sessions within this new group. However, these chimpanzees were far less aggressive with Cindy than her last group had been.

There seemed to be an initial communication barrier between Cindy and her new group. When the group would attempt to communicate with Cindy (or vice versa) the transmission would fail. Calls that elicited a certain response from Cindy elicited an entirely different response from a member of her new group. There were also the strange communicative sounds and gestures Cindy would make. None of the other chimpanzees knew how to take the raspberry sound and they certainly didn't understand what she wanted when she tapped on her head or folded out her lower lip. In time, the two communication systems would fuse together and Cindy would be able to communicate with her new group.*

---

* The advantages to having a communication system which can only be understood by your group would have enormous ecological implications. Such implications show why this

A few mornings after being moved to the new island, Cindy awoke to find that her baby had died in the night. The zookeepers would find the baby a few hours later when they came out to feed the chimps.

There was another female on Cindy's new island that had an infant. This new infant was of great interest to Cindy, especially after the death of her second baby. Cindy would gently approach the mother and infant. The mother would allow Cindy to touch and examine the baby. When the mother had enough, she would clutch the baby and walk away from Cindy. At this, Cindy would usually follow the pair around. If she ever became too intrusive, the mother chimp would give an angry hoot to Cindy, who would then back away.

One morning Cindy walked over to the mother and infant who were still sleeping. She touched the baby and examined her in her usual way. The mother woke up a bit to see what was going on. She saw that it was just Cindy and went back to sleep. Cindy put her hands around the baby and slowly pulled her from her mother. The baby screamed. The mother opened her eyes to see Cindy holding the infant. The mother screamed at Cindy. Cindy took the baby and ran. The entire group, by this time, was alerted to what was happening. They all began to chase Cindy around the island. Cindy clutched the baby tight and ran up the shelter to the highest point. She held the baby out and screamed.*

Meanwhile, across the park, Higgy and Peter were, once again, alerted to zookeepers rushing through the nursery looking for nets and cages. Higgy hooted loudly at the keepers as they came through.

---

phenomenon is naturally selected in so many primate species—culminating, of course, in human language.

* According to the records, Cindy only attempted to abduct an infant one time. Infant abduction occurs in most primate species. It is a misunderstanding to view it as having some universal purpose. Males will abduct infants to keep females, who are out of their alliance, from gaining more status (having an infant tends to increase a female's status). Some females, such as Cindy, will abduct an infant in order to raise the baby as their own. Still others, such as Clumsy, may just be murderers.

The public watched as Higgy created a massive display in his pen. The display caused Peter to become frightened and run to the other pen. Higgy ceased his display and watched as the zookeepers rushed out of the nursery to their trucks.

When the keepers approached the island, Cindy was still screaming on top of the shelter holding the infant. The other chimps had surrounded her on the ground and were looking up at her. The mother of the infant was screaming as well.

The keepers loaded up their boats and rowed toward the island. Cindy saw as the keepers came near. When they got close enough, Cindy threw the baby at the keepers' boat. One of the keepers caught the infant in his hands. The mother rushed over to the approaching boat. The keeper tossed the baby over to her mother. Fearing an angry retaliation, the zookeepers quickly paddled away. The other chimpanzees lunged at Cindy and threw her off the shelter.

By evening, peace had been restored on the island. Cindy was grooming the mother and had been accepted back into the group. When she was done grooming, Cindy walked over to the edge of the water and looked at the island next to her. Sitting across the water was Little Mama. The keepers watched as Cindy called out to her with a raspberry. Little Mama called back to her with a hoot. Cindy walked to the shelter and returned with an armful of straw. She made her nest beside the water. Little Mama did the same.*

---

* I used to love watching chimpanzees form relationships across the canal. Two chimpanzees I worked with would try to outdo each other across the canal by performing these amazing water displays. The displays would consist of a chimpanzee getting into waist-deep water and violently splashing around in a rhythm. It would amaze me how polite these exchanges were. When one was water displaying, the other would sit patiently across the water and watch. In another, very Shakespearean relationship, Peter was seemingly obsessed with a female across the canal. He would constantly wait for her to walk over to the shore and sit across from him. When his group would get fed, he would gather many of the preferred foods and throw them across the water to her. The female was quick to take advantage of his affections.

The next day, in front of Higgy's window, the director of the park was having a conversation with the zookeepers. The chimpanzee nursery was to be shut down. The chimpanzees inside had to be moved to an island. The director left it up to the keepers to figure out how to integrate the juvenile chimps with the rest of the population.

Peter wasn't going to be a problem. He could even be mixed with the group Cindy was with. Higgy, on the other hand, was a different story. The keepers knew that Higgy's dominant personality was going to be a problem. He was never going to submit to another alpha male. This would lead to battles and all sorts of injuries. It was decided that they would put Higgy out on an abandoned island and form a group around him with females. This would be his own group. They would have to choose females that wouldn't challenge Higgy for power. The first female that came to mind was Little Mama.

In the nursery, as Higgy vocalized to Peter, one zookeeper vocalized to another zookeeper. The guests outside the window vocalized to each other. On the other end of the park, Cindy vocalized to Little Mama. All of them were transmitting their own perception of the world, their own perception of the environment, and their own perception of information—all of them trusting that these perceptions were reality.

Each of us is so certain in our perceptions that we fail to grant that there may be other understandings of the same reality. We make broad and sweeping declarations, statements, and accounts of how the world works based on our own limited perceptions, never taking into account that these perceptions represent only our infinitesimally small understanding. We fail to grasp that there may be understandings outside the realm of our human comprehension. We see human perception as the ultimate benchmark of reality without seeing the limitations of our own cognitive functions. We don't accept that these perceptions are merely the product of an evolutionary process that developed the most survivable way to conceptualize our surroundings.

We are so sure, in fact, of our human view of reality that we impose our perceptions on other species. When another species fails to comprehend our understandings (as we would fail to comprehend theirs), we see that species as "below" us.

Soon, Little Mama and Higgy would be vocalizing together. They would use these mutually understood vocalizations to build a communication system of the group that would endure for decades. This communication system would be based on a chimpanzee understanding of the world and built by chimpanzee personal histories. Those that watched the chimpanzees would view this communication as nothing more than hoots and pants. They wouldn't understand that the hooting and pants they were hearing was a system of transmitting information every bit as complex as their own. They would watch, but not understand, that the chimpanzees in front of them were building a lexicon.

The world is my idea.

—ARTHUR SCHOPENHAUER

4

Gin

The screams and cries of a man perceiving imminent danger to himself reveal the foundations of his place in the natural world. These are the alarm calls of the human species. They have been granted to us, through biology, for being a member of the primate order. Thanks to their existence, primates have survived and thrived in their environment for the last 65 million years. They stand as a rare exception to primate behaviors in that alarm calls require no socialization or learning to be unlocked.

As with humans, the screams and cries of a chimpanzee's alarm call showcase the raw and unsocialized form of the individual. Unlike most chimpanzee vocalizations, alarm calls are not learned or acquired by experience, but genetically complete at birth. Alarm calls, however, are an exception to the rule. As with most behaviors, most chimpanzee vocalizations must be fashioned by experiences with other chimpanzees.

In 1981, the animal park was about to be introduced to another chimpanzee with no prior experience with other chimpanzees. This female chimpanzee, named Gin, would behave in a way that was unlike other chimpanzees. She would vocally communicate in the only way she was able to—the calls that required no learning or acquisition: unstructured screams and alarm calls.

Unlike Gin, the behaviors of Little Mama, Cindy, and Higgy were molded by social experiences. Though born into their worlds with the genetics necessary for survival (including the genetics for social behavior and communication), it was necessary for the chimps to socialize with others in order for these features to be unlocked.

It is tempting, at this point, to view this as a dichotomy of "nature" versus "nurture"—to think of who the chimps were at birth as their nature and to think of what the chimps had acquired as how they were nurtured. However, both are part of biology and a part of nature. How the primate brain processes experiences and how it uses these experiences to adapt to the given environment they find themselves born into is a biological adaptation. Acquisition and learning have evolved like any other biological traits.

As primates, we are genetically hardwired to acquire what we experience around us as we develop. We acquire methods of behaving with others, methods of parenting, methods of eating, methods of surviving the elements unique to our area, methods of creating, and methods of communicating. In this, we see that everything we learn and everything we create is merely a process of achieving biological fitness. It is a process that has allowed primates to adapt to an array of environments through socialization and learning.*

---

* Human culture is very much a part of this. As humans, we tend to view ourselves as separate and above the rest of the world through our use of specialized culture to adapt to our surroundings. Human culture is just another biological adaptation that humans have acquired through natural selection.

In order to truly explore what this process is and how it evolved over time, we must put it into context. In this, we'll see where it fits in with the rest of the natural world. Imagine that the entire timeline of the history of the earth is laid out across the United States. Let's put that timeline along Interstate 10, stretching from Jacksonville, Florida, to Los Angeles, California. The distance of Interstate 10 is roughly 2,430 miles. To accommodate the 4.6 billion year timeline of the earth's history, we'll let every 270 miles represent 500 million years.*

If we let Jacksonville represent the beginning of the earth and Los Angeles represent the present day, the first thing we'll notice is that humans don't diverge from the rest of the apes until about 3 miles before you reach Los Angeles. Modern humans develop a few blocks away from the center of the city. All of recorded human history would fit within the last 1/500th of a mile. However, if we look way back to about Gulfport, Mississippi, we can see the beginning of this process evolving. In fact, we'll see it with the very first living organisms on the earth.

About 3.7 billion years ago, the only living organism on the earth would have been single-cell prokaryote organisms (simple cells without a nucleus). No one knows for sure exactly what this organism would have been but we can make a guess, based on the state of the earth at the time. We can assume that it would have resembled and behaved much like bacteria do today. If you were to place a single bacterium in a nutrient-rich environment and wait for twenty-four hours, you would find that the bacteria have spawned billions of offspring. These offspring would be genetically identical to their parent. However, as the offspring encountered different environments, they

---

* Earth has always been the domain of the microscopic. In our timeline, visible life doesn't appear until Phoenix, Arizona.

would be able to chemically alter themselves into a more adaptable form. In this we see a living organism altering its essence to exist in a given environment.

Though we see a process of the external world causing an internal biological change, we aren't seeing it in a purely social form yet. Let's jump ahead on our timeline/map to Fort Stockton, Texas. It is here that we see the first complex single-cell organisms develop. With these organisms we begin to see complex behavior that depends a great deal on socialization. In fact, microbes such as these are shown to exhibit group-specific behaviors which increase their fitness in any given environment. Microbes in one environment will interact in one way while microbes in another environment will interact differently.* At this point, if you were to follow our timeline, you would begin to see the combination of social behaviors and the ability to alter individual constitutions and dispositions increase exponentially with each evolutionary step.

Now, let's jump way ahead in our metaphoric journey. By driving all the way to about 30 miles outside of Los Angeles, we move forward to just about 55 million years ago.† Imagine that you are standing in central Africa in the midst of a forest. In front of you is a large fruit tree with several different types of mammals occupying it. Most of these species are rodent-type animals. They are scurrying up and down the tree with relatively little regard for each other. As you look more closely into the tree, you begin to notice another type of mammal. These animals are in an almost constant state of interaction with

---

* For an extremely interesting account of microbial social behavior, read Gregory Velicer's article "Social strife in the microbial world" in *Trends in Microbiology* (2003).

† The beginnings of the primate order can be traced to at least 10 million years prior to that. However, these ancestral primates of 65 million years ago would not have been as noticeably different, in terms of eye placement and hand morphology, as they were 55 million years ago.

each other. They are touching each other, smelling each other, and calling to one another. They are moving extremely dexterously through the tree, leaping with ease and great accuracy from one branch to another. You also notice that they are feeding off of very small and very fast insects. You look for reasons as to why these mammals seem to be eating and moving so much more successfully than the other mammals. The first thing you notice are their hands which can grab hold of branches, allowing them to climb and maneuver through the tree very effectively. The next thing you notice is that their eyes are closer together than the other mammals in the tree. As we have already explored, this is allowing them to focus both eyes on the same scene giving them an extremely refined sense of depth perception. This depth perception is allowing them to correctly judge both the location of the tree branches and the small, fast-moving insects. These animals that you are seeing are early primates.

As you watch them, one of the primates descends to the ground. At the same time, you notice a large cat approaching from behind. At this point you begin to see, firsthand, the costs of having eyes close together. This primate is unaware of the silent cat behind him because his eyes are focused to the front. What he has gained in depth perception, he has lost in peripherals. As the cat gets closer, you brace yourself for the inevitable. Instead, one of the other primates calls out to him with a short, loud yelp. Instantly, the primate on the ground leaps to safety. In addition to this, the rest of the group scatters, leaving the big cat without prey.

What you have just witnessed is a primate alarm call. Alarm calls are the purely genetic root of all other vocal forms of communication in primates. The physical situation of primates losing their peripheral vision necessitates living in a social group. A primate's survival depends on having a close-knit group that will warn him of any danger approaching in his peripherals. Developing along with this social group is the primary alarm call which is a universal signal of imminent danger within a species. Infants, at birth, can both understand and create an alarm call. The alarm call, along with social behavior, is biology's compensation for the loss of peripheral vision.*

Primate alarm calls are extremely complex, despite the fact that they don't rely on learning or acquisition to be transmitted. I spend part of my year on the volcanic island of Ometepe, Nicaragua, studying the alarm calls of capuchin monkeys. What is incredibly fascinating about a capuchin alarm call is that it is specific to the predator it is signifying. There is a marked difference between the calls that signify predators in the air vérsus the calls that signify predators on the ground. Furthermore, there are more subtle differences in signifying exactly which predator it is. These significations are genetically understood and cause the appropriate defensive response within the species. In this way we see biology passing down a complex communication system without the aid of social learning.†

The ecological need for alarm calls has given rise to other calls. These more complex calls do, in fact, depend on socialization to be passed on. While the calls aren't signifying such grave and immediate concerns as alarm calls, their use and function is no less important to the survival of a species. These are the group-specific vocalizations

---

* The chimpanzees of Higgy's group live close to the docking port of a blimp. Anytime a blimp is needed, it must fly over the chimp islands, causing great distress in Higgy's group. Before the blimp is even in sight, the chimps begin to make an alarm call. Within seconds, almost every chimpanzee is alarm calling in unison at the blimp in the sky. Sometimes these alarm calls are coupled with throwing sticks at the sky and jumping up toward the blimp. For some reason, only the blimp elicits this response. Planes, helicopters, ultra-light gliders, and remote-control UFOs have all flown over the island to no response.

† Fascinating work has been done by Con Slobodchikoff concerning prairie dog alarm calls. According to Slobodchikoff, extremely specific information is transmitted in these calls. Prairie dogs are able to convey information about the characteristics of predators such as appearance. In fact, in experiments, prairie dogs were able to transmit information about the shirt color of humans they were calling about! (See Slobodchikoff et al., 1991.)

that some primate species use. The ability to create them, learn them, and use them is granted to a species through biology and natural history. Species depend on these communication systems for survival just as keenly as they depend on alarm calls. Human language is one such communication system. The lexicon of Higgy's group is another such communication system.

If individuals are secluded from socialization, they are left only with what is purely genetic. Such a chimpanzee was about to be thrown into the world of Little Mama, Cindy, and Higgy. The presence of this chimpanzee would forever alter both the social direction and the lexicon of the group she was about to join.

Little Mama, Cindy, and Higgy were about to encounter something entirely different from themselves. Who they were about to meet was a chimpanzee without the seasoning of socialization. They were about to meet a chimpanzee in her most raw and unpredictable form. They were about to meet Gin.

The ability to socially acquire traits allows us to alter our given natures in order to meld in with our environment and social group. These learned traits act like a smokescreen, concealing our at-birth selves from the rest of the world. With each learned or acquired trait the smokescreen gets thicker, allowing us to adapt more and more successfully with what is around us. Gin existed as a chimpanzee without that smokescreen. Her presence existed as savage behavior, savage vocalizations, and savage mind.

1981
Loxahatchee, Florida

Two men got out of the zebra-striped truck and looked over at the island. The situation was just as precarious as had been reported. The curator looked over at the keeper. The keeper began assessing the situation and trying to figure out how he was going to handle it.

At this point, it becomes necessary to introduce this zookeeper. His name is Terry Wolf and he had worked with the chimpanzees, in some way or another, since he was nineteen years old. He had remained fascinated by them ever since. Terry's long history of working "free contact" (without any protection) with these chimpanzees had given him a keen understanding of their individual behaviors.* He could sense when things were calm and he could sense when things were becoming dangerous. From his experiences, he knew that his present situation was the latter.†

The curator at the time, Bill, held the boat as Terry climbed in. He stared at the island as he approached it, slowly. On one side of the island were the five chimpanzees who had come to the island from the biomedical laboratory: Alvin, Spark, Nolan, Swing, and Doll. In the center of the island, lying facedown on the ground lay Doll's infant of a couple of months, Elgin. Even though Terry suspected that the infant was dead, he knew that taking an infant (even a dead one) from the group could elicit an extremely strong response not only from the mother but

---

* As should now be obvious, chimpanzees are extremely dangerous animals to take care of. Their intelligence coupled with their strength makes working with them one of the most dangerous jobs a zookeeper can have. Because of this, it is very rare for zookeepers to have full contact with them. Usually, animals are shifted out of exhibits while they are cleaned and food is set up. When the work is done the chimpanzees reenter the exhibit with the zookeeper safely out of harm's reach. In the event a chimpanzee needs hands-on care, there are protective measures, such as bars, squeeze cages, or other structures that protect a zookeeper from the extremely unpredictable behavior of a chimpanzee. However, the way the animal park was set up at the time necessitated the zookeepers working "free contact," which meant that they had no such protective measures. In order to survive such a job, a zookeeper needs a keen understanding of chimpanzee behavior. Failure to correctly predict a chimpanzee's mood can result in catastrophe.

† Terry Wolf's help in recounting these episodes cannot be understated. In his forty-plus years taking care of captive animals, he has witnessed amazing changes take place in the science of animal care.

from the entire group. As Terry banked the boat onto the island, the chimps looked over at him. Terry grabbed his fire extinguisher.

Elgin was the first infant born to this group of retired laboratory chimpanzees. His birth marked something of a triumph for a group that many had suggested would not be able to survive at all outside of a caged laboratory environment. They had become both a successful group and, now, a breeding group. However, Elgin was soon discovered to have some issues. Doll carried him lower on her back than most mother chimpanzees carry their infants (a sign that indicates an infant is not grasping as they are naturally inclined to do). His movements also seemed a bit odd. As the months went by, his condition seemed to deteriorate. Finally, on this day, he was found lying by himself in the middle of the island.

Terry attempted to show no signs of fear as he walked, with the fire extinguisher, over to the group of chimpanzees who seemed calm. Terry looked back at the motionless infant. He could, he thought, just grab the infant and run to the boat. The group may not even care.

No sense taking any chances, he thought as he raised the fire extinguisher.

Standing equidistant between the group of chimpanzees and the infant, Terry sprayed the fire extinguisher. This created a thick white wall of clouds, concealing him from the view of the chimps. When he was sure that the wall was thick enough, he silently approached Elgin. The infant chimp's body was, indeed, lifeless. As he picked him up, Elgin's head and limbs hung limply. Terry checked his cloud wall. It was slowly dissipating; however, none of the chimpanzees were making a sound. Terry stepped toward the boat when suddenly he felt Elgin's body tighten in his hands. He looked down to see the infant's eyes open. Terry immediately knew what was going to come next.

"Please don't," he whispered.

Elgin cocked his head and gave a short, loud alarm call. The sound reverberated around the island. Terry knew what was coming next.

Looking over at the white cloud wall, Terry saw a black silhouette appearing. Within a second, the silhouette transformed into an extremely angry chimpanzee. It was Doll, who was responding to the genetic alarm call produced by her infant son. No amount of white clouds could conceal Doll from her nature. This nature was to respond to an alarm call—especially one produced by her own offspring. Though she had apparently abandoned Elgin, instinct was taking over and she was not about to let Terry take the infant off of the island.

Terry ran, infant in hand, as fast as he could toward the boat. Realizing that he didn't have enough time to actually get both of them in the boat and get off the island, he placed Elgin in the boat and shoved it across the water toward Bill, who was standing on the other side. He looked back at Doll, who was screaming as she barreled toward him. He leapt out into the water as far as he could. As he jumped, Doll's arm swiped below his legs, just missing him. When Terry came up for air, in the middle of the canal, he turned to face Bill. The boat and Elgin had safely made it across. As Terry turned around to face the island he noticed, to his horror, that Doll was no longer there. She had launched herself into the canal and was now on the bottom. He could see her struggling to get to the surface. Terry knew that picking her up would mean death to both of them. The weight of a chimpanzee in the water is like a stone. Doll would inevitably grab him and they would both be stuck on the bottom. Terry turned to Bill, looking for help. Bill threw him a large cypress pole. Terry took the pole and attempted to push Doll toward the surface. Doll's weight in the water was too much and Terry could barely move her at all. With all of his strength, he managed to push her along the bottom of the canal and nudge her closer to the island. Even though Doll was now in shallow water, she was unable to get her head above the surface. Just when all seemed lost, Terry looked up to see Nolan, one of the males on the island, coming toward the water.

He's coming in after me too, thought Terry.

Instead, Nolan reached his hand in the water and pulled Doll up to the surface. Terry looked over at them. Doll was fine. She stood up and screamed at Terry, who swam quickly over to the shore.*

With Elgin safely in the truck, the two men sped to the hospital where Elgin underwent a series of tests which revealed him to have encephalitis. The swelling in his brain was causing him to have seizures. It was clear that the infant chimp would not be able to be returned to his group.

For the foreseeable future, Elgin would be kept in a hospital pen. It was not clear what could be done about his condition, what his future would hold, or if he would ever be able to live with chimpanzees again. As he was moved into the pen, the room beside him was being prepared for another chimpanzee. This chimpanzee had been a pet and would need to be quarantined in the hospital for a couple of months before she could be integrated with another group of chimpanzees. The chimp's name was Gin.

Gin had lived with an orange grove owner in central Florida. She had been born in central Africa around the same time as Cindy. As a very young infant she was caught and transported to the United States, where she was purchased at an exotic pet show. Since her capture, she had never been in contact with another chimpanzee. The orange grove owner had contacted the animal park in desperation to take the eight-year-old female chimpanzee off his hands. He explained that as she had gotten older, her behavior had become more and more unpredictable and increasingly erratic. The park agreed to take her in, believing that she would fit in with a group of chimpanzees. However, what they

---

* Doll's savior, Nolan, became a bit of a celebrity around the area. Every Christmas, a man in a Santa suit would come delivering presents to the chimp islands. Most of the chimpanzees were excited to get the boxes filled with treats, toys, and blankets. Nolan, however, was less than happy to see Santa. He became famous for throwing the presents back at Santa's head.

didn't realize was that Gin had missed her critical period of socialization with other chimpanzees. Gin was about to be thrown into the world of chimpanzees after having been denied much, if any, contact with the world that could unlock her nature. Her behavior would be just as erratic and unpredictable to other chimpanzees as it was to the orange grove owner. She would act and communicate in a way that was completely unseasoned by socialization.

Several weeks later, Elgin detected the presence of another chimpanzee in the room next to him. Gin was being moved in. The sounds of banging on bars and objects being thrown reverberated around the hospital. Elgin gave an alarm call. This caused the frightening response of Gin's extremely loud screaming. The screams had no structure. They were directed at nothing. These were not standard chimpanzee vocalizations. They weren't even alarm calls. They were simply loud screams. For the next several days, the screams could be heard at almost constant intervals.

1981
Mahale Mountains, Tanzania

Through the fog, the chimpanzee identified as Chausiku appeared without her infant. Prior to this, the last time the female chimpanzee had been observed was two months before. At that point she had just given birth. Now, two months later, she was without her infant. A baby chimpanzee of that age is normally always with his mother. There could be little doubt that the young infant was dead.*

Chausiku was part of a group that had been studied extensively by

---

* The following account of the Chausiku and Katabi event comes from the study done by Mariko Hiraiwa-Hasegawa and Toshikazu Hasegawa (1988).

primatologists in the Mahale Mountains. This community of chimpanzees had been named "Kajabala." However, Kajabala was not the only chimp group in the area. There was a much larger group that had been labelled "Mimikile." Though less studied than Kajabala, Mimikile was becoming more familiar to primatologists.*

It had been a little over a year since Chausiku had done what caused her to be of great interest to primatologists. She had left the Kajabala group to join Mimikile. That, in and of itself, was not unexpected. Chimpanzees are typically male philopatric, which means that females, when they come of age, disperse away from their groups and join other groups. What made Chausiku's case so interesting was that she had abandoned her five-year-old son in the process.

Before she abandoned her offspring, Chausiku was a fairly high-ranking female within the Kajabala group. She was frequently with the alpha male of the group, Kamemanfu, and mated with him frequently. Her son, Katabi, was always with her, never venturing over to any of the other chimpanzees without his mother.

During the period before he was abandoned, Katabi was observed to spend most of his time either being groomed by his mother or playing. Since his mother was frequently with Kamemanfu, the young chimp also spent a great deal of time with the alpha male.

Unexpectedly, Chausiku disappeared from the Kajabala group. In an instant Katabi's entire situation changed. He was, all of a sudden, left without a mother. Because he had previously spent all of his time with her, he was left to spend time only with Kamemanfu, who, being a good alpha male, appeared to take Katabi under his wing.

---

* Many accounts of the Mahale Mountain chimpanzees have been recounted and the stories of the Kajabala group and the Mimikile group are well known among those interested in wild chimpanzee behavior. Primatologist Toshisada Nishida has shed a considerable amount of light on our understanding of chimpanzees with his fascinating accounts of these communities.

The Mimikile group, where Chausiku was now residing, outnumbered the Kajabala group by about eighty to twenty. Chausiku was one of a number of females from Kajabala to join Mimikile. This, again, was not unusual. However, during this time males were also disappearing from the Kajabala group. Only they weren't moving to the Mimikile group. Rather, they were being murdered by raiding parties of the Mimikile group.* As the Kajabala males were being killed off, the females were beginning to defect. The Kajabala group was slowly being eradicated by the Mimikile group.

Meanwhile, young Katabi had become dependent on Kamemanfu. At night, he would make his nest right beside the elderly alpha male. In the morning he would wait for Kamemanfu to rise before getting up and following him for the day. The effect of redirecting his dependency had profound consequences on the chimpanzee.

Katabi had begun to alter his behaviors. He now spent about half as much time playing as he previously had spent. Perhaps the protection of a mother had afforded him more time to spend in this type of social activity. In addition to his playtime being cut, his time being groomed was also significantly lower. This was due, in part, to the fact that his mother had been mostly the one grooming him. Now that she wasn't present, it was left for others to groom him. The others weren't so willing, and he was seldom groomed. He replaced the time spent in these behaviors by approaching others and grooming them. In this behavior it appeared that he wanted to be groomed in return. Unfortunately, it rarely happened.

Katabi was now being bullied by the other chimps in the group. Without his mother, Katabi's social status had diminished significantly. As one would predict, when there was any competition for food, he

---

* Richard Wrangham and Dale Peterson discuss raiding parties in their classic book, *Demonic Males,* which explores the roots of human violence.

would be attacked and lose out to the others. In addition to this, there were also acts of aggression that were completely unprovoked. If this had happened when his mother had been around, she would have protected him by staying close and making certain vocalizations at anyone antagonizing him. Now that she was gone, Katabi had no one to depend on.

Katabi was beginning to act in a bizarre manner. The Mahale primatologists at times would offer bananas to the chimpanzees. Katabi would grab the banana, peel it, throw away the fruit, and eat the peel. Such a behavior had never before been seen in this area.

This period of time was also beginning to have a physical effect on Katabi. During this time he lost almost 20 percent of his body weight. He acted lethargic, increasingly resting more and more as time went by. This sedentary existence would have taken its toll both physically and socially.

One day, as the Kajabala group was moving through the forest, they encountered some members of the Mimikile group. One of these Mimikile chimps was Chausiku. When Katabi saw Chausiku he immediately ran to her and instantly began grooming her. The exchange, however, was very brief. Chausiku showed very little interest in her abandoned offspring and hardly returned the grooming. After a while, the two groups separated, with Chausiku remaining with her Mimikile comrades and Katabi following Kamemanfu and the rest of his group. The exchange appeared to affect Katabi even more with him losing more interest in play activities and spending less time attempting to groom others.

Though Katabi was, chemically, the same chimpanzee inside, his altered behaviors had created a very different individual. These altered behaviors are nature's response to a change in environment. The adjustability of Katabi's behaviors has evolved in the same way as his chemical makeup inside.

There are two types of traits that nature has endowed to the living. There are obligate traits, or traits that cannot change based on the environment. There are also facultative traits, or traits that respond to environmental variation. Obligate traits are the ones we normally think of when we consider genetics. These include things like blood type, eye color, organ structure, body plan, and anything else that resists influence from the outside world. If all traits, however, were obligate, living organisms would be extremely unadaptable. Facultative traits are how nature has compensated for the obligate. These traits can alter themselves based on what's going on in the environment. These become especially useful when the state of the environment is variable within the lifetime of an individual. Primates, along with other social mammals have an extremely useful facultative trait: the ability to learn, use, and choose an array of behaviors.*

Katabi could not go about acting as if his mother was still present in the group. He had to alter his behaviors to survive in the world around him. He had to adjust to become dependent on different individuals. In this case, he had made the wise choice of a high-ranking individual that he was already extremely familiar with, Kamemanfu. He also had to adjust his behaviors based on the fact that he had lost his mother's protection. He had to become submissive in food competition. He had to be vigilant in looking out for unprovoked attacks. Katabi was learning how to become a different chimpanzee.

The same process that occurs in social behavior also occurs within social communication. Primates alter their methods and styles of communication based on both the natural environment and the social

---

* Of course this all goes back to the original prokaryote organism. When this prokaryote reproduces, the genetic structure of its offspring are the obligate traits. The ability of these offspring to chemically alter themselves to compensate for their environments are the facultative traits. Behavior and, more specifically, communication are merely the primate forms of these facultative traits.

environment they live in. Chimpanzee vocalizations respond to this the same as humans do.

Prosody, the rhythmic and intonational aspect of speech, determines how a vocalization sounds. In human language, prosody determines dialect. Prosodic features include the way syllables are accented, the speed in which sounds are voiced, and the pitch in which sounds are produced. Prosody is determined by both obligate and facultative traits. The obligate traits that determine prosody are factors like larynx structure, palate structure, and labial structure. These cannot be changed unless something is damaged or physically altered. The facultative traits that determine prosody are factors like the sounds one learns to make, the influence of other individuals on speech, and the alterations one makes on speech to accommodate different acoustics. Though no such research was performed, I would hypothesize that Katabi's prosodic features during this time were being altered by the extreme changes in his social environment. Not only would his facultative behaviors be altered, but also his facultative prosody.

In humans, these prosodic changes are how dialects evolve and change over time. In the long run, it is how different languages are formed. Let's imagine that a plane carrying a group of strangers crashed into the ocean. The survivors of the crash find themselves stranded on an unknown island indefinitely. In this case, a number of things would begin to affect their prosody. First, the stress of being in a plane crash would have an emotional affect on the way they are speaking. They would probably speak more rapidly, drop sounds that were less useful than others, and speak in a higher pitch.* Even after the stress of the crash dissipated, the prosodic footprint would remain in their lexicon. The next thing that would happen is that the group of strangers would

---

* Much research has been done on the effects stress can have on prosody (see Cowie et al., 1999; Fernandez and Picard, 2000; Kienast et al., 2000; and Wichmann, 2001).

begin influencing each other's speech. Individual idiosyncrasies in the way some would speak would begin to diffuse throughout the population. At some point, a few social leaders would emerge from the group. These leaders would have an even greater influence on the speech patterns of the castaways. Socially, each leader would probably have his or her own group of followers. The followers would begin to identify themselves by their allegiances and, subconsciously, speak even more like their leaders. Eventually, one leader would assume complete dominion over the population. This would probably happen after either a political or physical battle. At this point, the speech patterns of the victorious leader and his or her followers would be the upper-class dialect on the island. The speech patterns of the losing leader and followers would be the lower-class, or hick, dialect. As time goes on, the island's common dialect would continue to evolve. After many generations the dialect would be completely unique to that island.

Let's now imagine that hundreds of years and many generations later, the descendants of the group of castaways are rescued. As they are brought back to their country, they would immediately realize that their dialect had evolved on a separate path from their parent population. They would be, in effect, speaking a completely different language from the rest of the country. At this point, they wouldn't be able to understand anyone outside of their own group. They would probably, at this point, return to their island, where they could remain with their own community and their own lexicon.*

Katabi, like any primate facing extreme social change, had completely adjusted to adapt to the new situation. Unfortunately, sometimes this adaptation can create an entirely new and more profound set

---

* For a more complete picture on how languages change, I recommend anything by the linguist William Labov. His series of books *Principles of Linguistic Change* give a great glimpse into the inner workings of what drives language evolution.

of problems. Such was the case when Chausiku returned to the Kaja-bala group.

Chausiku was noticeably pregnant when she returned. Though accepted back into the community by Kamemanfu, the situation would prove to be different. This difference would lie in her relationship with Katabi. When she would try to groom Katabi, he would not groom her back. In fact, Katabi had stopped grooming anyone, even Kamemanfu.

Having his mother back seemed to have negatively affected Katabi. He had become even more lethargic and more sedentary in his behavior. He lost more weight and appeared sickly. In the few times he would get up and move around, he was unable to walk in a straight line. Finally, three months after Chausiku returned to the group, Katabi died.*

Soon after Katabi's death, Chausiku gave birth to a new baby. After the birth, she disappeared with the baby for two months. The next time she was observed, she was coming out of the fog without the infant. In a few months, Chausiku had lost both Katabi and her new baby. Chausiku was alone.

1982
Loxahatchee, Florida

Elgin awoke to horrendous screams coming from the next room. The screams were combined with the sounds of metal being hit, objects being thrown, and zookeepers shouting at each other. All at once, the sounds ceased. Elgin peered out from his pen to see the chimpanzee he had only previously heard being dragged outside of her room. Gin

---

* The actual cause of Katabi's death was undocumented.

had been sedated by the veterinary staff and wasn't moving. Hoisted up by three zookeepers, she was loaded onto a truck and driven away from the hospital.

Gin was being moved out to the preserve. She was about to interact with a world she hadn't experienced since infancy. That world, of course, was the world of chimpanzees. Everything about Gin's life was about to change. Not only were her physical and social environments about to change, but the very species that Gin was about to interact with would be entirely new to her. Normally, facultative behaviors would allow an individual to adapt to such changes. Unfortunately, the facultative behaviors that Gin would require the most would be the ones that depend on socialization during an individual's critical period. Since Gin had no socialization during her critical period, she was unable to use these facultative behaviors. Therefore, being able to socially adapt or socially communicate would be impossible.

After the truck pulled up to the islands, Gin was loaded into an animal carrier. The carrier was placed in the rowboat. A zookeeper got into the rowboat and took Gin over to the small island. Watching intently from her perch on top of the small island was Cindy.

Gin's carrier was placed on the island with the door opened. Gin was inside sleeping, still apparently sedated. The chimpanzees on the island were immediately curious and surrounded the carrier. Cindy took the initiative. She approached the carrier and looked inside. As she got closer and examined the sleeping chimpanzee, Gin's eyes flew open and she screamed. She slashed Cindy across the face with her fingernail and charged out of the carrier. Cindy screamed and charged after her.

Gin ran around the island screaming. Anytime she got close to a chimpanzee, she would swipe at them. Finally, a chimpanzee named Old Man, the alpha male of the group, ran at her in an apparent attempt to subdue her. Gin climbed up to the top of an eighteen-foot-high shelter. Old Man, Cindy, and the other chimpanzees surrounded the base of the shelter. Gin screamed louder. The chimpanzees on the ground vocalized back. Gin kept screaming at them.

Cindy climbed up the shelter after Gin. As she did this, Gin jumped from the top all the way to the ground. The fall caused her to roll down the mountain. As she hit the water, she gave an alarm call and jumped back to the shore. Old Man and the other chimpanzees ran at Gin. Finally they caught her. Screams turned into wails as the chimpanzees bit her. After a few seconds, the chimps got off of her. Gin sat on the ground screaming.

Gin had been thrown into a world completely foreign to her. This fact was clearly coming through in the behaviors she was exhibiting. In an instant she was being faced with a chimpanzee world and a chimpanzee social structure. She had no understanding of the female dominance hierarchy that was being established with Cindy. She had no idea of the role of an alpha male chimpanzee like Old Man.

Gin continued to scream for hours. As time went by, Old Man approached her in a nonaggressive manner. He attempted to groom her. Gin either didn't understand the behavior or didn't care. She jumped up and began screaming at him. This pattern continued throughout the day. Old Man would approach Gin. Gin would scream. Sometimes Gin would swipe at or bite him which would lead to a short violent exchange—which sometimes included the entire group.

There is a structure to chimpanzee aggressive behavior. Violence, as unpleasant as it may seem, fulfills a necessary social function in chimpanzees. There are two types of violence. In the first type, the goal of the aggressive act is to kill another individual. In the second type, the goal of the aggressive act is to communicate. The first type is lethal while the second type is nonlethal. Nonlethal violence is extremely prevalent in chimpanzees and communicates rank, alliances, and social politics. The communication that nonlethal violence provides is necessary when two chimpanzees are introduced to each other. Without this communication, rank is never established and, therefore, the two can never live together in the type of socially viable alliances that chimpanzees depend on for survival. Chimpanzees acquire the function of nonlethal violence the same way they do other complex communication systems: by a mix of genetic hardwiring and social molding.* A problem occurs when a chimpanzee has never had the social molding for this type of communication. The chimpanzee won't understand the information being transmitted. She will merely understand the raw violent acts. Gin, of course, was such a chimp.

When two chimpanzees are introduced, the following pattern generally takes place. First, the two examine each other. After a certain period of time, one chimpanzee will make an aggressive act against the other. The two will fight, sometimes to the point of severe injury. After the fight, the chimps will separate. This will probably repeat several times. However, at some point, the two will meet again and begin to groom the injuries they have inflicted upon one another. What I have just described is what a human observer sees. What the chimpanzees are communicating, however, is key to their social survival together. First of all, rank must be established. The fighting will continue until one of them acts submissively. With this submissive act, the chimpanzee is communicating that he or she is willing to let the other have the dominant rank. Once this has been established, the dominant chimpanzee begins to groom the injuries of the submissive chimpanzee. The message being communicated is that the submissive chimpan-

---

* And speaking of chimpanzees being genetically hardwired for nonlethal violence, Richard Wrangham compared the rates of lethal and nonlethal violence between humans and chimpanzees. Rates of lethal violence were about the same. Rates of nonlethal violence were much higher in chimpanzees. This seems to suggest a greater ecological need for the function of nonlethal violence in chimpanzees than in humans (see Wrangham et al., 2006).

zee will be taken care of by the higher-ranking chimpanzee. The submissive chimpanzee accepts this status by returning the grooming. At this, at least for a little while, peace is achieved. If neither submits, the fighting can continue until the nonlethal violence becomes lethal. In either scenario, peace is achieved.

In Gin's case, she had no understanding of what was being communicated by Old Man. She would neither submit nor act aggressively enough to warrant his submission. All she would do was swipe at him and run. Every day the same cycle repeated itself.

After a few weeks, it was determined that Gin would never be able to integrate with Old Man's group. There was another option, however. The new island that Higgy was about to occupy was nearing completion and they were still trying to decide on the group of females which would make up Higgy's group. Higgy's personality was so dominant that perhaps he could subdue Gin. It was decided that Gin would become part of Higgy's group.

1982
Mahale Mountains, Tanzania

Chausiku sat alone. In her hand was a blade of grass. As she examined the blade of grass, she noticed that, running up and down, were small ants on the stalk. Slowly, Chausiku raised the grass to her lips and ate the ants. She stood up and looked around. In her vicinity were other members of her now permanent group, Mimikile.

Several months prior, Chausiku had been seen with Kamemanfu for the last time. Without Katabi or her recently deceased infant, Chausiku would have occupied a different social role within the group. Having no living offspring, Chausiku would have needed to be in a group with more viable mates. Kamemanfu was old and the other males in the group were subadult. Therefore, a couple of weeks after the death of her infant, Chausiku moved to the Mimikile group indefinitely.

Though she was in a large and dynamic group, Chausiku was spending time alone. After eating the ants, she made a nest on the ground. Laying in the bed, she grabbed a branch that was in her reach. Making a chimpanzee's play face, she began wrestling with the branch. The wrestling became more and more exaggerated until, finally, she was vocalizing to it. She slapped the branch and rolled around with it. The primatologists who observed this behavior noticed that they hadn't seen her do such movements since she had her infant. These were the games Chausiku would play with her offspring. Now that all of her offspring were dead, Chausiku had yet to erase the behavior.*

There are moments when organisms cease to adapt. There are times when facultative traits appear to become fixed. Chausiku had adapted to a number of different social situations, all of which demanded her to accommodate her behaviors accordingly. She had traveled back and forth between groups. She had been a mother during some stages and without a dependent offspring at others. These changes in her area, social group, and status caused her to continually adapt to these different situations. It was possible now that Chausiku had merely stopped adapting. She was acting as the mother of an offspring—a social role she no longer had any reason to hold.†

---

* A similar account of solitary play was recorded in Hitoshige Hayaki's study, "Social play of juvenile and adolescent chimpanzees in the Mahale Mountains National Park, Tanzania" (1985). In the paper, Toshisada Nishida recounts to Hayaki that Chausiku had been observed in a similar type of solitary play. This play was similar to the way she had played with her recently deceased infant.

† It is important to note that this conjecture on Chausiku's behavior and her inability to adapt yet again is entirely my own. To me, play (which this is considered) is a mirror into the inner workings of a social animal's consciousness. An individual that is playing alone can tell us a great deal as to what is occurring as far as his or her social adaptations are concerned.

1982
Loxahatchee, Florida

Gin stretched out her arm, reaching across the canal, to the zookeepers on the other side. As she held her arm in that position, she emitted the hoarse screams that had been an almost constant sound on the island. She watched as the zookeepers and veterinarian loaded up their boat with carriers, dart guns, and nets. The zookeepers slowly passed her island and moved over to the island next to her. The other members of her group ran to the other side of the island in order to view what was going on. She watched the veterinarian hold up his dart gun and aim it at Little Mama. Little Mama screamed as the dart hit her. Cindy hooted from across the water as the zookeepers dragged Little Mama onto the boat. The zookeepers then turned their boat toward Gin's island. She watched a dart hit Edwina, another female on the island. This caused Cindy to run around the island and deliver an alarm call. As Gin finally heard a call that she could understand—that there was imminent danger—she felt the dart go into her leg. In an instant all was dark.

When she awoke, she examined her surroundings. She was on a completely different island in a completely different area. Surrounding her were three other chimps. Edwina, a small female who had been with Gin on the other island, was walking the perimeter of the island. In the center of the island, Little Mama was just waking up. Gin turned around to see a large male chimpanzee approaching her. She screamed and ran to the edge of the water. This male, Higgy, kept coming toward her. Gin reached out her arm and screamed to him. He got close to her and put his forehead up to hers. Gin held her mouth open. Her screams were no longer audible. Higgy held this position for a few moments. Gin closed her mouth. As Higgy walked away, Gin followed him. This time, however, she did not scream, she did not swipe at anyone, and she did not run. It appeared that Gin had finally connected with another chimpanzee.

Societies exist, in social animals like humans and chimpanzees, because of our ability to seemingly mask our nature with what we learn. We alter our behaviors, alter our appearances, and alter our vocalizations. In doing so, we are able to coexist in a social group—without which, we wouldn't be able to survive. We acquire mannerisms, gestures, and dialects to be able to become a working component of our social order. As humans, we acquire conduct, rituals, and what to say in order to make ourselves more palatable to others in our group. We learn codes of ethics, concepts of right and wrong, and beliefs which further mold our nature in the image of our society. Without these acquisitions, we are left exposed for what we truly are. Without these acquisitions, we are like Gin.

However, who we truly are *includes* what we learn and acquire. The ability and the method by which we retain our experiences are as much a part of our nature as our physical construction. We are genetically predisposed to both how we learn and acquire and what we learn and acquire. No matter what type of social traits we use to disguise our nature, we are exposed because those very social traits are part of the very nature we are attempting to conceal. Each social trait we acquire, each moment in our history, and each genetic trait we are born with combines to form the complete picture of our individual natural selves. All three are imprinted on the way we look, the way we act, and the way we speak. Each of us is exactly as nature has created us; through genetic code and experience. An individual's nature is neither *good* nor *evil*. An individual's nature is merely *working*. In the end, our nature is who we are, what we've ever been, and who we'll ever be. It is how we survive and what we do to enable that survival. Social experiences or not, we are all raw nature. We are all Gin.

Like a group of castaways from different lands, Higgy's group met for the first time on that afternoon in 1982. As Higgy's group was beginning in Florida, the Kajabala group was ending in the Mahale Mountains. The last remains of Kajabala sat together. Two adult females, an adolescent male, and an infant were all that was left. The once vibrant group now existed as a monument to an everchanging world that requires everchanging actions. In months, the group would be completely gone. The social traits, social hierarchies, and vocal lexicon that had sustained a population would soon be extinguished from the earth forever.

Talk of mysteries!—Think of our life in nature,—daily to be shown matter, to come in contact with it—rocks, trees, wind on our cheeks! the solid earth! the actual world! the common sense! Contact! Contact! Who are we? where are we?
—HENRY DAVID THOREAU

5

Elgin

I once worked with a chimpanzee named Oz. Oz was an extremely large, extremely round, teenage chimpanzee who resembled a gorilla more than a chimp. Oz lived with his father, his sister, his sister's juvenile female offspring, and an unrelated but very submissive male.* The small group was extremely laid-back. In fact, because there was no observable social hierarchy, there was no way to tell who was in charge. Because of this, there was little to no competition for dominance in the group. Fights were pretty much relegated to Oz frustrating his sister by chasing her, very slowly, around the island. These episodes would last until Oz's sister would get so frustrated that she would scream continuously. At

---

*This male was Peter, Higgy's old buddy from the nursery window.

this point, their father would lose his patience and aggressively end the game.*

The only time that real competition would take place would be if there were special treats around their island. Because there wasn't a whole lot of rank difference between the individuals, there wasn't a clear pecking order in who would get the treats. Therefore, special treats would lead to fighting, thievery, and a lack of sharing.

On one particular Halloween, I decided to give the chimps some pumpkins to play with. Knowing that chimpanzees don't get very excited about pumpkins (it is just a large orange squash, after all), I hollowed them out and filled them with treats (peanuts, popcorn, gummy bears, etc.). I placed the tops back on the pumpkins, concealing the treats inside. I then scattered the treat-filled pumpkins around Oz's island (along with their daily meals). As I had suspected, the chimps walked by the pumpkins without paying them any attention. As Oz walked by one of the pumpkins, he grabbed it by the top. In trying to pick the pumpkin up, the top came off, revealing the treats inside. Oz looked into the pumpkin then around the island. None of the other chimps had seen. Slowly and silently, Oz placed the top back on the pumpkin and picked it up. He then, without any sound or vocalization, walked around the island, picking up every pumpkin. By the time he gathered them all up, he had six large pumpkins in his arms. He walked to a secluded part of the island and took the lids off the pumpkins. Very quietly, he chirped to himself as he ate all of the treats.

What Oz had done here was to demonstrate something remarkable. In this act of withholding information, he showcased one of the bedrocks of the complexities of chimpanzee communication. At the same time he realized that the pumpkins were special and contained hidden

---

* Oz's father was an old curmudgeonly chimp. When he would end these little games between his two offspring, he would approach them, yell, throw his hands up, walk away, turn back, and yell at them again from a distance.

treats, Oz understood that he was the only chimpanzee that was possessing this information. Furthermore, he made a decision not to transmit this information to the rest of his group. In doing so, he kept all of the resources for himself and benefitted from his surreptitious behavior.

Such is the way of chimpanzee communication. Unlike many communicative species, chimpanzees are able to consciously choose which information to transmit and which information to conceal. They can also transmit false information in order to benefit their situations. This feature of communication is extremely beneficial to their survival and has evolved accordingly in any species that has complex social systems.

In order for Oz to cover up the information about the pumpkins, he had to understand himself as a separate individual from his social group. He also needed to understand that others in his group possessed their own consciousness about the world that was different from his. Without such understandings, communication can be little more than raw responses to information and stimuli—it would transmit only unreflected consciousness.

When Oz first perceived the pumpkins, he was conscious of only the basic information attached to the pumpkin. He had yet to reflect on the pumpkin or give it more of a meaning than had already been supplied by his genetics and memory. When he picked up the pumpkin and the top came off to reveal the treats inside, he looked over at the other chimpanzees. It is at this point that Oz had reached a state of reflected consciousness. His perception of the pumpkin completely changed. This change is due not just to the fact that the pumpkin had revealed new information about itself but also to the fact that he knew something about it that the other chimps didn't know. In order for him to have gained this consciousness about the pumpkin, he had to reflect on the others and reflect on himself. In doing so, he could now attach new meanings onto the pumpkin. In this act, he became aware of himself, the others, and the situation. In understanding this, he was able to make a conscious and self-aware decision to conceal information from the others. Without the social presence of the others, Oz would be unable to reflect on himself as a unique individual capable of possessing his own information. Without his understanding of the others and his understanding of himself, Oz would be unable to make the decision to hide information and, therefore, would lose out on the resources he had obtained.

Everything that we are conscious of, we perceive as a reflection of ourselves. When Oz looked at the other chimpanzees, he was not actually perceiving what was going on in their minds. Instead, he was perceiving his own mind in a similar situation. He was making the connection that, if one of the other chimpanzees had made a similar discovery (without him knowing), that other chimp would be able to freely eat the treats without his interference. In order for him to be able to perceive this about himself and the others, he had to have close social bonds. Socialization allows an individual the ability to reflect themselves onto another and, in turn, to understand their own limitations as an individual and the limitations of others. This socialization drives and builds our communication systems.

This drive to form close social bonds is synchronic with a drive to understand ourselves. Social bonds create self-awareness. Self-awareness creates a reflected consciousness which can perceive information in the most survivable and fit manner in a social species. This is another reason why socialization is crucial to survival in primates. Communication is the glue that binds social groups together.*

In the early 1980s (as Higgy's group was forming and its members were cementing their social bonds together) a three-year-old chimpan-

---

* The foundational function of vocal communication is individual identification. All other complex features and functions derive from this essential purpose. An infant identifies its mother by the sound of her voice. A group member identifies another group member by individual vocal characteristics. Likewise, strangers are identified by the fact that their voices do not sound like anything familiar. Stemming from individual

zee, Elgin, was spending the beginning of his life in a hospital pen without any social bonds at all. Isolated from all other chimpanzees since infancy, Elgin was like a child growing up without ever seeing a mirror. Without a sense of the other, he would have no sense of the self. Without a sense of self, he would have no idea of how to attach his own individual understandings onto information. These features are not just beneficial, they are essential to survival. Elgin's history is the story of a chimpanzee's struggle to achieve a place in the social world. It tells of how a social bond can make even the most unfit individual thrive and survive. Elgin is the embodiment of all who are finding companionship and the desperate measures to maintain that companionship through communication. We will explore how two individuals, who are socially bonded, become a reflection of each other and how they mold their behaviors and interactions to adapt to their companion.

Our companions in life allow us to understand who we are and what our place is in the world of others. They allow us to know our limitations and, in turn, their limitations. Our companions build the methods in which we see ourselves, the methods in which we see the world, and the methods in which we interact with the world. They build our lexicon.

1982
Atlanta, Georgia

A historical meeting of primatologists had descended on the Colony Square Hotel. The meeting, hosted by the Yerkes Regional Primate

---

identifications are individual perceptions of information. These perceptions, added with the identifications, give the transmission its full meaning. Information coming from one individual may mean something different when coming from another individual. In chimpanzees, information being transmitted from individuals of different ranks can carry far different meanings.

Research Center and Emory University, was the largest ever of its kind. Three of the largest societies relevant to primatology were combined in one massive conference. These were the International Primatological Society, the American Society of Primatologists, and the International Society for Human Ethology.

The combination of the three groups led to an eclectic array of the different types of primate studies. Some of the sessions dealt with the behavior of primates in the wild. Others dealt with primate physiology. Some of the sessions were purely biomedical and dealt with laboratory primates. Occupying a large portion of the conference, however, were presentations on cognitive studies done with primates in behavioral labs. Cognitive studies can include anything from how well primates perform at various puzzles to primates doing math tests. Cognitive studies also include attempts to teach primates to use human language. Despite the doubts cast by Project Nim, there was still a community of academics dedicated to this study.*

Noticeably absent from the conference, however, was a presentation of one the most groundbreaking papers published that year in primatology. That paper, by a psychologist named Gordon Gallup, was entitled "Self-awareness and the emergence of mind in primates." In the paper, Gallup combined his studies from the last two decades into a theoretical framework of primate consciousness. These studies, simply enough, were experiments to see if primates could recognize themselves in a mirror.

The idea for the study came to Gallup as a grad student in the mid-1960s. One morning, as he was staring into a mirror shaving, he

---

* And still to this day, language-trained studies persist. Since apes seemed to fail at sign language usage, studies have been done using symbols which apes can point to in order to make a sentence. These studies have found far greater success than the sign language studies. Apes can be trained to do all sorts of amazing things. I'm far more interested in what they are teaching themselves to do, however.

started to ponder the psychological mechanisms that allowed him to recognize himself in the mirror. Furthermore, not only was he able to recognize himself, he was also able to use the mirror reflection to manipulate an aspect of himself (shave the whiskers off his face). He began to contemplate what it would be like to not have this ability and what that would mean to his consciousness. He wondered if other species had this ability as well.

He, therefore, began a project which would define a large part of his academic career. He initially conducted his study with three species of monkeys (stump-tailed, rhesus, and crab-eating macaques). Anytime any of the monkeys would look at the mirror, they appeared to think that the reflection was another monkey. Even after three weeks of mirror exposure, the monkeys still viewed the reflection as an unfamiliar monkey. The other aspect of the test was to anesthetize the monkeys and apply red dots to their faces. When the monkeys woke up, Gallup would present them with mirrors to see if they would understand that they had red dots on their faces and attempt to remove them. Again, after weeks of exposure, the monkeys showed no signs of understanding the reflections or understanding that the red dots were on their faces.

After the monkeys failed at self-recognition, Gallup attempted the same project with chimpanzees. After a brief period of acclimating to the mirror, chimpanzees were always able to both recognize themselves and understand that the red dots in the mirror were actually on their faces. Repeated tests with chimpanzees showed that they were routinely able to understand the principles of reflection and to understand that the images they were seeing were of themselves.

Later tests confirmed that orangutans could also recognize themselves and the red dots on their faces. These results suggested that mirror self-recognition could possibly just be an ape phenomenon. Perhaps self-awareness emerged with the evolutionary lineage of apes.

However both gibbons and gorillas failed the test.* These results led Gallup to further contemplate what mirror recognition meant to the mind of primates. Are only those primates who can recognize their reflection self-aware? If so, what is the consciousness of species who are not self-aware?

Gallup came to the conclusion that the species who were able to recognize themselves in a mirror had a clear concept of themselves as individuals. These animals could distinguish themselves from the rest of the world and make choices based on that level of self-awareness. In addition to this, animals capable of recognizing themselves would be capable of recognizing that what they perceive in the world is uniquely their own perception and others, likewise, possess their own perceptions as well. Such a cognitive awareness would have profound ecological consequences. Highly social animals could devise ways to act based on the hierarchy they live in. Politics, for example, would be impossible without this level of self-awareness. One must know how to play to the will of others. In order to do this, one must realize that others, like oneself, possess their own individual minds.[†]

In his 1982 paper, Gallup devised a table distinguishing the mind of animals who showed no signs of self-awareness (those that had failed the mirror test) versus those that showed clear signs of self-awareness (those who had passed the mirror test). Those who were not self-aware were relegated to what Gallup referred to as "hard-wired analogs." These consisted of genetic reactions to other indi-

---

* Since this time, several attempts to "prove" mirror self-recognition in these species have been undertaken with various degrees of success (or peer-reviewed acceptance). Most of the gibbon positive results have been anecdotal at best. As for gorillas, Francine Patterson was quick to show Koko recognizing herself (see Patterson & Cohn, 1994).

† Several hypotheses have been floated around as to why this degree of self-awareness would have evolved. These have ranged from the need to understand one's weight when jumping around on branches to knowing how *not* to make your neighbor angry. I tend to be more convinced by the latter.

viduals, mimicry, and alarm calls. Hardwired analogs can also consist of behaviors that seem very conscious and complex such as pretending (a frog may pretend to be dead) in order to avoid predation. Also included are genetic responses to alarm calls. This is contrasted with what Gallup referred to as "instances of mind" which depend on self-awareness. Such instances of mind consist of conscious intentional behaviors (such as distorting or withholding information), selectively offering aid (and behaving in order to gain reciprocal behavior), comforting others in distress, reconciliation, and complex deception.

Chimpanzee communication, like human language, depends on these instances of mind. In order to communicate about such things as a planned attack, a planned escape, a reconciliation after an altercation, or any of the other instances we have explored, chimpanzees must be in constant possession of self-awareness. Without self-awareness, complex communication is impossible.

I would add to all of this the fact that self-awareness and what emerges as "mind" don't come about without complex socialization (and, therefore, complex communication). In order for an individual to be truly self-aware, one must be conscious of the presence of others. An isolated chimpanzee (such as Elgin) has no self-awareness until he forms a conscious bond with another chimpanzee. Therefore, without complex communication, the mind never emerges from a human, chimpanzee, or any other sentient species. These two cognitive evolutionary developments, self-awareness and complex communication, are mutually dependent on each other. Without either, a species that depends on intricate social systems to sustain itself would not survive.

Though a chimpanzee like Cindy created social bonds with humans early in her life, she failed to understand herself as a chimpanzee until she bonded with other chimpanzees. This is evidenced by her behavior upon entering the animal park. Her burgeoning self-awareness as a chimpanzee would allow her to begin to socially thrive in her environment. There is a direct correlation to Cindy's well-being (and even the well-being of her various offspring) and Cindy's level of socialization with other chimpanzees. The more social bonds Cindy created, the better she survived.

Contrast this with Elgin who had *no* social bonds and was *barely* surviving.

1983
Loxahatchee, Florida

The rowboat inched closer to Old Man's island as the zookeepers attempted to get a better look. The morning sun was glaring so brightly against the surface of the water that it was difficult for them to see. As the zookeepers squinted, they could make out Cindy's large figure in front of them.

Cindy sat at the edge of the island, holding an infant that had been born overnight. Knowing the history of the health of Cindy's infants, the zookeepers were keen to examine the infant as best they could without upsetting any of the chimps. As they approached, Cindy opened up her arms to reveal the new female chimpanzee on her chest.

The infant appeared to be healthy. Her eyes were open, she was clutching onto Cindy very firmly, and she was nursing. Sitting behind Cindy and the baby was Old Man. Due to how close Cindy had become with Old Man, he was determined to be the infant's father. Looking around to the other chimpanzees, the zookeepers could find no sign of any aggression from the others. Everyone was sitting fairly peacefully at different ends of the island. The zookeepers returned to the shore feeling good about the infant's chances of survival. They decided to name her Rachel.*

Since joining Old Man's group, Cindy had formed some close social bonds. Now that Gin had left the island, peace had been restored and there seemed to be no serious conflict among the group. Since Little Mama had left the other island to join Higgy's group, Cindy spent more time interacting with her own group instead of across the water. Finally, Cindy was fulfilling a social role within a chimpanzee group. Her new offspring helped to solidify this mantle.†

The apparent health of Rachel was good news to the zookeepers who already had their hands full with one chimpanzee in a hospital pen—a chimp whose sole interactions with the outside world were with zookeepers. This was, of course, Elgin.

1983
Mahale Mountains, Tanzania

A female chimpanzee named Watendele sat with a one-month-old infant clutching onto her chest and a five-year-old at her side. Both of the small chimpanzees were males and they both belonged to her. The three of them sat on a mountainside overlooking a valley at the edge of Lake Tanganyika. All three were estranged from the group they had only recently joined, Mimikile.

It had been ten months since Kamemanfu disappeared from the

---

* By all accounts, Cindy was a very attentive mother with Rachel. Cindy's large stature coupled with her new infant was helping her status within Old Man's group. Rachel was well protected.

† Chimpanzee females tend to ascend to a higher rank within their social groups when they have offspring. Keep in mind, however, that since females are responsible for forming the alliances that put males in power, many males do not *want* certain females to climb any higher.

Kajabala group, leaving it without an alpha male and therefore vulnerable. Since Kamemanfu was the last of the group's reproductively viable males, his disappearance (seemingly at the hands of the Mimikile group) doomed the present generation of Kajabala to be its last. A month after his disappearance, Watendele, like Chausiku before her, left the remnants of her group and joined Mimikile. Unlike Chausiku, Watendele brought her five-year-old offspring with her.

Watendele's history with the Mimikile group was brutal. In 1974, as a member of Kajabala, she had bore a male offspring. Two years later members of Mimikile raided Kajabala and killed the juvenile. This attack occurred toward the beginning of an eight-year series of attacks by Mimikile which, in the end, wiped out the males of Kajabala and assimilated the females. Watendele would endure these attacks and remain with Kajabala until the end. Kamemanfu's disappearance, however, made it impossible for a female to remain. A month later, Watendele, with Masudi, her five-year-old, would join Mimikile.*

Masudi had been born in 1977. His history with Mimikile had also been rife with violence. In 1981, Masudi was alone with his mother when they were both viscously attacked by Mimikile. The attack was led by the Mimikile males Ntologi (the alpha male) and Kagimimi (the third-ranking male). While the other Mimikile males joined in on the attack, two of them stayed back and didn't participate. They were Bakali, the second-ranking male, and Musa, the fourth-ranking male. The attack continued until primatologists who had witnessed the attack interfered, allowing Masudi to flee with his mother.†

---

* It may seem, from these accounts, that Mimikile was somehow an inherently evil and violent group. Rather, it may have been that Mimikile was a group in social flux. The group was growing and with growth comes changes in social hierarchy. With social changes come conflicts.

† Interference is a troubling dilemma for those studying the natural behaviors of animals. Many would argue that interfering in any natural behavior creates a divergence from the

Ten months later, the situation repeated itself. Again, Watendele and Masudi were attacked by a group led by Ntologi and Kagimimi. Again, Bakali and Musa did not participate. Again, primatologists interfered, which stopped the attack long enough for Watendele and Masudi to flee. Due to these incidents, it must have been with great trepidation that the mother and her offspring joined Mimikile when they were forced to do so.

Surprisingly, when they initially joined the group, there weren't any attacks. In fact, Watendele was accepted to the point that males began mating with her almost immediately. She became pregnant soon after and gave birth to another male seven and a half months later.

Sitting on the mountainside Watendele and her two offspring were still seemingly isolated from the rest of the group. She was unaware that a group of Mimikile males, who were at the banks of Lake Tanganyika, had suddenly changed their direction and were venturing up the mountainside. This group of males included (among others) Ntologi, Kagimimi, Musa, and Bakali. As the males got closer to Watendele, the other females in the vicinity quickly ascended into the trees.

Watendele was caught by surprise when the large group of males came charging up the mountain at her. As they charged the females in the trees began to vocalize aggressively. Quickly, Watendele crouched into a ball, protecting her infant with her body. At this, Kagimimi attacked Watendele brutally. Within moments, Watendele's face was covered in blood. The attack continued as Kagimimi tore Watendele's anus. Soon all of the males, with the exception of Musa and Bakali, had joined in the onslaught.

For over twenty minutes, Watendele sustained these attacks. Finally,

---

natural order of things and therefore makes a situation much worse. Some would go further and say that even the presence of an observer on a group of animals disturbs the true nature of that species, causing a disruption within the natural behaviors of the focal species as well as invalidating all data.

Ntologi came from behind and grabbed the fur of her back. He succeeded in lifting Watendele up, leaving the infant exposed. He then dropped Watendele, grabbed her infant, and carried the infant, by the skin of his back, in his teeth. With the baby in his mouth, he ran into the bushes, with the other males following him. Two minutes later, the infant was dead.

Masudi sat beside his bloody mother. He began crying and vocalizing. The vocalizations, described as a "waao, waao" sound, were not directed at anyone and received no response.* Masudi had escaped much of the attack and, unlike his mother, was uninjured. He got up and walked into the bushes where Ntologi had gone with his brother. As he disappeared into the bushes, Watendele got up and left the area. It would be weeks before she was seen again.

In the bushes, Ntologi was eating the infant's carcass. He did this by grabbing a handful of dead leaves and eating the leaves with the meat of the dead chimpanzee.† Kagimimi approached Ntologi and vocalized. The alpha male ignored him and continued to eat the infant's wrist. Within five minutes, he had eaten the wrist and had moved on to the face. As he continued, Masudi got closer. The five-year-old stared at the alpha male eating his brother. None of the males attacked Masudi or paid him any attention.

It is at this point that Masudi would have to reach a new point of self-awareness. He was left by his mother to watch his old social bonds being, quite literally, devoured in front of him by the group he would be forced to join. He would have to alter his perceptions of the others

---

* Twenty years after this episode I would have the opportunity to hear such a vocalization. This would come from Higgy. More on that in chapter 9.

† It is interesting that this chimpanzee had to mix the meat with leaves. It makes sense, as the meat of a chimpanzee would not be something that would be naturally palatable to another chimp. Dead leaves would dilute the taste. This really exemplifies the political nature of such an attack.

around him and alter his understanding of himself in a new social situation. This would alter everything about his behavior and interactions with others. Through ecological necessity, his communication with the world around him would have to change. We can imagine that as Masudi stood staring at Ntologi, he was attempting to understand the situation. We can imagine that he was, in effect, reflecting on the perception in front of him. His previous cries had failed him. He had received no reassurances through communication. He had received no alliance or protection through his cries. He was left to find socialization in any way he could, even if that meant staring at his antagonist. He was forced, at that moment (through the biological need to communicate and socialize) to truly get to know the members of the Mimikile group.*

Kagimimi stayed near. As pieces of meat would fall to the ground, he would pick them up and eat. Other males followed his example and began to eat the scraps that Ntologi had dropped. Kagimimi soon grabbed the infant's leg and bit it as Ntologi held the carcass. Ntologi didn't seem to mind as he had moved on to the inside of the skull.

With his brother dead and his mother having disappeared, Masudi had no choice but to stay within the social territory of Mimikile. Though almost certainly Mimikile would have been a stressful situation for Masudi, the alternative was to live in solitude. A solitary chimpanzee cannot survive. Since the Mimikile males did not seem interested in harming Masudi at this point, he remained with the group. The next day, the group migrated south.†

---

* So, in order to have a fully functional vocal communication system, one has to be able to recognize individuals. Once this is accomplished, one can recognize oneself as a parcel of the greater environment. After this, an individual can attach meanings to identifications and the information transmitted by these identifications. One can also alter their messages depending on who they are communicating with. Without any of these abilities, one cannot fully integrate in a social system.

† For a complete account of the incident, see Takahata, 1985.

Days later, Masudi was seen grooming Musa. A minute later, Musa began to reciprocate and groomed Masudi. After grooming, the two found some fruit and ate together. They were beginning to form a bond. With such a bond, Masudi was now truly a part of Mimikile. Without his mother or brother, he was forced to bond with one of the males. Through this bond, he was able to immerse himself within the group and survive the stormy social environment of Mimikile. In order for Masudi to survive his new environment, he must alter his behaviors, his interactions, and his communication.

In turn, having devoured everything that had been Masudi's world, Mimikile must alter itself, as a group, to accommodate its newest member and the changes he would bring to their social group.*

1983
Loxahatchee, Florida

Elgin spent the day recovering from another tonic-clonic (or grand mal) seizure. The encephalitis that he suffered from as an infant had left him epileptic. His moves were shaky and quivering. Every action was undertaken very slowly. Because of all of this, it was uncertain when, if ever, he would be able to integrate with other chimpanzees. It was becoming clear that there was a real possibility of Elgin having to spend his entire life in a hospital away from all chimpanzee companionship.

The zookeepers and hospital staff who were in charge of taking care of Elgin took great pains to minimize his isolation. They would

---

* The infant that was killed and cannibalized was sired by a Mimikile male. Masudi would have been fathered by a Kajabala male. The Mimikile males appeared to have absolutely no interest in killing Masudi, only the new infant. Questions remain about the motivation behind this attack.

play with him every day, allow him to watch television, and groom him. When Elgin would attempt to groom them back, he would emit a unique vocalization. In fact, most chimpanzees, when they groom, produce a unique vocalization. Elgin's consisted of pushing air through his lips (much like Cindy's raspberry sound) at three-second intervals. Chimpanzees often produce vocalizations for the sole sake of identifying themselves. Furthermore, all vocalizations have a self-identification aspect and may have stemmed from the ecological need for identification through sound.

During this time, a paper was published in the *Psychological Record* which detailed this very idea. The paper showcased the role of recognizing other chimpanzees in vocal communication.* The star of the paper was Nim Chimpsky. After Nim had underperformed with Terrace, he was moved from Terrace's Manhattan apartment to the Institute for Primate Studies in Norman, Oklahoma. There, he was integrated with other juvenile chimpanzees and provided fodder for more behavioral studies.

In this study, Nim was shown black-and-white photographs of the chimpanzees he lived with at the institute. Recordings were then played of the chimpanzees vocalizing. At this point, Nim was asked to point to the individual producing the vocalization. Sure enough, the results showed that he displayed a competency in being able to recognize the caller. Efforts were made to perform the same task with the other chimpanzees by using recordings of Nim's vocalizations. However, since Nim never vocalized like a regular chimpanzee, that was impossible.

The results show not only the function of facial recognition in chimpanzees but also the function of vocal recognition. A chimpanzee can recognize other individuals even without seeing their faces. In

---

* See Bauer & Philip, 1983.

THE SONG OF THE APE / 134

a species where social hierarchy is so important to the survival of the group, the implications of these results are profound. The ability to recognize each other as individuals allows for a retained knowledge of social rank, social roles, and alliances.

Chimpanzees are constantly engaged in showcasing their individuality. In addition to traits that cannot be altered (such as physical features and chemical emissions), chimpanzees have conscious ways of showing who they are to others. Every individual has his or her own styles of displaying. Every individual has his or her own characteristics of calling. Every individual, like Elgin, has unique grooming vocalizations. For Elgin, this was the last remnant of an individual trademark he was holding on to.

Elgin existed in a world where there were no other chimpanzees to recognize. Since Gin's departure from the hospital pen, Elgin had not heard another chimpanzee's voice. He had no way to recognize another chimpanzee individual and therefore could not recognize his own individual nature as a chimpanzee.

Attempt, for a moment, to view the world like Elgin. The last time you saw another of your species, you were an infant and too young to remember. You are very familiar with three or four individuals of another species. However, you cannot communicate with them. Your only perception of the outside world is your television (which you cannot understand), these individuals, and any toys you are given. Imagine your view of yourself. Can you even perceive of yourself as an individual? Are you self-aware? Imagine, then, being self-unaware. You are still intelligent. You still have all of your given cognitive faculties. However, you cannot comprehend yourself as an individual living in the world in front of you. The world, instead, exists as a sort of a motion picture working on all of your senses. You react instinctually to stimuli but not as an individual conscious of the consequences of your actions.

Because you have no perception of yourself as an individual entity, the communication you utilize is far different from what you would naturally use. You would have no need for self-identification in your gestures or vocalizations because you wouldn't realize that you were separate from the rest of the world. Likewise, because of your lack of self-awareness, you would have no ability to recognize other individuals. They, too, would exist as part of an amalgamation of the world in front of you. Also, because of your lack of self-perception, you would be unable to consciously choose your actions or methods of communication. All of this would, therefore, be left up to instinct. Even your choices would appear to you to be beyond your control and part of the world you were watching.

However, Elgin still had his individual trademark: his grooming vocalization. This was a small sign that all shreds of his individual nature had not been vanquished by his solitude. He still had time to recognize himself and others. In the meantime, Elgin sat in his hospital pen—shaking, weak, and unable to affect the world around him.

1983
Mahale Mountains, Tanzania

Masudi inched closer to the Mimikile infant female. In an instant he grabbed her and wrestled with her. Making a play face, the two chimpanzees rolled around, seemingly having great fun. A three-year-old female approached the two chimpanzees. She tackled Masudi. Masudi spun around and pinned her to the ground. The vocalizations of happy chimps engaged in play filled the air. For ten minutes the fun continued. Without warning, one of the lower-ranking adult males appeared. This male, Kasangazi, was one of the males who had participated in the attack on Masudi's mother and brother. Kasangazi had also taken part in the cannibalism of Masudi's infant brother. The adult male tackled Masudi. The young chimp screamed and tried to flee. At this, Kasangazi grabbed Masudi by the wrist and bit him hard. He then kicked him and dragged him by the wrist. As quickly as he had appeared, Kasangazi left. Masudi sat alone and began to groom his injuries.*

According to the observing primatologists, it appeared that Masudi had begun to depend on Musa for solace. In the turbulent social situation that Masudi has been thrown into, Musa had become his companion. In addition to grooming each other, they would eat next to each other. In fact, Musa was the only male that would eat with or groom Masudi. It wasn't, however, for lack of trying on Masudi's part. He had attempted to groom other adults (such as Kagimimi and Kasangazi), however none of them reciprocated.

One month after the killing of her infant, Wantendele returned to Mimikile. When this occurred, Masudi quickly shifted his social dependency from Musa back to his mother. However, things were different with his mother. She had restarted her reproductive cycles and was in estrus when she returned. Because of this, the adult males would approach and mate with her. When this occurred, Masudi would avoid the situation. However, when Ntologi attempted to mate with Wantendele, Masudi tried to stop the act. As Ntologi mounted his mother, Masudi began vocalizing and touching his mother's back. The interference, however, was not successful, and Masudi gave up.

As time went on, Masudi began to occupy more of a social role within Mimikile. In addition to his social bond with Musa, he began to interact with Bakali. Masudi would greet Bakali when he saw him

---

* The transfer of Masudi from Kajabala to Mimikile has been documented in Hitomi Takahata and Yukio Takahata's fascinating paper, "Inter-unit group transfer of an immature male of the common chimpanzee and his social interactions in the non-natal group" (1989).

by standing directly in front of him and vocalizing. Bakali would respond by touching his head.

During this time Watendele became pregnant again. By June of 1984, she had bore another male offspring. Masudi had a new brother. Although he preferred playing with his other companions in Mimikile, Masudi would also play with the infant.

Masudi had begun to mate with other females. However, his status in the group was still extremely low ranking. Thus, the mating always occurred far away from the rest of the group. At one point, the female he was mounting vocalized loudly. Ntologi heard it and ran toward the sound. Finding them, he ran at Masudi and broke up the mating session.

Because Masudi had established social bonds within the group, he was aware of his role. For example, he knew that he had to hide in order to mate with any of the females. He knew which males to stay away from. In knowing these things, he was able to survive the very volatile group situation he was in. As he altered his behavioral patterns, we can imagine that he communicated based on this knowledge of himself and his relationship to the others. Such factors influence the means in which an individual communicates. Eventually, this changes the way an individual vocalizes and, in turn, helps shape the dialect of the entire group.

1986
Loxahatchee, Florida

A decision had been made. Elgin's quality of life was at stake. He had spent the majority of his life drugged up in a hospital pen. This was not the life for a chimpanzee. Therefore, Elgin was going to be united with other chimpanzees. Either he would find a social niche or else he wouldn't be able to survive. Either way, it was better than the alternative—an isolated life of medication and boredom.

The decision to integrate Elgin with other chimpanzees was not made lightly. The obvious choice of which chimpanzee Elgin would be introduced to was the one who had done so well subduing Gin. Higgy had proven to be an excellent alpha male. His group (even with Gin) was peaceful and orderly. He was judicious with his aggression and was never excessive with his power. In addition, both Edwina and Gin had given birth in the last two years. So now, Higgy was showing his ability to lead a group that contained mothers and juveniles. Both Gin's nine-month-old baby (appropriately named Tonic) and Edwina's two-year-old female (named Cashew) spent a lot of time with Higgy. He was extremely gentle with them and would play with the young females throughout the day. The fact that Higgy was maintaining a group that contained two nursing juveniles, a fifty-year-old (Little Mama), and an extremely unpredictable and erratic chimpanzee (Gin) was testament to his power as an alpha male. Also, it would be good for Higgy to have another male chimpanzee on the island. Higgy had done exceptionally well with Peter in the hospital pen, so it was reasoned that another male would fit in with Higgy's group very well. Therefore, it was decided that Elgin would go to this group in the hopes that the alpha male would take him under his wing.

In 1986 Elgin was weaned off of his medication.* After several months of observation, it seemed that he had learned to control his seizures. There were times when he would sort of hug himself and rock back and forth. This may have been his way of controlling seizures. Outside of these episodes, he seemed to do fine without the

_____

* Keep in mind here how much of Elgin's reality was beginning to change. Having been on medication for the better part of his development and being isolated in a hospital cage, it would almost have been as if he was entering the world for the first time.

medication. Soon Elgin was packed into an animal carrier and rowed out to the island. Elgin was about to be introduced to Gin, Higgy, and Little Mama.

Elgin's carrier sat closed on Higgy's island. One of the zookeepers opened the door and Elgin slowly walked about. He looked at the ground as he stepped from the plastic carrier onto grass. Shaking, as he always did, he sat down and looked around. Around him were other chimpanzees.

The images and sounds perceived meant very little to him. They all existed as snapshots of unreflected consciousness (the only way Elgin ever perceived anything).* The chimpanzees in his sight had no identities. The sounds of chimp calls had no inherent meaning. The sky, the feeling of the wind, the water around him, and all other observations had no other significance above the sensations they provided. As the three chimpanzees approached him, Elgin had an instinctual drive to flee the situation—which he did. Running as fast as he could (which wasn't very fast), Elgin tripped and rolled down the island. He sat up and looked around. There were two chimpanzees still approaching him. He couldn't see the third.

At that point, Elgin felt a sharp pain across his back. The cause of this sensation was Gin, who, with Tonic clinging on to her, had rushed up from behind him and slashed Elgin across the back with a fingernail. Elgin screamed as he looked at the female chimpanzee. As he looked at her face, she opened her mouth and sunk her teeth into his

---

* The best way I know to imagine unreflected consciousness is to compare it to having a horrendously boring person talk to you at a cocktail party. If you are like me, you tune them out and function on "autopilot." You are hearing their words, seeing their movements, and are aware of how close they are to you. Yet, you place no meaning on what you are seeing or hearing. At the same time, you may nod or say something like "ummm hmm" out of instinct. At the end of the conversation you have no idea of what was said. This, to me, is how an individual without the ability to reflect on what is being perceived sees the world and communicates with the world.

ear. Elgin cried out and reflexively tried to push Gin away. Gin screamed at him as she held onto his ear with her teeth. As he pushed her and Gin released her bite, he could see another chimpanzee. This chimp was a much smaller individual wrapped up in a burlap cloth. It was Little Mama and she was distressed. Little Mama was calling to Higgy, who had now gone out of Elgin's sight. She then turned to Elgin and reached out her hand toward him. Before he could do anything, Gin lunged toward him again. This time, she clamped down on his foot. Elgin howled as he closed his eyes. When he opened them he saw another chimpanzee charging toward him. This chimp, Higgy, was rushing at Elgin and Gin with his right arm raised. As he ran, he was calling out. Elgin perceived the image of the male chimpanzee running toward him, the image of the chimp's right arm in the air, and the sound of the chimpanzee vocalizing. Again, these perceptions lacked any greater substance to Elgin other than the sensations they elicited. Elgin covered his face with his arms. Higgy brushed past Elgin and brought his arm down on Gin's back. Gin screamed and ran away. Higgy followed her. At this, Elgin ran back into the animal carrier.

When he was safely inside the carrier, Little Mama slowly approached him. She popped her head inside the carrier and vocalized softly. Elgin opened his mouth and lunged at her. Little Mama yelped and ran far away from the carrier. Elgin embraced himself and began rocking back and forth inside the carrier.

Higgy appeared outside of the carrier. The alpha male reached inside and pulled Elgin out. Elgin screamed. Higgy grabbed each of Elgin's hands and pressed his forehead against Elgin's. He gave a series of short hoots. Elgin looked at Higgy up close.

It is at this point that, I believe, Elgin reached a point of chimpanzee self-awareness. After experiencing chimpanzees for the first time since his infancy, Elgin could become conscious of himself as an individual. As horrifying as these few moments were for him, he could instinctually relate to these three animals. In this instinctual relation, he was able to consciously understand them as three unique individuals. He could then understand himself as an individual. As Higgy and Elgin stared at each other, eye to eye, he was able to understand that Higgy was protecting him. He was able to be conscious of himself as a chimpanzee, able to be hurt by Gin and able to be protected by Higgy. He could see three different parts of himself reflected in the three chimpanzees he had come in contact with.

When Elgin created a social bond with Higgy, he could consciously understand that he could utilize another chimpanzee in helping him to survive. The instinct to survive had taken over and had driven this form of conscious self-awareness. He could now be as dependent on Higgy for survival as he was on his own instinctual responses. This realization led to his self-awareness and the emergence of Elgin's mind. Elgin had a genetically hardwired need to be protected from Gin. The protection came from another chimpanzee. This brought about the genetically hardwired need to be conscious of the other chimpanzee in order to utilize him for survival, at that point and in the future. This consciousness gave rise to his own self-awareness which, in turn, would aid him further in survival. The instinctual drive to survive, the instinctual drive to be protected, and the instinctual drive to socialize gives rise to the conscious awareness brought about by a social bond.

Later that day, when the sun was beginning to set, things on Higgy's island had calmed down. Higgy and Elgin sat together. Throughout the day, anytime Higgy would get up, Elgin would rise and follow him. It appeared that Higgy tolerated this dependency. In fact, when Higgy would walk away, he would stop and look back at Elgin following. It was almost as if Higgy was checking to make sure. For Elgin, Higgy had become an extension of himself. Without Higgy, Elgin was

vulnerable to everything else in his new environment. As they sat together, Elgin began to groom Higgy. As he groomed, he produced his
strange grooming sound. Higgy turned around and began to groom
Elgin back. For the first time, Elgin heard another chimpanzee's
trademark grooming sounds. Higgy's vocalization was far different
from Elgin's and sounded like he was clicking his tongue. Little Mama
came and sat behind Higgy. She began to groom Higgy's back as he
groomed Elgin. She produced her own sound (which sounded an awful lot like Higgy's). After a few moments, Gin and Tonic approached
the three chimpanzees. With Tonic on her back, she sat down beside
Elgin's feet. She picked up the foot she had bitten and began to groom
the wound she had inflicted. Elgin closed his eyes and began mimicking the soft vocalizations Little Mama had made to him as he hid in
the carrier. Little Mama, from behind Higgy, returned those vocalizations back to him.

That evening, as Higgy's group continued to form stronger bonds,
the opposite was occurring in the Mahale Mountains of Tanzania. A
chimpanzee was living alone. This chimp (unnamed and unknown to
primatologists) was living within the Kajabala area and exhibiting
ranging patterns as if he were living within the Kajabala group. Kajabala, however, had been extinct for close to four years. Primatologists
later found this chimp to be a Kajabala male they were familiar with.
They had thought that, like all the other Kajabala males, he had been
killed by Mimikile. The male, exhibiting as if Kajabala still existed, was
seemingly unable to sever the bonds of his group, even though the group
had long since disappeared. Even though the social bonds had been extinguished, the behaviors that the social bonds granted this male were
strong enough to cause him to lead a completely solitary lifestyle. The
chimpanzee now lived alone in the wild—without a group, without
social bonds, and without communication. As Elgin was exiting a
world of isolation and entering a world of social bonds, this chimp, a

hemisphere away, had left the social world he had been raised in to lead a solitary existence.

At the animal park, the next morning, zookeepers found that four nests had been made on the ground. All four nests were neatly nestled right beside each other.*

> *All friendship is desirable in itself, though it starts as a need for help.*
>
> —EPICURUS

---

* You may wonder, at this point, where the nest was of the mother and juvenile, Edwina and Cashew. Their nest was actually far away from the four on the ground, up in a shelter. Clearly, these two hadn't been included in the initial group bonding session.

6

The Leap of Faith

The structure of the communication system of Higgy's group had been built, piece by piece, by the histories of each individual within the group. When Little Mama was thrown into a world of humans from her natural world of chimpanzees, we were able to see the adaptability of the structure that she had brought from Africa. When Cindy was suddenly integrated with other chimpanzees after being raised as if she were a human child, we were able to see how this structure is acquired. When Higgy became socially indispensable to Cindy (and every other chimpanzee he came into contact with) and was able to interact with her (unlike her human caretaker), we were able to see how the structure of a chimpanzee communication system depends on a shared chimp perception of the outside world. When Gin was unable to relate to any other chimpanzee, we were able to see the raw and useless form of an unsocialized structure of a communication system. When Elgin stood head to head with Higgy, we were able to see how the communication system relies on social bonds in order to be unlocked. In all of these cases, we see evidence of a linguistic structure to chimpanzee communication. However, a linguistic model relies on more than just structure. A linguistic model relies on its conscious usage.

Imagine, for a moment, that a child is sitting alone in a room with a hot iron. Away from the protective watch of his mother, he crawls over to the iron and places his hand on the hot side. Reflexively, two things happen at once: he pulls his hand away from the iron and he yelps. Both actions occur without a conscious decision by the child. Both actions occur purely on instinct. Both actions, for the child, function as a way to survive. The reflex to pull oneself away from a painful situation is obvious. If the child didn't have this reflex, his hand would remain longer on the hot iron while he consciously decided to remove it. Likewise, the yelp that the child produces has a purpose which is just as beneficial. When the child yelps, his mother runs into the room and picks her child up—away from danger. This reflex would occur in any painful or dangerous situation the child—or any individual for that matter—would find himself in. The reflex to cry out is an unconscious and insentient communication system.

Now compare this with a conscious communication system, a system quite different and far removed from the insentient system. Let's imagine that the child is, again, alone in a room. Only this time, there isn't a hot iron. Instead the child is lonely or bored and wants his mother's attention. In an effort to communicate this to his mother, he lets out the same yelp. The mother, once again, comes running to him and scoops him up. In both incidents, the child produces the same call. In both instances, the call produces the same results: the mother running in and picking up the child. However, there is a profound difference between the two events. The first event is a purely instinctual and unconscious act of communication. The second event is a highly complex and conscious transmission of a message.

Freedom of choice distinguishes a conscious communication system from an insentient communication system. The ability to choose such features as a message to send, a way of conveying that message, a channel to send that message through, and a receiver to direct a message toward is the cornerstone of a linguistic system. Humans communicate through both conscious and unconscious systems. When the child yelps from touching the hot iron, it is not a consciously chosen piece of communication. It happens by reflex along with other reflexes (such as pulling his hand away). This unconscious communication alerts his mother to the fact that her child is hurt and causes her to run to him and help. There is no freedom of choice in sending this message. The child isn't choosing the yelp, isn't consciously directing that yelp at anyone in particular, and isn't selecting from any other ways to convey that message. The message comes without the aid of any conscious effort on the child's part. However, in the second scenario, the form of communication has gone from being an unconscious response to being a complex form of conscious communication. The child has chosen a certain message, conveyed that message by yelping, and directed it at his mother (who then comes running).

Linguistic communication systems rely on this freedom of choice to function. In language, we choose a message and a receiver. We also choose whether to send that message verbally, gesturally, or in written form. Within each one of these choices, we have more conscious decisions. For example, if we chose to send a message verbally, we have to choose which sounds we are going to combine to create that message. This decision may be based on who we are directing the message to, the environment we are in, how we want to present ourselves, or any other conscious reason that might be applicable to the situation or message. As humans we rely on this freedom of choice in language to survive our social systems and our world.

What about chimpanzees? Do chimpanzees utilize this freedom of choice in their communication systems? If so, is it linguistic? Is it language? Up until now, we have danced around using the term "language" to describe chimpanzee communication. Indeed, the definition of language is a touchy subject. Some linguists have gone to great lengths to declare that the phenomenon is an exclusively human trait. Some anthropologists have taken this to the next level and determined that the very thing that makes the human species unique from the rest of the animal world is its ability to use language.

I, however, feel confident in granting language to chimpanzees. Not, of course, in what we can teach them (or not teach them) in a lab, but by how they are communicating in the wild. As we have explored, the histories of Little Mama, Cindy, Higgy, Gin, and Elgin demonstrate the structure of the language of chimpanzees. What we must look at now is their ability to consciously use this structure. That usage depends on intentionality—or the conscious freedom of choice.* Chimpanzees do, in fact, make conscious linguistic choices. When the chimpanzee, Oz, found hidden treats inside a pumpkin and chose not to vocalize to his group-mates, we see a conscious linguistic choice.† Yet, this choice was limited. Oz was merely making a conscious choice not to communicate. He was not making a decision on the manner in which he would communicate. Moreover, the choice

---

* When we look at the foundations of what makes a communication system, we divide the system into its structure and its usage. The structure consists of the manner in which the system is transmitted, the manner in which different meanings are attained through different combinations, and the learned lexicon of definitions. The usage is the conscious way the structure is applied. In other words, the structure is the sounds, grammar, and definitions while the usage is how we choose to use them in everyday life.

† See chapter 5.

Oz was making had clear consequences. If he had chosen to communicate, he would have lost his treats. Since he had chosen not to communicate, he was able to keep all of the treats for himself. Most conscious linguistic choices do not have such apparent results. In fact, in some choices, the results are ecologically equal and therefore require a much more complex decision-making process.

The following accounts detail chimpanzees in the process of making conscious decisions. Unlike Oz's pumpkins, the choices within these decisions don't necessarily have apparent ecological benefits. The decisions made by the chimpanzees don't necessarily seem to make any ecological sense. Rather, what they show are chimpanzees as cognizant organisms faced with the same dilemma humans are faced with—that, instead of relying on instinct, they must consciously make a choice without knowing the consequence of their action. Language relies on the ability to rise above instinctual calls and make conscious choices about the messages, channels, and receivers. Being saddled with freedom of choice means that one is aware that a wrong decision could have grave consequences. In language, a wrong choice can also have dire consequences to a species which relies upon socialization for survival. Freedom of choice in language, and every other conscious situation, requires faith in one's knowledge of the world, one's memory of relevant situations, and one's intuitive impulses. The leap of faith is the abhorrent side effect of having the cognitive complexities that grant us language.

1988
Loxahatchee, Florida

Rachel jumped down from the shelter and ran to the edge of the island. Cindy, her mother, was there watching as trucks, backhoes, and barges lined up in front of the large island beside her. As Cindy watched, Rachel did somersaults in front of her. Cindy grabbed her by the leg and pulled her close. The five-year-old female playfully bit her mother's hand. As the two wrestled on the side of their island, they kept an eye on what was occurring across the canal.

In front of the large island, Terry Wolf stood in waist-high water, holding a fire extinguisher in his hands and facing the group of chimps on the shore. Behind him was a growling backhoe, dredging up dirt from the bottom of the canal to create a land bridge to the island. As the land bridge expanded, both Terry and the backhoe got continually closer to the island's shoreline. With each step, Terry would lightly spray the fire extinguisher in the air, causing the chimps to move back.

The purpose for all of this construction was to divide the large island into four smaller islands. These four islands, combined with the island that Cindy's group occupied, would make five islands on the large canal. This would enable the park to move Higgy's group and Romeo's group to the canal (thereby locating all of the chimpanzees into one section). With four groups and five islands (Doll's group of ex-lab chimps would stay where they were), they would have an additional empty island to use in case any chimps needed to be removed from their group for any reason.

Such a move was not without concerns. As we have seen with the Mimikile and Kajabala groups in the Mahale Mountains, the closely knit social groups of chimpanzees are extremely territorial. Any unwelcome chimpanzee trespassing onto the island of another chimpanzee group could result in violent consequences. An entire group mixing with another group would be disastrous. Because of this, dividing these islands was quite a chore. It required the backhoe to slice through the island in three different places with each slice conforming to certain dimensions. Since there were about to be four separate chimpanzee groups living right next to each other, each slice had to be deep enough and wide enough to ensure that no chimpanzees would be able to go from one island to the other. This was not as easy as it sounds. Chimpanzees can jump extremely far. Due to this, each slice had to be at least five meters wide. Also, since these chimpanzees had provided evidence against a natural fear of water, the slices had to be deep enough to guarantee that a chimp couldn't wade across the canal. Keep in mind that all of this was occurring with a group of chimpanzees on the very island that was being sliced up—the backhoe being defended by one man and a fire extinguisher.

Meanwhile, at the other end of the park, Higgy's group was peaceful. Unaware that they were about to be uprooted to another island surrounded by other chimpanzees, they were only concerned with their own social world. Within the group, Elgin had been taken completely under Higgy's wing. If Elgin was ever antagonized, Higgy would retaliate for him. No one was allowed to steal from Elgin, threaten Elgin, or harm Elgin. No one, that is, except for Higgy himself. Though Higgy prevented others from terrorizing the neurologically impaired chimp, he occasionally took to roughing Elgin up in order to display his power to the other chimpanzees.* At times, when the group was silent, Higgy would begin making a slow and deliberate call. The call would become louder and louder until it would climax with Higgy screaming and running toward Elgin. The other chimpanzees would scatter out of the way and watch as Higgy would smack Elgin across the back. Elgin would scream and reach out to Higgy. After a few moments, Higgy would walk over to Elgin and groom him.

Another interesting dynamic that was developing within the group

---

* Though this seems barbaric and mean of Higgy, it's actually a necessary practice which enables an alpha male like Higgy to retain his status. Without these displays (which sometimes have to carry with them a bit of violence) the alpha male is vulnerable to alliances being created behind his back. If such an alliance were to happen within Higgy's group, he could easily lose his power. This would make chimps like Elgin, Little Mama, and the babies very vulnerable to the other members of the group.

was the raising of the island's two juveniles, Cashew and Tonic. A year apart in age, the two were frequently together. Edwina was an extremely attentive mother to Cashew. Now four years old, Cashew was becoming more independent. The times she spent away from her mother were spent playing with either Higgy or Tonic, who was now three. Tonic's mother, Gin, had been a considerably less attentive mother. In fact, when Tonic was an infant, Gin would frequently lay her down in the middle of the island and climb up a shelter or go to the other side of the island. When this would occur, Edwina would pick Tonic up and take care of her. After a while, Edwina began spending more time with Tonic than Gin was spending with her. She would carry her and Cashew around at the same time, play with both of them, and sleep with both of them. When it was time for Tonic to eat, Edwina would calmly walk Tonic over to her mother and push the infant up to Gin's chest. Gin would grab hold of Tonic and allow her to nurse. When Tonic was done, Edwina would walk over and pick her back up.

Little Mama had also begun to fill a new role within the group. She would take care of the two juveniles when Edwina needed a break. Oftentimes, Edwina would fall asleep during the day, leaving Cashew and Tonic with Little Mama. She was an engaging caretaker and would play with them throughout the entire time she had them in her care. Games she would play included lying on her back and holding a juvenile up in the air with her feet. Both Tonic and Cashew would make high-pitched squeals as they rode on Little Mama's feet.

Looking at the dynamics of Higgy's group at this time reveals the dynamics of how the free will of a group of chimpanzees could work together in one system of survival. First, you had the structure of the group. This structure consisted of the chimpanzees themselves—the physical presence of Little Mama, Higgy, Gin, Elgin, Edwina, Cashew, and Tonic. The structure also included the environment they lived in—in this case, an island isolated from other groups of chimpanzees.

Finally, the structure was formed by the social roles each chimpanzee was playing—Higgy as an alpha male, Elgin as a low-ranking male, Edwina as a mother, Little Mama as a caretaker, Gin as an aberrant agitator, and Cashew and Tonic as the juveniles of the group. The usage of this structure depended on the individual wills of each chimpanzee. The will of each chimpanzee was realized by choices they were all making; choices which may or may not have been within their best ecological interest, but which satisfied the usage of the group's structure. Even though Edwina had to spend energy and time with an infant that wasn't hers, she still chose to take care of Tonic in addition to Cashew. The same was true of Little Mama's choice to take care of the juveniles. She expended time and energy on an activity with no immediate benefit to her own survival.

As Higgy's group had both a structure and a usage, so did the communication system of Higgy's group. There was the basic structure. This consisted of the meanings associated with each call. These meanings, possibly originating from Little Mama's group in Sierra Leone and modified by each additional member of the group, were learned and specific to Higgy's group. The structure of this communication system also included the way the calls were produced and how they sounded, their prosody. This prosody was influenced equally by each member of the group and bore the imprints of their individual histories. The prosody of Higgy's group was built by the times of turmoil, peace, social change, and environmental change that each chimpanzee had undergone. This structure had been involuntarily saddled upon the group. Yet, there was a usage to this structure that was entirely voluntarily. The chimpanzees were able to manipulate the structure. They were able to choose which calls to make, modify the prosody of each call to achieve an effect, and choose whether or not to vocalize at all. This usage was based on the cognitive free will of the chimpanzees. The structure and usage of the communication system of Higgy's group maintained the structure and usage of the group dynamics. In addition to normal communicative functions, social roles and identities were maintained by these linguistic choices. Though both the group dynamics and communication system were maintained by the apparent randomness of chimpanzee free will, somehow both worked in an extremely complex system which enhanced the fitness of the group.

All in all the group was extremely stable. They lived without competition, without threats of danger, and without much intragroup conflict. Higgy had proven to be a good and effective leader, able to govern a group of chimpanzees with extremely disparate temperaments and histories. The stability of the group, however, was about to be tested by the fact that they were going to be moved beside other chimps. The proximity to other chimpanzees would create other roles within the group's hierarchy. Even though they would be separated by water, the chimps on the other islands would present a perceived threat to the security of the group, a perceived threat to their access to resources, and a perceived threat to Higgy's power. These threats would have consequences and the dynamics of the group would change.

As with all changes to the group dynamics, these would lead to changes within the communication systems; changes that would stay with the group and alter its vocal evolution. If you imagine the evolution of a language or any vocal communication system as a straight line, you can see how any slight change to the situation of a group would have a profound effect. This straight line represents vocal evolution in a state of equilibrium (no changes in social hierarchy, environment, or stress). The vocalizations evolve very gradually based on natural phonetic inclinations.* Any change to the equilibrium al-

---

* It is unclear what natural phonetic inclinations there may be within chimpanzee vocalizations. In typological studies, we can see human phonetic inclinations that appear to dictate change

ters the straight line and causes it to veer off its original path. Even if the change is minimal, it forever alters the course of those vocalizations. With that in mind, suppose Higgy's group remained on their original island for generations. Suppose, also, that Higgy remained as alpha male and each of the other chimpanzees maintained the same social roles. In addition, imagine that there were no real times of stress within the group and everything was functioning free from incident. This would be the real-life linguistic equivalent of our straight line. Now suppose a new chimp, a female, were to join this stable group. The addition of this female, at first, would cause a stressful period within the group where everyone was calling a bit faster and a bit higher in pitch. Also imagine that the other females, in order to showcase their rank and role to the new female chimp, were making different choices in the usage of their vocalizations. The effect may cause them to make different calls or make different prosodic choices. Higgy would also display different choices in his vocalizations. He would, almost certainly, have to display his rank as alpha to the new chimp. This would cause him to use all sorts of different vocalizations which would portray him as unquestionably in charge. Even though these social changes would, most likely, only cause temporary upheaval, the linguistic imprint would be permanent. Some of the prosodic changes would stick around based on the fact that each chimp's social roles would change in some way. Also, the two juveniles, at this time, would be acquiring all of the vocalizations that they were hearing. Even a temporary shift in the communication system would be acquired by these juveniles and would forever affect the way they

---

regardless of language. These inclinations are based on such things as the ease of making certain sounds, the ease of having one sound follow another, or the expense of energy in making overly long sounds. Chimpanzee natural inclinations, like human inclinations, would be based primarily on the morphological operation of making sounds (something that would be very different between the two species).

communicated. They, in turn, would pass along these vocal changes to their offspring. So, the addition of a new chimpanzee would shift the straight line of vocal evolution in Higgy's group, making each change something that builds the way the group calls.

Across the park, work was finishing up on cutting up the large island. There were now two islands dividing Old Man's group from the other group. Cindy and Rachel had stayed on the edge of their island the entire time. Cindy was about to have a lot more chimpanzees to watch; most of whom she had come into contact with before. What was not realized, at that time, was that Cindy was pregnant again.

1988
Campo Animal Reserve, Cameroon

A termite mound had been disturbed. It was clear from both the marks on the mound and the chimpanzee-crafted tools lying around the area who had meddled with it. It had been a group of chimps who had been indirectly studied by a group from the Primate Research Institute at Kyoto University. The reason they were only able to be studied secondarily was that the group was not habituated to human presence and was unable to be observed without their behavior being profoundly affected by the presence of a researcher. This, however, was not an issue for the current study—the chimpanzees' choice of termites to eat.

It was in 1960 that Jane Goodall discovered chimpanzees in the Kakombe Valley (later Gombe National Park) of Tanzania making and using tools to take termites out of their mounds and eat them. These termite mounds are impressive structures with a thick concrete-hard surface. Termites can successfully enter these mounds and remain safe from all outside predators. In order for the chimps to get to these termites, they have to fashion a tool out of the thin branches of nearby trees.

They form these tools by picking off any leaves or divergent branches, leaving them with a thin long stem. They then take this stem and insert it into one of the holes of the termite mound. When a chimpanzee does this, the termites cling onto the stem. The chimp slowly pulls the stem out of the mound and eats off all of the termites that were holding on. Juvenile chimpanzees have been observed watching the older chimpanzees perform this feat then trying it themselves.* In one fascinating film clip from Gombe, both chimpanzees and baboons surround termite mounds. The baboons, who do not know how to use these tools, can only eat the termites on the surface of the mound. After all of the termites disappear from the surface of the mound, the baboons retreat and leave the area. The chimps, however, can eat the termites that are inside of the mound and, therefore, outcompete the baboons for a food source.†

Until this discovery, conventional wisdom determined the uniqueness of the human species to be its ability to manipulate its environment for greater survival. Anthropologists pointed to the ability of humans to make and use tools as evidence for this. Jane Goodall's discovery would throw a wrench into this line of thinking. Not only were chimpanzees making and using a tool, but they were passing the technology down from one generation to the next. It was later discovered that different groups of chimpanzees were using different tools.

---

* The fact that older chimpanzees pass down a technology to the younger generation of chimpanzees has profound implications on our views of the rest of the animal world. The ability to pass along beneficial traits was long thought to be the hallmark of human culture. What Jane Goodall witnessed pioneered the other studies of chimpanzee culture—including our current exploration of the language of chimpanzees.

† At one point a fake termite mound was built on one of the chimp islands at the animal park. Inside the mound was honey, mustard, and other condiment-type items that the chimps enjoyed. Around the mound, thin branches were scattered. None of the chimpanzees seemed to understand how to get to the treats. Only a wild caught ex-lab chimp, Inky, immediately understood what to do. The others were quick to catch on after watching her.

Sometimes this was based on the environment they lived in, sometimes not. In fact, many groups of chimpanzees who live around the same type of termite mounds have not learned the technology to "fish" for termites in this way. Because of this, the tool-manufacture-and-use definition of human uniqueness had to be questioned.*

The termites and chimpanzees currently studied at the Campo Animal Reserve had a different type of situation. There were two species of termites. One of the species constructed the mounds with the thick cementlike surface. The other species constructed towering mounds with a much weaker surface. These mounds would have been easy for the chimpanzees to merely knock over and collect all the termites without much effort and without the use of tools.

The differences between the two species seemed not to go much further than that. Nutritionally to chimpanzees, the termites were identical. As far as taste goes, they also seemed similar. Both species displayed the same seasonal activity and both had a similar distribution. Because of this, one would naturally think that the termites in the tall mounds with the weaker defense would be the species of choice at the Campo Reserve. Instead, the opposite was true. All signs pointed to the fact that the chimpanzees ate the species that lived in the mounds requiring the tools much more often than the species that lived in the mound that could just be broken open by hand. This group of chimpanzees was choosing to go through the expense of energy and effort to make and use a tool to eat a species of termite with the same payoff as a species which was much more easily available. The scientists at Campo wondered about these results.

In addition to the seemingly strange choice of termite species, the primatologists also noticed that the chimpanzees displayed a prefer-

---

* It would be replaced by language. Humans, it was determined, are the only species capable of language.

ence in which type of branch they used to make termite fishing stems. The chimpanzees always made tools from branches that had a certain shape and fiber and would go far away from the termite mounds to find these preferred configurations.

An ecological reason for these choices could not be determined by the Kyoto primatologists. Energy expense alone should dictate that the chimpanzees select the termites in the easily accessible mounds. If, for some reason, the termites which require tools are selected, it would make ecological sense to select nearby branches instead of taking the time to hunt for far-away branches that have to be brought back to the mounds. Yet, the chimpanzees displayed a strong preference for the opposites.

These random preferences have their roots in the conscious free will of cognitive species like chimpanzees and humans. So, if free will can cause a randomness to group behavior which is not beneficial to survival, in what scenario would it have been selected by evolution to develop? Free will can be made beneficial to a social organism through complex and abstract communication.

The philosopher Jean-Jacques Rousseau famously pondered a scenario involving two hunters. The hunters have a choice to go after either a large stag or a hare. The hare is easily caught but only yields a small amount of meat and reaps a small reward. The stag, on the other hand, can only be caught by both hunters working together. However, it yields a large amount of meat and reaps an extremely large reward (even with the two hunters sharing). The dilemma is that neither of the two can know what the other is choosing. Therein lies the predicament. If both hunters choose the stag, they both work together and reap a large reward. However, if one hunter chooses the stag but the other hunter chooses the hare, the one that chose the stag will be unable to catch it on his own and will go home with nothing. If both choose the hare, they both go home with a small reward. This is how conscious free will must make a decision that determines one's survival. Without knowing what the other hunter will choose, both hunters will inevitably choose the hare and miss out on the large reward. This choice is the only one that ensures that they are not left empty-handed. Now, let's throw the ability for complex communication into the mix. Suppose that the two hunters are able to communicate with each other. Now the ability for conscious free will can work to the benefit of both hunters. If they can communicate their intentions, they can communicate plans to choose the stag and both will go home with a large reward. This is how complex communication endows cognitive and social organisms to make complex choices together and end up with the best possible outcome.*

We can't know the reason that the chimpanzees at Campo Reserve constantly chose the termite that is more difficult to obtain. Nevertheless, what we can know is that these chimpanzees are capable of communicating complex situations to each other and that, through a shared decision-making process, they have made a choice which they have communicated as being beneficial (for a reason unclear to us). It is in this way that communication makes having the ability for free will more beneficial than not having the ability. Though this ability leads to randomness that, on the surface, should not be beneficial to the ecological fitness of a group, abstract communication coordinates this randomness and allows it to become systematic and, therefore, advantageous.

---

* Game theorists have expanded upon Rousseau's scenario and developed several other "games" which seek to understand human behavior. These games showcase our behaviors to not be as random as they appear to us. One of the games supposes two prisoners are given the same choice—they can either confess or deny the crime. Like in Rousseau's scenario, the two do not know what the other is choosing. If both confess to the crime, they both receive a six-month sentence. If they both deny the crime, they both get five-year sentences. If one denies the crime and the other confesses, the denier gets to go free while the confessor has to serve a ten-year sentence. Because they can't be sure what the other is going to do (they can't communicate), both will inevitably deny the crime.

In order for abstract communication (such as language) to be able to achieve this, it must also have a component of free will and freedom of choice in its usage. By choosing what to communicate and how to communicate, we can manipulate our group environment to better our predicaments. We can ally ourselves with some in certain situations and with others in different situations.

Let's expand on the hunter's predicament. Let's say that one hunter wants the other hunter to go hungry. Let's also say that the second hunter is a tyrant and any weakening of this hunter is beneficial to the first hunter. The first hunter can choose to communicate that he will hunt the stag with the other hunter, but, in reality, hunt the hare. This way the first hunter can still have a small reward while the tyrant hunter goes poor. This freedom of choice, which determines both what is communicated and what is acted upon, benefits the individual.

The chimpanzees at Campo, like many chimpanzees, have made choices that go beyond the comprehension of their human observers. These choices, though making little sense to us, worked for this group of chimpanzees. The answer may very well have been buried in what they were communicating to each other.

1989
Loxahatchee, Florida

Five animal crates sat on an otherwise empty island. Surrounding this island were four other islands—three of which were filled with chimpanzees. The last group had finally been placed on the last island. It would only be a matter of time before the seven chimps would wake up from their sedation and venture out of the crates one by one.

Watching from the next island over was, of course, Cindy. She was clutching her newborn infant who had been named Smiley. Beside them was Smiley's older sister, Rachel. The first island was occupied by Little Mama's original group. The second island was now occupied by Bashful, Michael, Romeo, Clumsy, and Clumsy's offspring, Two-Nine. The third island was the one that now contained the five animal crates. The fourth island contained Cindy, her two offspring, and the rest of Old Man's group.

Cindy had watched the process of Bashful's group being unloaded onto the second island. She watched, from two islands over, as the keeper had rowed the group over. The keepers had dragged the animal crates from their boat onto the island. Once settled, they opened the crate doors, went back to their boats, and left the island. After a matter of minutes, the chimps emerged from their crates. As each member of this group appeared, Cindy shouted at them. The biggest reaction from Cindy came when Clumsy appeared. Cindy jumped repeatedly into the air screaming. Clumsy, too disoriented to notice, huddled close to Michael.

Now, watching the third island, Cindy was still. Smiley nursed and Rachel played. One of the crates abruptly began shaking back and forth. Out of the crate crawled Edwina holding (a still sleeping) Cashew. Cindy hooted at Edwina, who stumbled around while examining her surroundings. Moments later another mother and sleeping juvenile came into view. This time it was Gin and Tonic. Unlike Edwina, Gin barreled out of her crate. She shouted at all of the chimpanzees that were surrounding her on different islands. After walking the perimeter of her own island, she handed Tonic off to Edwina. Edwina, who was already holding one sleeping juvenile, reluctantly accepted. Cindy held Smiley tightly as she moved closer to the edge of her island to get a better view. What she saw next was a trembling hand appearing out of the next crate. Attached to the trembling hand was Elgin, who slowly crawled out onto the island. Elgin's appearance largely went unnoticed by the chimps on the surrounding islands.

They were still watching Gin (who was now running around the perimeter of the island and screaming at the other islands).

All of the chimpanzees had to adjust to an extreme change in their environment. Even Old Man's group, who was still occupying the same island, now had to deal with being surrounded by new chimpanzees. There would now be greater perceived threats and competition. This would lead to more exaggerated displays. This would also lead to a marked change in vocal prosody and usage.

After Gin had finally settled down a bit, the next chimpanzee exited her crate. It was Little Mama. As soon as Cindy saw Little Mama, she began to call out loudly. With Smiley on her chest, she jumped up and down and reached out her arm to Little Mama. In a move that showed that she recognized Cindy, Little Mama walked over to the edge of the island and returned the call. The two vocalized back and forth. They continued this exchange until something monumental distracted Cindy from Little Mama.

Higgy swaggered out of his crate. Cindy yelped. Higgy smelled the ground and surveyed his group. All the chimpanzees, including the infants, were now awake. He looked around at the other islands. He saw Cindy who was, once again, jumping up and down holding her arm out across the canal. Before he vocalized to anyone, Higgy walked around the perimeter of the island. Unlike Gin, he was slow and methodical in his patrol. When he arrived at the edge of the canal across from Cindy, he looked over at her. He reached his arm out to her and vocalized. Little Mama walked over beside him and also called out to Cindy. As they called to her, Cindy continued to leap into the air. The exchange continued until nightfall.

The next morning keepers arrived at the new chimp islands. When they stopped in front of Old Man's island, they noticed something was wrong. Rachel was pacing nervously back and forth at the far end of the island. The other chimps were looking over at Higgy's island.

Scanning the group, the keepers could not find Cindy or Smiley anywhere on the island. They ran over to look at Higgy's island.

Higgy's island appeared calm. Gin was sleeping on top of a shelter with Tonic sprawled out on top of her. Edwina was at the bottom of the shelter with Cashew in front of her. Elgin was sitting on the ground in the middle of the island staring at the ground. The keepers looked over at the edge of the island where the realization of what had occurred was on display. Higgy and Little Mama sat together grooming Cindy. There was no sign of Smiley anywhere.

A new situation had arisen overnight—a situation that established Cindy as a member of Higgy's group, Smiley as missing, and Rachel as an abandoned juvenile. Since the change happened overnight, we are left to speculate as to what had occurred. We have to piece it together based on what we do know.

When the keepers left the chimps that evening, Higgy and Little Mama were at the edge of their island calling to Cindy. Cindy was jumping up and down with Smiley clinging onto her chest. Rachel had lost interest and was playing by herself. The other members of Higgy's group were busy exploring their new surroundings. The rest of Old Man's group, like Rachel, had lost interest in Higgy's arrival and were back to minding their own business. None of the chimpanzees in the surrounding groups were taking much notice of what was occurring on Higgy's island or Old Man's island.

When the keepers arrived the next morning, Cindy was on Higgy's island. She was dry by this point. Unlike Cindy, Smiley could still not be found. Little Mama and Higgy were both displaying extremely affiliative behavior toward Cindy and there seemed to be little aggressive posturing from anyone. Across the canal, Rachel was still pacing very close to the water's edge.

I speculate that, after the keepers left that evening, the exchange between Little Mama, Higgy, and Cindy became more intense. Cindy probably began pacing along the edge of the island as she watched Little Mama and Higgy reaching their arms out to her. Rachel would have been too busy playing to notice any change in the exchange. At this point, Cindy would have walked over to the edge of the island, clutched Smiley tightly to her chest, and leapt out as far as she could jump toward Higgy and Little Mama. As far as she could jump would have only propelled Cindy to about the center of the canal. Landing in the water, she would have sunk very rapidly to the bottom. She would have hit the depths of the canal with Smiley still on her chest. Due to the fact that Smiley's lung capacity would have been much less than his mother's, he would not have lasted long at the bottom.

The bottom of the canals, having been newly dug, would probably have been irregular and rocky. I think Cindy would have pulled herself along the rocks toward Higgy's island. In this process, Smiley would have lifelessly fallen off of his mother. He would have ended up in the deepest part of the canal. Cindy, in the meantime, would have climbed up the bottom rocks leading up to the surface. As she would have reached an area close to the island, Higgy would have reached her and pulled her up the rest of the way.

At this point, Cindy would have been with the very first chimpanzee with whom she had ever established a social bond: Higgy. She would have also been with her friend across the water, Little Mama. Some other chimpanzees in Higgy's group were also familiar to Cindy. She had already lived with Edwina, who had been part of Old Man's group before being taken to Higgy. She had experienced Gin from across the water. This alone probably wouldn't have kept Gin from being aggressive. However, I imagine that Higgy would have been displaying a protective posturing. That would have certainly kept Gin from going after Cindy. During the entire episode, I imagine that Elgin didn't move much. He probably glanced over and watched for a while, but it is doubtful that he would have gone over and involved himself in the situation. Elgin always preferred to watch rather than get involved. The juveniles would have probably greeted Cindy more with curiosity than anything else.

I imagine Rachel, when she first realized that her mother was gone, would have become extremely excited. Seeing Cindy on the other side of the island would have caused Rachel to yelp and cry out in a long and laborious cry. All at once, Rachel's life had changed drastically. No longer would her mother be around to offer her protection or reassurance. Rachel would have to choose to bond with others in her group or live in relative isolation. She would now be viewed by the other chimpanzees as a low-ranking adult instead of a juvenile who was protected by a higher-ranking mother. She would have to choose to adjust her behavior, the way she related to others, and the way she communicated with others. Her survival in the group depended on her choices.

It is impossible for us to understand why Cindy would have made the choice she did. Ecologically, it makes no sense at all. She had a good social ranking in her current group and was successfully breeding and feeding herself and her offspring. She chose to end this situation and leap to an unknown situation. She chose to join with a chimpanzee she had not seen since both of them were juveniles. She chose to do this at the expense of both of her offspring. Instinct would have warned her against jumping into deep water with her infant. Instinct would have also warned her against abandoning her older offspring. Yet, her free will rose above these instinctual calls and caused her to jump over to Higgy's island. We are left to imagine that whatever was being communicated to Cindy was enough for her to decide that the benefits of joining him outweighed the consequences. Just as the two hunters in Rousseau's scenario were able to communicate to each other to make the less sound but more lucrative choice, Higgy's communication with Cindy possibly conveyed a hidden benefit to her decision—a benefit that was worth killing her baby and abandoning her daughter.

As cognitive animals, we, like Cindy, are forced to make choices in almost every instant. Ultimately, everything in life is our decision. Even if all of the choices that we are presented with are dire, there are always choices. Each choice, however small at the onset, can have a profound effect on the path our lives take. As social animals, in order to make the choices that achieve the greatest benefits, we communicate with others. This communication tempers the randomness of our free will and streamlines our decision-making process into the system of our group dynamics. Abstract and complex communication is how a social organism capable of conscious free will survives together and achieves the greatest possible benefits for survival.

Abstract and complex communication relies on the same conscious free will and decision making as everything else. The ability to consciously decide on the usage of communication allows us to manipulate our interactions with others to reach the greatest possible benefits for our survival. The usage of a language is dependent on the user's intention. In this, freedom of choice is put squarely back on the individual. Everything we decide shifts the pathway of both our lives and our social group. Even the slightest shift forever alters the destiny of the group. We are ultimately responsible for each situation we have manipulated ourselves into. We are faced with a new set of realities every day and must make choices on how to handle these realities. Some make choices that benefit the group as a whole. Some make choices that benefit themselves instead of the group. Still others decide to do nothing and allow the present realities to take over.

Such was the case with Rachel. Rachel choose to do nothing to deal with the new reality she was faced with. She neither attempted to join her mother nor attempted to establish bonds with the rest of her group. Four months later, she was found dead on Old Man's island.*

---

*The cause of death remains a mystery.

Our social groups, our languages, and our situations are the result of the collective individual choices we make. Chimpanzees, humans, and all other conscious organisms are forced to act cognitively in life instead of relying on instinct. These acts are when individuals, in social situations and in language, slip out of the comforts of group membership and act as the sole entities they are. These acts form a collective that, when seen together, create a functioning group dynamic and language that is beneficial to everyone. The free acts that we are forced into are part of the grand scope of nature which relies on individual randomness working together to create a larger picture. When viewed from far away, you can't see the individual random elements; you see one functioning image of a social group or of a language. Yet, examining the individual elements showcases the random acts that create the image. These random acts are the free choices we make at any given moment.

In the end, in the world, we are on our own.

We are the pawns of an irresistible force, and never for an instant is it within our power to do anything but make the best of our lot and forge ahead along the path that has been traced for us.

—The Marquis de Sade

7

The General's Will

Legend tells of a dying World War I doughboy. Lying on a hospital gurney in France, he was slowly succumbing to the effects of mustard gas poisoning. In the three weeks that this young enlisted man had spent in the medical tent, his skin had blistered, his eyes had swelled, his breathing had become more labored, and he had begun to lose his mind. He suffered from wild delusions—one of them being that he was a general in charge of the entire army. He was so certain of his position that he would scribble war strategies on scraps of paper and ask the nurse that they be delivered to his lieutenant generals in the field. When they complied, the dying man would commend the nurses and thank them for their contributions to the war effort. The hospital staff began referring to him only as "the General."

In a short amount of time, the General's condition would get even worse. The pain in his lungs would cause him to convulse, resulting in him being strapped to his gurney. His eyelids had become so swollen and stuck together that he could no longer see. The blisters on his skin had yellowed. His throat was closing, making it extremely difficult to swallow or breathe. He spoke with a low whisper, able to get only a few words out at a time. Five weeks after entering the medical tent, the General faced his merciful last day.

With his eyes closed, the General motioned for a nurse. When the nurse approached him, he attempted to vocalize but could only produce a choking sound. Frustrated, he began to whisper one word at a time. The nurse bent down so that she could hear. With a series of painful whispers, the General informed her that he had an infant boy at home that he had never seen. He knew he was about to die and wanted to leave something for his child. Quickly, the nurse grabbed a pad of paper and a pen and began to write down what he whispered to her. After several agonizing minutes, the General had finished. He asked if the nurse had written everything down. She responded that she had. The General gasped one last time and sank into the relief death provided. The nurse looked at the dead soldier. She then looked at what she had written. She didn't quite know what to do with the madness on the paper in front of her.

The General's will began by stating that the world was a cruel and bloodthirsty place. Indeed, the desolate landscape of war that the General had known throughout the last period of his life was hellish. The trenches and burnt terrain of the First World War were inescapable to the young soldier. The perceptions of death were all around. Men survived by killing each other. The only solace from this bitter condition was his fellow soldiers and the interactions he had with them. These soldiers, like all soldiers, had made a pact to fight to protect each other from the war around them. This pact declared that the survival of their platoon, their alliance, was more important than any individual's survival. Also secondary were the inclinations and aspirations of the individual to the alliance. The strength of the alliance would boost the strength of each of the individuals. The alliance's survival bettered the chances of the individual's survival. In order to boost the odds of survival and the strength of this alliance, the soldiers developed codes of behavior. With this came rules of how to interact with each other or the outside world. These rules helped to establish a chain of command which was crucial to their survival within their the war-torn environment. These rules established customs which, to others, may have seemed frivolous, but were critical to those within the alliance. Finally, the alliance created forms of communication that only they understood. This would allow them to communicate with each other in front of any outside force and be understood only by each other.

The General, assuming that his child had been born into such a vicious and merciless environment, bequeathed his alliance of soldiers to his child. They were to report to his child, teach him their customs, their codes of conduct, their ways of interacting, and their forms of communication. The alliance was to keep the child with them and include him into their pact. This was the best way to ensure the child's survival in the ruthless world. The General, having nothing material to pass on, had something vastly more important to give: his method of survival.

We cannot choose what we inherit. At our entry point of existence we are saddled with the world we are given. Though we may attempt to escape, the arena we have assumed is with us in some way or another throughout the course of our lives. Some elements define us, some protect us, and some color our perceptions. At birth, every organism is given a genetic construction, an environment, and other organisms sharing its world.

Like the General's son, our parents, whether or not we know them, pass along to us our genes. The genes we inherit give us both our abilities and our limits. In this, our most defining aspect, we have absolutely no choice. We must learn to work within the confines of our genetic parameters to survive whichever environment we are thrown into. Whether we are born into a tropical forest, an icy tundra, an island surrounded by water, or a suburban neighborhood, we must make our genetic construction adapt or we die. Part of this environment is the community of others we are surrounded by. We inherit this community, not by choice, but by birth. The community is made up of individuals who, like us, must survive their environment by any means necessary. That survival would be at the expense of other individuals were it not for an advantage held by social organisms: the alliance. This alliance is a social pact wherein everyone agrees to follow the will of the group rather than the will of the individual. The survival of the individual becomes tied to the survival of the alliance and is, therefore, stronger.

The role of the alliance is not just to protect each other. The alliance also forms a collective of knowledge on how to survive in a given environment. The trials and errors of each individual get passed along so that others in the alliance don't have to make the same mistakes. Each individual innovation also gets passed along so that the alliance shares the benefits together.

The strength of this alliance, at its core, is how strong its communication system is. Alliances that have complex communication can transmit more complex ideas of innovations, trials and errors, and traits that aid in survival. Communication systems that are coded for only that group have the benefit of being unintelligible to other groups. This allows the alliance not to have to share information with the outside world and to outcompete the outside world with its knowledge.

The General, with his delusional assumption that his child was inheriting the same war environment that he was living in, wanted to pass along the best way to survive that particular environment. He did this by giving his alliance. With his alliance came all of the collective knowledge, the communications system, and the protection of the pact—all geared toward survival in this particular environment.

Let's assume that the legend was true. Let's also assume that the General's alliance heard of their comrade's dying wish and, out of sympathy and sentimentality, returned home and found his child. Once there, they would teach the child all of their knowledge, their codes, and offer him protection. However, the child wouldn't be living in the environment of the First World War. Chances are he would be living in a peaceful community far removed from the world his father had died in. This alliance would not be helpful. In fact, it would seem insane. The presence of his dead father's group would actually be a social hindrance. He would, most likely, be ostracized by his actual community for following these strange codes of behaviors, bestowed upon him by his father's pact. He would be an outcast, experiencing his world as a social pariah.

Specific environments carry specific needs. Different environments require different behaviors. In social organisms, these behaviors include different ways of interacting and communicating. Certain communication systems only work in precise environments. When environments change, communication systems must change with them. Communication that relies on learning, such as language, is able to adapt quickly to new or changing environments. Such learned communication makes a species highly adaptive and, thus, more successful.*

We inherit what we physically are, how we are able to learn, the

---

* Both purely genetic behaviors and learned behaviors are subject to natural selection. In the same way that instincts and reflexive actions that are maladaptive don't survive, the same goes for behaviors that we learn. If the maladaptive qualities of the behaviors that we learn outweigh the adaptive qualities, we tend not to pass them down.

environment that dictates what we learn, the others that we learn from, and the limits of what we can do. What has been passed down to us is everything we are and everything we'll ever be, and in that, we have absolutely no choice.

1990
Mahale Mountains, Tanzania

The environment was beginning to change for Ntologi. The once un-disputed alpha male was now contending with an uprising young male named Kalunde and a crumbling alliance of females. The coalition he had depended on for power was slipping away from him. Despite dis-plays of power and aggressive posturing, his days as the chimpanzee in charge of the Mimikile group were numbered. He produced a loud call which reverberated through the forest. The call was answered and returned by another male.

The male returning the call was Masudi. In the years since the vicious attack on his brother, Masudi had ascended in rank and become a key figure in Mimikile. Now thirteen years old, he was the sixth-ranking male in the social hierarchy of the group. The call he returned was similar in structure to the call Ntologi had given. It began with a few indistinct hoots. This was followed by a quick se-ries of pants, each one a bit louder than the last. These culminated in a high-pitched scream. The scream then descended into another quick series of pants—only these became progressively softer. The call, along with the other calls of the day, was being recorded by pri-matologists who were observing the chimps. These recordings would be the beginning of a new understanding of chimpanzee communica-tion.

On the surface, chimpanzee calls can fit into broad categories based upon their structure. In much the same way that we can categorize human vocalizations with such classifications as cries, screams, words, laughs, and whispers, we can make similar assessments of chimpanzee calls. The calls given by Ntologi and Masudi were typical of loud chimpanzee calls. The structure of these calls may contain any of the following elements: an introduction (the series of sounds at the beginning), a buildup (the series of progressively louder pants), a climax (the high-pitched scream), and a descent (the progressively softer pants at the end). Both of the calls that had been recorded by the two chimpanzees contained all four elements.

Interested in studying the role of these vocalizations, primatologists analyzed these calls (along with 164 other calls from the Mimikile chimps) and compared them with another group of chimpanzees from Gombe National Park (just north of the Mahale Mountains). The implications of what they found would set off a far-reaching debate about the communication systems of other species and question the very notion of the uniqueness of humans.*

The Mimikile chimpanzees of the Mahale Mountains were producing different loud calls than the Gombe chimpanzees. The way in which this was determined was to convert the vocalizations to a visual representation of sound called an audio spectrogram. Spectrograms represent the structure, intensity, and frequency of a sound. They appear as smudges on a graph with the vertical axis representing frequency, the horizontal access representing time, and the darkening of the smudge representing intensity (the louder the sound the darker

---

* John Mitani, who wrote the initial paper on this vocal analysis, would continue to weigh in, assess, and reassess the role learning may play in chimpanzee vocalizations. The debate that his research encouraged has been highly influential to anyone looking at chimpanzee vocal communication and the relationship between nonhuman primate communication and human language. Mitani's work helped shift the focus from what could be taught in a lab to what was actually occurring in nature.

the smudge).* It's very easy to look at a spectrogram of a chimpanzee call and clearly see if there is an introduction, buildup, climax, or descent. It's also easy to compare the length, volume, and pitch of different vocalizations. Through the analysis of these spectrograms, it was determined that the Mimikile group was producing loud calls that had a shorter and faster buildup phase and a higher-pitched climax than the Gombe chimpanzees.

Another comparison was made by a primatologist working at the Kibale National Park in Uganda (almost four hundred miles away from the Mahale Mountains). Again, these particular loud calls were compared, this time with all three groups. This revealed greater differences. While the buildup phase of the call was different between the Gombe chimpanzees and the Mahale Mountains chimpanzees, the buildup phase was oftentimes completely absent with the Kibale chimpanzees. Whereas the comparison between Gombe and the Mahale Mountains chimps revealed a difference in pitch and duration, the comparison with the Kibale chimpanzees showed a structural change. This finding was significant, in that it showed groups using entirely different calls in the same situations.

There was no question that chimpanzees from different areas produced different calls. What was not clear, however, was the reason why this was occurring. The papers published on these studies pointed to a number of possibilities. One possibility that could not be ruled out was that the differences were due to vocal learning.

One year later, Ntologi had lost his status as alpha male. Kalunde was now in charge. Like an overthrown tyrant, Ntologi was exiled from the group. He was banished to live alone in the Mahale Mountain forests.

---

* Audio spectrograms are an extremely informative representation of sound. If a spectrogram were produced on a person saying a familiar word, a well-trained reader of spectrograms could discern which word had been spoken.

1990
Loxahatchee, Florida

It was Christmas Eve day and a holiday crowd had gathered around the chimpanzee islands. It was the only day of the year that guests were allowed to step out of their cars and watch the animals. Terry Wolf appeared in his boat from behind the first island. In front of him, standing on the bow of the boat, was a man dressed in a Santa Claus suit. In the center of the boat was a bag filled with wrapped presents that were to be thrown to the chimps. Inside the packages were toys, puzzles, and candy treats. This ritual happened every Christmas. The chimpanzees anticipated it as much as the onlookers. When the boat appeared, both the crowd and the chimps went wild. Higgy began a display by rocking back and forth, stomping one foot, and making a series of loud calls. Elgin began jumping up and down. Little Mama held out both her hands. Gin swayed at the top of the shelter, bobbing her head up and down. Tonic and Cashew tackled each other. Noticeably absent from the gathering were Edwina and Cindy. They were inside the shelter with their two new babies. Edwina was cradling her new female infant, Kathy, and Cindy was holding her new male infant, Hank.

Kathy had been born three months before. As she had been with Cashew, Edwina was an attentive mother. Unlike with Cashew, she wasn't also raising Gin's child at the same time. Cashew was keenly interested in her new little sister. The six-year-old would sit patiently beside her mother and wait for Edwina's permission to hold Kathy. She watched intently as Edwina would vocalize softly to the infant. Cashew would study the pair as Kathy would nurse while Edwina gently held her head. Cashew would pay close attention to her mother when Edwina would groom her infant. Often Edwina passed the infant over to Cashew. Kathy would cling onto her older sister while

Edwina sat extremely close. Cashew would cradle her sister and try to groom her. She would vocalize softly, the way her mother had done. She would spend just a few moments with Kathy before her mother would take the baby back.

Cashew was learning from her mother. She was watching her mother handle and care for her new baby. She would then handle the baby herself and care for her the same way her mother had. This is a trait that Cashew was acquiring which she could hold onto until she, herself, had an off-spring. This knowledge, passed down from Edwina to Cashew, would help ensure that Cashew would give her offspring attentive care. In doing so, Edwina helped strengthen the survival of her lineage. Contrast this with Gin. Gin had never had the ability to learn from another mother chimpanzee. Since she was a very young infant, she had been isolated from such things. Due to this, Gin lacked the ability to care for Tonic.

Sitting beside Edwina and Kathy, Cindy was holding her first off-spring since the deaths of Smiley and Rachel. Hank was just a few weeks old. The helplessness of the newborn chimpanzee was tempered by his already larger stature. Hank, as a neonate, was already larger in size than three-month-old Kathy. Cindy's hulking body plan had very obviously been passed to her son. Though Cindy, like Gin, had been isolated as a pet during her juvenile years, she had been exposed to other chimpanzees at a younger age. On top of this, Cindy had always seemed to have a keen natural ability in caring for young chimpanzees. She first showed this with Higgy in the nursery pen. She continued to show it with Hank.*

As the Christmas boat moved in front of Higgy's island, the chimps

---

* Even beyond this, Cindy was always a source of comfort for the younger chimpanzees. Anytime there was trouble on the island, the juveniles would all run to Cindy. She would respond by embracing them. Chimpanzees like Cindy and Little Mama fulfill a sort of child-care role and make themselves more valuable to the group in this way. They improve their status and build tight alliances with other females.

shouted at each other and at the boat. Cindy, with Hank clinging onto her chest, climbed out of the shelter and slowly made her way down to the banks of the island. She patted her head twice, folded her lip down, and made a raspberry sound at the man dressed as Santa. When a wrapped package was thrown to her, she quietly and gently picked it up and carried it with her as she went back into the shelter where she opened a box with candy and called out excitedly.

That night, as darkness covered the islands, everything was still. The crowd had gone home, preparing for their own Christmas morning. In each household, the families who had come to see the chimps were planning on celebrating the holiday in different ways. Some of them had opened presents that evening. Others waited until the next morning. A portion of them went to church services. Some went to parties. Others didn't celebrate at all. Many of them spent the evening with their families. Some of them spent the evening alone. The chimpanzees on the island spent the evening in silence. Like all chimpanzees, they spent the night sleeping. In the morning, they would wake up to another day on the island. When they woke, they would communicate and interact in a way that suited their group. Christmas morning, like all mornings, would be a time spent surviving together.

1991
Mahale Mountains, Tanzania

The primatologists watched as Ntologi circled the perimeter of the Mimikile group's range. He was completely alone; unable to socialize with his old group mates. In a relatively short amount of time, he had gone from being the alpha male to being an exiled solitary chimpanzee.

Far away from Ntologi, the Mimikile group was functioning with its new alpha male, Kalunde. The alliance that had put him into power was still intact. However, all social groups have those members that never quite mesh with the others. One such individual was a male named Jilba. The sixteen-year-old would frequently attack females and would never really ally himself with any other males. This was evidenced by his lack of using a certain type of vocalization with the other males. This vocalization was a soft grunting directed at another individual. These calls differ from the very loud calls in that they seem to serve a different function. The loud calls are frequently directed outwardly to no one in particular. The softer grunts are more deliberate and have a dialogue quality to them. These vocalizations are used in an affiliative or nonaggressive way. Therefore, using them to another chimpanzee not only conveys the information contained in the vocalization, but also conveys an alliance or, at the very least, a nonaggressive interaction. Jilba never used these vocalizations with any of the males in his group. He had not even vocalized in this manner to Kalunde. When an individual doesn't show any sort of affiliative communication with the alpha male, that individual can be in trouble.

In addition, Jilba would frequently use visually aggressive gestures to the other males. When he would pass them, his hair would stand erect and he would maintain a facial expression that conveyed frustration to the group. At one point, the second-ranking male took such offense at Jilba's attitude that he chased him until Jilba vocalized a grunt back to him. Outside of this forced incident, Jilba was silent with the other males.

One morning, Jilba was left out of a group activity. The rest of the Mimikile adults were hunting a red colobus monkey (something chimpanzees are known to do).* When chimpanzees hunt these monkeys,

---

* Chimpanzees often hunt these monkeys. It's an interesting phenomenon because chimpanzees are mostly vegetarian. They certainly don't require meat in their diets for sustenance. Yet, they will go through the very costly and dangerous activity of hunting red colobus monkeys. Primatologist

they are known to hunt cooperatively. Each hunter has a job and they work together, resulting in the capture of one or more monkeys. Usually this involves a cooperative team of hunters so that the monkey or monkeys can be cornered in the forest. A cooperative hunt may go something like this: one or more red colobus monkeys are detected in an area of the forest. One or more chimpanzees silently occupy the forest floor or lower canopy underneath the area that the monkey is occupying. Another chimpanzee rushes toward the monkey, causing the monkey to run in the opposite direction. In that direction, another chimpanzee is positioned to block the monkey. Yet another chimpanzee may then ambush the monkey from the side. The hunt concludes with the monkey either falling or attempting to escape to the lower canopy where the silent chimpanzees await. These chimpanzees grab hold of and kill the monkey. The meat is then shared. The eating of monkey meat is something that fills a social niche within a chimpanzee group. The meat is distributed by high-ranking individuals to lower-ranking individuals. The distribution helps to solidify the hierarchy. The hunts are extremely complex and not only do they require the ability to predict the movements of the red colobus monkey, they also require a great deal of communication in order to coordinate the attack.

The Mimikile chimpanzees were involved in this type of cooperative hunt. While most of the hunting party were high up in the canopy ready to attack the monkey, Kalunde sat silently below. After a great deal of chasing, blocking, and ambushing, the red colobus monkey fell directly into Kalunde's hands. He killed it and took it up the tree. The rest of the adults surrounded him as he began to eat it. Occasionally, he would share the meat with the rest of the group. For almost an hour, the chimpanzees sat in the canopy, peacefully eating the red colobus monkey.

Craig Stanford has devoted much of his research to this question and his book *Chimpanzee and Red Colobus: The Ecology of Predator and Prey* is a fascinating read.

After a while, Jilba appeared and disrupted the gathering. He approached the group and began to display to them. Abruptly, Kalunde charged him. Jilba jumped to the ground to escape but while he ran, he got caught in a bush. The other chimpanzees in the hunting party sounded loud vocalizations to the rest of their group. Soon seven chimpanzee aided Kalunde and descended on Jilba. Within moments, Jilba fled the group and disappeared into the forest. The other chimpanzees continued to produce a call for fifteen minutes after he had left. Jilba was now exiled from the group, sentenced to live alone in the forest.

Jilba had failed to honor the behavioral customs of his social group. His presence in the group was maladaptive to them and, therefore, he was exiled. A social group only functions when one puts his own will second to the group's will. Jilba had not done this. He had refused to recognize the hierarchy and had refused to communicate with the others in the group. He was aggressive with the females and had assumed the role of pariah. The last straw appeared to be when he approached the group after a hunt. Rather than waiting for meat to be distributed to him, Jilba had aggressively approached the group. This resulted in the attack by Kalunde and Jilba's banishment.

Jilba went out into the forest alone. Later, he encountered Ntologi. For three months the two of them formed a two-member alliance and lived together as refugees from Mimikile. During this time, three young males would occasionally defect from Mimikile and spend time with Ntologi and Jilba. At the end of this period, Ntologi and Jilba reappeared at Mimikile together. Their alliance of two with the help of the three other males was strong enough to allow their reintegration into the group. Before long, Ntologi was alpha male again.*

---

* The Mahale Mountain chimp dramas, as reported in the last several chapters of this book (initially studied and documented by primatologists from Kyoto University headed

1994
Loxahatchee, Florida

Hank followed Higgy around the perimeter of the island. Higgy was going through his ritual of walking the boundaries of his group. When he did this, he would frequently stop to sit and watch the other groups. Higgy's presence was such that the other groups would take immediate notice of Higgy's watch and act nervously until he moved on. Following closely behind, Hank would attempt to match Higgy's swagger. He would also walk at exactly the same pace and sit when Higgy sat.

Hank had become Higgy's shadow. When he wasn't with Cindy, he could always be found within a few steps of Higgy. He would watch as the alpha male would tend to the group. Higgy's actions were always powerful and reaffirmed his position at any given moment. Hank, at four, was acquiring these movements and mannerisms.*

Higgy's group was extremely orderly. If ever a dispute got out of hand, Higgy would quickly put an end to it by giving a certain vocalization. If the vocalization didn't work, Higgy would charge at the fighting chimps. This would almost always end the dispute. Higgy would show any displeasure with the group's behavior with massive displays that included loud calls and violent gestures. The displays would end with one of the chimps (usually Elgin) getting charged. The charging would

---

up by Toshisada Nishida), make up some of the most fascinating primatological studies one could ever read. This book offers a mere glimpse of what these primatologists witnessed in this area during these times. The journal articles on the Mahale Mountains chimpanzees give a complete (and, indeed, more graphic) account of everything that ensued with these groups.

* Hank had also begun to resemble his mother even more. Besides the fact that he had inherited Cindy's large size, he had also received her strange heart-shaped head and her half-closed eyelids. Even though he seemed to be attempting to look like Higgy in every way, he could not escape what genetics had given him: a replica appearance of his mother.

culminate in a slap across the back. These charges were not so much physically violent as they were spectacles of power. Across the water, the other groups would watch Higgy display his authority. Higgy was so powerful that he could affect the behavior of the other groups. If there were fights in the other chimp groups, Higgy could, oftentimes, end the assault by carrying on in this fashion.

Higgy continued to protect the weaker individuals in the group and control the aggressive ones. Elgin was still very much under Higgy's protective wing. Though an easy target, Elgin was untouchable to the rest of the group. Higgy was the only one allowed to act aggressively toward him. Little Mama, also low in the social hierarchy, also benefitted greatly from Higgy's powerful protection. Both Little Mama and Elgin, without the strong protective backing of Higgy, would have been treated aggressively and eaten only scraps. Instead, they ate what everyone else ate and they were protected from aggression. Without Higgy, or the fully functioning social group that Higgy represented, they would not survive.

Higgy's actions as alpha male included more than just displays of power. He also spent a great deal of his time with the juveniles. He played with them, groomed them, and slept next to them. He groomed their mothers while they were nursing. He was extremely protective with them and was always near any of the juveniles who had ventured away from their mothers. One such mother was Gin.

Ten years after the birth of Tonic, Gin had given birth to another offspring: a female named Nana (short for Banana). Watching Edwina with Tonic had apparently been good for Gin, who was now raising Nana all by herself. This was not without its problems. Gin hadn't quite gotten the knack of holding her infant. In Nana's early infancy (when most infant chimps stay on their mother's chest), Gin had flung Nana on her back to carry her around. Nana would frequently slide off her mother, which would make Gin nervous and cause her to scream and react wildly. Sometimes she would carry Nana around backward on her lower back. Also, Gin would carelessly put Nana down on the ground and venture off somewhere else. Since Higgy was always keeping a watchful eye out for the children, he was never far behind. He would scoop Nana up and bring her back to Gin.

As all of these events occurred, Hank was watching and learning how to be a protective male chimpanzee. What was also being passed along to him was how to be a powerful chimpanzee. He was learning how to maintain alliances, use displays to maintain status, and how to receive consent from others to rule them. What Higgy was, inadvertently, teaching Hank would prove to be the ultimate undoing of his group.

1994
Mahale Mountains, Tanzania

Ntologi's vocalizations were, once again, being recorded by primatologists. The loud calls he was producing were the subject of a deeper exploration into chimpanzee communication. His calls, along with the calls of the rest of Mimikile, were part of another group-to-group comparison.

The last few years had been a time of social upheaval for Ntologi. He was, once again, the alpha male of the Mimikile group. His re-acceptance into the group had hinged on a number of things. In addition to his exiled alliance with Jilba, Ntologi had apparently been following the group dynamics by eavesdropping on the vocalizations that he was able to hear in the periphery.* In listening to the calls being produced by his old group, he was able to determine that Kalunde's status

---

* This was reported by Toshisada Nishida and included in his "Review of Recent Findings on Mahale Chimpanzees" in the book *Chimpanzee Cultures*. He reports that Ntologi was listening to the "pant-hoots" of his old group while he was roaming alone and plotted his return based on this.

as alpha male was constantly being challenged by another male named Nsaba. In gathering this information, Ntologi chose the right time to reappear to the group. Kalunde, who needed an ally, had accepted Ntologi back. Ntologi used the chaos of a power struggle to manipulate the situation. Before long, Ntologi was, again, the alpha male. Nsaba was still the second-ranking male. Kalunde, who had trusted the wrong chimpanzee, had lost much of his social status and was lingering at the bottom of the social hierarchy.

That Ntologi had used the vocalizations he heard to map out a strategy shows the complexity of information being transmitted between individual chimpanzees. He was able to divine what was occurring within the social situation of the group, who was aligning with whom, and how solid Kalunde's power was. He was able to use this information and act on it in a way that best suited his own survival. The question that the observing primatologists were pondering was if this information was understandable to all chimpanzees or just the Mimikile chimpanzees. In other words, was the information contained in these vocalizations something that had to be learned or was it genetically ingrained in all chimpanzees?

More loud call vocalizations had been recorded from the Mimikile group to explore whether or not chimpanzees learn some of their calls. The paradigm-shattering discovery that the chimpanzees of the Mahale Mountains, Gombe, and Kibale were all using acoustically distinct calls was eclipsed only by the fact that the reason for these differences was that chimpanzees were learning vocalizations from each other. Chimpanzees being shown to learn vocalizations from each other would end the notion that humans were the only species to do so. The conventional wisdom that all other species communicate with merely that which is genetically programmed would have to be rethought. If learning, in fact, was the reason that chimpanzees were producing group-specific vocalizations, the line between chimpanzee calls and human language was becoming one of debate. However, the newly recorded vocalizations, and a deeper look at them, would cast doubt on this.

The new recordings were compared with the recordings from Kibale. Because the previous comparisons between the Mahale Mountain chimps and the Kibale chimps had differed from the comparisons with the Gombe chimpanzees, another study was needed to look deeper into the phenomenon. It is important to remember that with the Gombe comparison, the chimpanzee calls were differing in their pitch and durations; the Kibale comparison showed that the vocalizations were structured differently. In finding that the Kibale chimpanzees were using one less element in their calls than the Mahale Mountains chimpanzees, the data suggested that the chimpanzees were learning a different call rather than just a way to produce the call. This finding was what was driving this new comparison.

Though the differences may sound trivial, they are profound. The loud calls of two groups that differ in pitch and duration but not in structure (and fulfill the same function) may just be accounting for differences in the acoustics of an area. For example, if one group of chimpanzees live in a rocky location, where sound reverberates, and another live in a densely forested area, where sound is absorbed, the two groups are going to produce the same call differently. The chimpanzees are merely shaping their genetic calls to conform to the acoustics of an area. Learning would not necessarily be involved. However, if a group is producing a structurally different call, learning would almost certainly be a factor. A different structure would imply a different call, not one that would be genetically programmed at birth.

The original study of the Kibale chimpanzees revealed that they were using a different structure in their loud calls. Whereas the Mahale Mountain chimps were using an introduction, buildup, climax, descent structure, the Kibale chimpanzees were leaving out the buildup. The buildup, being a very large portion of the vocalization, is a key element. Not having any sort of buildup completely changes the structure of the call. The study had also confirmed that the pitch and duration of the individual elements differed between groups.

The new study differed from the previous study and questioned learning in chimpanzee vocalizations. The Kibale chimpanzees were found, in fact, to be utilizing a buildup in their vocalizations, only dropping them out occasionally. Thus, the notion of a completely different call was disputed. It was also found that the Mahale Mountains chimpanzees were occasionally switching around the structure. This meant that structural variation was occurring within the group, making a case that, since the structure of a call should be uniform within a group, learning was, in fact, not occurring.

There were, however, still differences between groups that the new study found. These differences occurred acoustically in pitch and duration. As we have discussed, these variances could very well be to compensate for different acoustic environments. Another reason proposed was that since the chimpanzees were from different lineages (Kibale and the Mahale Mountains are too far away to assume much relatedness between groups), they would have different physiological features which would account for differences in voices between the two groups. Just like a human family who all sound the same when they talk, the same thing could be happening within a group of chimpanzees.

This reassessment of group-specific calls in chimpanzees had given rise to a skepticism of chimpanzees learning calls.* A new study was

---

* Interestingly enough, this skeptical reassessment of learning in chimpanzee calls was authored by the primatologist who had first suggested learning in the Mahale Mountain chimpanzee population, John Mitani.

needed that could control certain variables. Two groups of chimpanzees needed to be studied where the acoustics of the two environments were similar. The lineages of these groups must also be known in order to ensure that there wasn't enough relatedness between group members which would cause a similarity in voice. Also, a more in-depth look at the structure of vocalizations was necessary. Up until this point, only loud calls had been compared. Was there a difference within other categories of calls? Some of these answers would begin to be revealed when two captive groups of chimpanzees were studied a year later. This study provided a setting where relatedness was known and the acoustics were similar. The two groups of captive chimpanzees would show, definitively, whether vocal learning was occurring. One of the groups was living on an island in Loxahatchee, Florida.

1996
Loxahatchee, Florida

Higgy's group sat silent and motionless as they watched the zookeepers slowly row away from the island. Cindy stood staring at the boat, her knuckles buried into the ground. In front of her, Cashew clutched her sister, Kathy. Tonic paced wildly in front of the two juveniles. The zookeepers reached land and docked their boat. Gently, they lifted the body of a chimpanzee out of the boat and into their truck. As they drove away, they heard Higgy calling out from the top of a shelter. Edwina, mother of Cashew and Kathy, caretaker of Tonic, was dead.

Edwina, being an older chimpanzee, had died of natural causes. Her death marked a radical change in the dynamics of Higgy's group. Kathy, at six, was still very young. She had been very dependent on her mother until the end. Though she would still have her older sister, Little Mama, and Cindy, she would be forced to become more independent.

Gin, who was dealing with the two-year-old, Nana, would have to stop relying on Edwina for child-care help. When she would fall short in her maternal responsibilities, Little Mama or Cindy would now have to step in.

The following weeks of transition were marked by the increased presence of human observers around the island. These observers weren't typical park guests. These were primatologists who were there to record any loud call from the chimps that they heard. The project, in response to the last study at the Mahale Mountains, wanted to look for evidence of vocal learning in a controlled captive environment. The chimps at the animal park were being compared with the chimpanzees at the North Carolina Zoo.*

The acoustics of the islands at the animal park were similar to the acoustics of the North Carolina Zoo. Therefore, it was reasoned that if there were call variances between the two groups, acoustic compensation could be ruled out. Additionally, the relatedness of all of the captive chimpanzees was known. With the exception of the juveniles, the chimps at the animal park, as well as the chimps at the North Carolina Zoo, all came from diverse genetic backgrounds. This fact would rule out genetic family vocal similarities. If the two groups were using their own calls, learning would have to be ruled the best explanation.

While the chimpanzees on the islands vocalized, the primatologists recorded the calls. Once recorded, they were compared with the North Carolina Zoo calls. Similarly to how the calls were compared in the Mahale Mountain studies, spectrograms were used to

---

* The study had been conducted by a senior anthropology student at Harvard University, Andrew Marshall, as his senior thesis. The study would have such profound implications on our understanding of chimpanzee vocal communication that it would be published several years later in *Animal Behaviour*. It would also, obviously, have a great influence on the study I would do with these chimpanzees years later.

determine the structure, pitch, amplitude, and duration of the calls. What was found was a clear indication that chimpanzees were learning their calls.

The data would show that not only did the Florida chimpanzees differ from the North Carolina chimpanzees in pitch and duration, but they also differed in structure. The Florida chimpanzee incorporated a long buildup phase, while the North Carolina chimps usually didn't include them. The North Carolina chimps seemed to replace these buildups with long introduction phases. This contrasted with the Florida chimps, whose introductions were very short. There was enough vocal similarity within the communities and enough vocal difference between them to show that each group was, indeed, producing their own loud call.

What this study had achieved was an exploration of the arbitrary nature of a chimpanzee call. There was no ecological need for the Florida chimps to produce a different loud call than their North Carolina counterparts. There were no acoustic barriers that existed in one setting that didn't exist in the other. There was no large related family of similarly voiced chimps in either group. Therefore, the explanation that remained was that the members of each group were learning these loud calls from each other.

The quest to understand chimpanzee communication and its relationship to human language had led primatologists to seek answers from this small group of captive chimps living on an island in an Everglades animal park. Here the quest would stay and the journey would continue. The chimpanzees themselves, of course, had no idea that what they were doing was of any importance to their relationship to humans. They were merely surviving in the environment they had been given; surviving by communicating in the way that they had learned. They used this communication to govern their group, raise their offspring, help each other during times of need, alert each other in times of danger, maintain their social roles, and create alliances when they wanted something more from the group. Each of them were experts in the learned behaviors, learned social traditions, and learned communication systems unique to their group. They were experts in them because without them they wouldn't be able to survive. These learned traits were viable nowhere else but in their own unique situation.

As humans, like chimpanzees, we rely on the learned traits and learned communication systems of our social groups. We rely on them because they work in our own unique situation. From our vantage point, within our situations, these traits seem like the best way. Like the General, we are sure that everything else in the world functions the same way our own little world does. Like the General, we tend to try to inflict our own learned behaviors on those outside of our situations. We do this with outside cultures and outside species. In the same way that we assume a culture in another part of the world would function better if its people adopted our own cultural traits, we assume that chimpanzees are members of a more relevant species if they act and communicate just like a human. This is why we put them in films, make them learn sign language, watch them ice-skate in circuses, and make them dress up for tea parties in zoos. This is why we are surprised when, in the end, they don't quite act like little humans. This is why we are shocked when a chimpanzee gets violently aggressive toward a human caretaker. This is why we are disappointed when we realize that a chimpanzee really *can't* use sign language in any meaningful way. However, when we look at chimpanzees relating to each other and their own given environments, we see the miracle of a species inheriting, teaching, and surviving by learned behaviors that fit their own situations.

Like chimpanzees, it benefits us to live within our social groups and follow the social hierarchy, learned customs, and communication systems therein. Our own desires, our own will, are secondary to the general will of the group. It is the group, as a whole, that allows us to survive better than we would if we were on our own. If, at some point, the social group ceases to be beneficial to our own survival, we have a choice. We can attempt to change the group and teach new learned behaviors to each individual, or we must leave the social group and either find a new group that fits our needs or create our own social group out of our own desires.

In Higgy's group, there was an established hierarchy, established code of behavior, and established communication system. These were benefitting the entire group. Thus far, nothing had challenged these established traits.

The primatologists, having recorded everything they needed, began to pack up. Late in the evening, after the primatologists had left with their data, a zookeeper observed Hank and Cindy standing next to a sleeping Higgy. The nest Higgy had made was enormous. As an alpha male, Higgy was always entitled to the most hay and branches which he would use to make these very massive, thronelike nests. The nests were a sign of his status. The zookeeper wondered why Cindy and Hank were standing by Higgy watching him sleep. After a while, the zoo-keeper left. The next morning, Higgy was lying on the bare floor of the shelter. Hank and Cindy were sharing an enormous nest beside him.

Individualism is the most modest stage of the will to power.

—FRIEDRICH NIETZSCHE

8

Alpha Falling

1998
New York, New York

It was almost seven o'clock. I pulled the cord out of the phone and plugged it into the computer that I shared with my three roommates. I had told them earlier that I was reserving the computer (and the phone cord) from seven to eight o'clock. I had been anticipating this computer event for several days. That night, on America Online, Koko the gorilla was going to hold a chat with her fans.

I had just recently graduated from college and was working at a bookstore in New York City. I had absolutely no idea what I wanted to do with my life and had moved to New York hoping that something would materialize. Unfortunately, nothing had. That evening, however, strangely enough, watching Koko's chat would change all of that.

I had been fascinated by Koko ever since reading about her in *National Geographic* as a child. My interest in apes had only increased over the years and the thought of actually being able to talk back and forth with a gorilla was something I had only dreamt about. Knowing that there would be thousands of other people in the chat room, I wasn't under any delusion that I would be able to actually ask Koko a question, but seeing the exchange would be almost as good.

This chat was to be a bit of a reintroduction for Koko. It had been fourteen years since her *National Geographic* cover story. Since Project Koko had begun, she had been introduced to other gorillas. The first was a male named Michael. It was claimed that Koko taught Michael to use sign language. She apparently had taught him so well, in fact, that Michael was supposedly able to recount the death of his mother at the hands of poachers in Africa. It had been hoped that the two gorillas would mate and spawn a sign language–using offspring—taught by Koko and Michael. Hopes for this faded when Koko and Michael wouldn't mate. It was then decided to introduce Koko to another male. This time they allowed Koko to pick the mate herself through a sort of video-dating arrangement. Koko would watch males on a video and make a sign as to which one she desired.* The male she picked was named Ndume. Unfortunately, Koko must have had second thoughts because, as with Michael, the two never mated.

While waiting for the computer to connect, I went to the kitchen and poured myself a whiskey over ice. I arrived back at the computer

---

* Even outside of the absence of video screens and sign language, this is a bit different from how gorilla courtship occurs in the wild. Gorillas live in patriarchal groups with one adult male (a silverback). When young males come of age, they leave their natal group and travel around to neighboring groups. While there the young male communicates to other females vocally and gesturally. If he's successful, the female leaves her group and follows the young male around. After a while, the male has acquired a group of females. They live together with their offspring—with the silverback very much in charge.

to see that the chat was beginning. It all began smoothly enough. The chat room host started off by explaining how the chat would work. Koko and Dr. Francine Patterson were in a room with a telephone. The host would tell Dr. Patterson the posted question. Patterson would translate the question to Koko in American Sign Language. Koko's responses would be typed into the chat by a typist who could see what the gorilla was signing. Finally, it was time for the first question. I took a sip of my whiskey and waited. Posed by a user named "MInikitty," Koko was asked if she was going to have a baby in the future.

"Pink," responded Koko.

Luckily, Dr. Patterson clarified the response. Apparently she and Koko had just been having a "discussion" about colors and Koko's mind was still on that. The question was repeated to Koko.

"Unattention," replied Koko.

To me, this was even more confusing than "pink." Patterson came on again to help us understand. She explained that Koko was covering her face which meant that pregnancy hadn't happened and wasn't going to happen.

A few more questions later (after Koko had responded that the name of her second kitten was "Foot"*), a question was posed that really began to show me the truth about what I was witnessing. Koko was asked if she liked to chat with other people.

Koko's response was cryptic: "Fine nipple."

Again, Patterson was quick with an explanation. "Nipple" rhymes with "people" so Koko was doing a "sounds like." I sat in front of my computer screen wondering how "nipple" and "people" rhyme in American Sign Language. Was Francine Patterson suggesting that Koko was transposing a rhyme she had heard in English into sign language? Perhaps, but wouldn't

---

* It wasn't. The cat's name was "Smokey."

there be a better rhyme for "people" than "nipple"? Maybe I had just had a bit too much whiskey and this would make a lot more sense later.

The chat became progressively more weird from there. Toward the end, Koko was asked about her first male companion, Michael. The person asked how she felt about Michael.

"Foot foot good," said Koko.

What about Ndume, her second companion?

"Toilet," replied Koko.

At this point, two of my roommates came into the living room and complained about my hoarding the computer *and* the phone line. I looked at my roommates then looked at the computer screen. Koko was in the process of saying, "Koko loves that nipple drink, go." I turned back to my roommates, downed my whiskey, and gave up the computer. I was done.

I felt like I had been taken. Koko wasn't having a dialogue. Koko wasn't using language. Koko was making random gestures based on the training she had received. It didn't bother me so much that Koko was speaking gibberish. What I really didn't like was the way that Francine Patterson seemed to be covering for her. Was she deliberately attempting to deceive the public, or did she actually believe that Koko was using sign language? Either way, the implications were far-reaching. I began to wonder how much of what I had read about apes, or any other animal, was real. From an early age I had immersed myself in reading about animals. As a child, I had a wide range of animal interests. Books about whales, snakes, alligators, and jellyfish were stacked next to my bed. However, nothing fascinated me more than the apes. With this interest, I couldn't escape the stories of the "talking" apes. The idea of another species that could talk to us in our own language captivated me. I had been fascinated to read about animals like Koko and what she could do. The reports I had read about Koko, Washoe, and other apes supposedly using some form of human language had not just come from popular sources like *National Geographic*.

These projects were actually written up in peer-reviewed academic journals. In one very brief online encounter, I had lost all faith in these reports. All at once, I no longer trusted what I had read, heard, or seen on a show.

Every once in a while we come across circumstances that consume us. These circumstances can take the form of an occupation, a family, a hobby, or an interest. For me, it was an interest in the apes. When we are faced with these circumstances, we look for leaders. We look for mentors. We expect to follow these leaders down a path that will bring us closer to whatever it is that's consuming us. For me, it was the scientists who had written about apes, the papers I had read, and the animals that they had reported on. We use our mentors as candles to follow in the dark. When we find out that these leaders are flawed, we experience a crisis. The light they once carried for us begins to flicker and fade. We find ourselves left alone; stranded on the path that we had followed them down. We begin to doubt everything about what we had worked toward. At this point, we can stay in the same spot or forge ahead on our own path (and hope that it's right). Or we can take a third option; we can turn back and begin a new path altogether.

As I plugged the cord back into the phone, I made a decision. I was going to experience for myself the way other animals lived. In particular, I was going to study apes firsthand. I was no longer going to rely on what others were reporting. I was going to see with my own eyes what they could do, how they did it, and what it all meant to their survival. It was this decision that would bring me to an animal park in south Florida.

2000
Loxahatchee, Florida

I stood outside the gates of the animal park, waiting to be picked up by my new boss. Out of the distance appeared a zebra-striped truck.

When the truck stopped in front of me, the door opened and a towering figure got out.

"Are you the new keeper?" he asked.

I nodded. I was, in fact, the new keeper. Being a zookeeper was part of the mission I was on—the mission to experience the apes on my own terms. I would go to graduate school and specialize in primatology. At the same time, I would work with chimpanzees as a zookeeper.* While my classmates would spend their time away from the classroom reading textbooks and articles, I would spend my time directly with chimpanzees. As I no longer trusted the textbooks and the articles, I would read them with an air of skepticism. I would draw the main source of my knowledge out of my experiences with living chimpanzees. Working with chimpanzees every day would give me an insight into their behavior, the inner workings of their groups, and their communication. This was an experience I could only get as a zookeeper. Even field research in the wild couldn't offer me the same type of constant exposure. By working with chimpanzees every day, I felt that I would truly get to know them.

"Get in. My name's Terry Wolf. We'll drive through the preserve on our way to the chimps."

I got into the truck, moving aside a large net, a box of plastic gloves, and a large fire extinguisher that occupied the passenger seat. Before the door was completely closed, Terry took off. As we drove through the preserve Terry filled me in on the chimp section. He told me how it had all started in 1967 when he was a teenager. The park was looking for a way to house chimpanzees without a cage. He explained how they came up with the idea to put chimps on an island, since they couldn't

---

* This, of course, is frowned upon in graduate school, where they don't want you having a full-time job. I hid my employment as long as possible. I became an expert in changing my clothes while driving. At all times, I smelled like the chimp islands, leaving many of my classmates to question my hygiene practices.

swim. When they had finally moved a group of chimpanzees onto the island, they were elated with how well the system worked. The chimpanzees did a really good job of managing themselves. They formed their own social hierarchies and policed their own behavior. With only a few exceptions they raised their own young. In fact, with the exception of food delivery and medical care, these captive chimps were self-sufficient. Part of the reason for this, Terry explained, was that the park allowed them to be free to establish their own political systems. The chimpanzees would accept those they wanted and ostracize the ones they didn't. Terry said that they tried as much as possible to not interfere in this process.* When a chimp was ostracized, he or she would be moved to other groups to see if they could be integrated there. So far, there had been a group for everyone. It all worked out for the best because the groups operated like groups in the wild. When there was a strong alpha male, the group was strong. Weaker alpha males led to groups falling apart. He then mentioned the most dominant alpha male they had, Higgy. This alpha, he said, was so dominant that he had never even been challenged. There was something about his demeanor that exuded power and authority.

After what seemed like a long ride, we entered the section of the preserve where the chimps lived. The section was a large field with herds of zebras and giraffes wandering around. In the distance were the chimpanzee islands. As we got closer to them, I stuck my head out the window, trying to get a glimpse of the animals I would be working with for the foreseeable future. I saw five islands and four groups. Terry explained to me that this setup was new. At first, there had just been one extremely

---

* This can be something that is difficult to get used to but vastly important. Allowing chimpanzees to "fight it out" is key to how they survive. The fighting and, later, reconciliation by grooming is the way these social groups exist and survive. To interfere would be to destroy the cornerstone of the fabric of their social groups.

large island. Sometime later, the islands were divided. Finally, a few years ago, the park had decided that the chimpanzees should be able to travel from island to island. In order to do this, they placed drawbridges between each island. Each day, the zookeepers would connect the first group to the empty island with the drawbridge. Once they were all safely on that island, the keepers could clean and set up food, branches, and hay for the next group. They would then connect the second group to that island. They would keep doing this until all the chimps had moved over one island. This system had the benefit of keepers being able to clean and set up an empty island, rather than one with chimpanzees on it. This also allowed the chimpanzees to maintain a nomadic lifestyle—something extremely important to their behavior in the wild. The results were cleaner islands and even more wild-acting chimpanzees. When each group ventured onto their new island, they would forage around for food, gather up branches and hay for nest building, and patrol the boundaries.

Behind the islands, the park was constructing a building. This building, Terry told me, was to be an indoor chimpanzee facility. Once completed, we would be able to bring the chimps inside for brief periods of time. This would be the first time that many of them would have ever been indoors. Those that had been indoors before hadn't been in many years. The park would construct a new drawbridge, leading from the back island into the new chimp house.

As we drove past each island, Terry pointed out each chimpanzee and told me a bit about their histories. Each chimp group was named after the alpha male. First there was the group of retired laboratory chimps. This group, known as Nolan's group, was led by its highly aggressive alpha. Due to their histories, the chimps of Nolan's group displayed highly erratic behavior and oftentimes had difficulties in socialization. The alpha male of the next group was named White Ass. Juvenile chimpanzees have a white tuft of hair on their backside. This white patch stays with them until they are about seven or eight years of age. White Ass was so named because, when he came to the park as an adult, he still had the white tuft of hair. After White Ass's group, we saw Bashful's group. Bashful was enormous. Terry explained to me that Bashful was in danger of losing control of his group. There was an up-and-coming male named Ian that was constantly challenging Bashful for power. Ian had put together a strong alliance of females and was ready to overthrow Bashful any day.* Finally, there was the largest group of chimps. That was Higgy's group. Terry stopped the truck in front of the island.

"Get out," he said.

Opening the door of the truck revealed the island in full view. In the center of the island, slowly rocking back and forth, was a magnificent-looking chimpanzee. I stepped out of the truck. My boots sunk into the swampy ground. I stared at a chimpanzee who was directly across the water from me and he stared back. I knew, before Terry said anything, that this was Higgy.

Higgy stood up, revealing his immense size, and gave an extremely loud call into the air. At this, the rest of the group emerged around him. From the top of a shelter came a female chimpanzee with an infant on her back. She bobbed her head violently up and down as she shouted at me. Below her, coming out from the inside of the shelter, was the largest female chimpanzee I could have ever imagined. She sat down, hanging one leg outside the shelter, and made a raspberry sound to me and clapped once. From behind the island came a much smaller chimpanzee wearing a burlap sack around her head. Following behind her was a slow-moving male, shaking as he walked. The burlap-clad female approached Higgy and sat to his left. The slow-moving male

---

* Ian was in fact successful at this. In a matter of years, Bashful would be overthrown and kicked out of the group (he would later join Nolan's group). Ian proved to be a very poor alpha male. His group was extremely volatile with very violent fights happening on a daily basis.

made it to Higgy a few moments later and sat to his right. As I looked around, I realized that an enormous assemblage of chimps seemed to appear from nowhere around the island. Between infants, juveniles, and adults, there were eighteen chimpanzees on this island.

Terry appeared to my right, holding a notebook full of labelled chimp pictures in one hand. In the other hand was a pair of binoculars. He shoved both at me. My boots sank deeper into the mud.

"Here you go," he said. "Learn 'em. In a little while, your coworkers will come by on the boat to pick you up." At that, he climbed back into his truck and drove off.

I stood alone in a large field, surrounded by zebras and giraffes. In front of me were five islands, four of which contained chimpanzees. I looked down at my boots. They were now completely submerged in the ground. I struggled to pull them up but couldn't. I looked across the canal at the chimps, who were seemingly taking a great deal of interest in the fact that I was stuck. All eighteen silently watched as I unlaced my boots and stepped out of them, leaving them stuck in the mud. Standing in wet socks, I opened the notebook and began to look through the binoculars. My introduction to the chimps had begun.

What at first seemed overwhelming turned out to be easier than expected. With the photos, the chimps were easily identifiable. Along with their pictures, I had their names, birth dates, and who they were related to. Using Higgy as a starting point made it all seem easier. The second chimp I identified was the large female who turned out to be Cindy. Cindy's adolescent son, Hank, was also easily identified. He looked exactly like her and, like her, was enormous. I watched the two of them interact for a while.

At one point, Cindy and Hank approached a group of females. Using the pictures, I was able to identify these females as Nana, Kathy, and Cashew. Nana was a juvenile, while Kathy and Cashew were older. Both Kathy and Cashew had infants on their chests. I was able to identify Kathy's infant as Chuckie and Cashew's infant as Kipper. Cindy walked over to Cashew and hit her hard in the back of the head. Cashew screamed and held her infant tight. Kathy backed up. Nana came charging at Cindy and started hitting and biting her. Cindy, who was clearly big enough to hold her own against little Nana, screamed and covered her head. Seeing that she was cowering, Kathy and Cashew joined Nana and also began beating Cindy. Cindy screamed louder and reached out to Hank. Hank stood motionless for a moment, then started to hoot. He charged at Nana, Cashew, and Kathy. Cashew and Kathy, having infants to protect, ran away. That left Nana and Hank to fight. The two screamed, hit, and bit each other. I noticed that as the fighting continued, Cindy calmly walked away. By the time she had made it to the other side of the island, Higgy had stepped in. Higgy descended on the fighting pair with his hand raised high into the air. This was all that needed to be done. Hank and Nana quickly split apart. Higgy sat down exactly where the fight had occurred. Peace had been restored. Cindy watched from a distance.

About five minutes later, Higgy stood up and climbed to the top of a shelter. He greeted the female with the infant (who had shouted at me earlier) with a low grunt. He laid down behind her. My photo book revealed this chimp to be Gin. The book also showed her to be the mother of Nana, Irene (her infant), Juniper (a three-year-old), and Tonic. I flipped to Tonic's picture to see if I could pick her out. Tonic's striking resemblance to Higgy made her fairly easy to identify. She was sitting in the front of the island with her offspring, a one-year-old named Prime. Crawling around in front of Tonic, Prime seemed awfully independent for a one-year-old. While I watched them, Hank walked over and sat beside them. Prime, seeing Hank, jumped into his lap. Tonic stood up and grabbed Prime, placing him on her back. She walked over to the shelter with Hank following her. She climbed up the ladder with Prime on her back toward Higgy, Gin, and Irene.

Hank climbed up after her. In moments, all six chimpanzees were sitting together on top of the shelter. Higgy began to groom Hank.

At the front of the island was what was known as "the feeder platform." On the feeder were buckets filled with fruit, vegetables, and biscuits* that had not been scattered around the island. This was food that could be eaten all day by the chimps, anytime they got hungry. Sitting on the feeder platform were the slow-moving male and the small female with the burlap around her head. Using the photos, I determined these to be Elgin and Little Mama, respectively.

Little Mama immediately caught my attention. She ate with the burlap around her head. Every once in a while she would look over and shake her hand at me. I'm not sure what she was trying to convey but it seemed friendly enough (unlike Gin's greeting earlier). As she ate, Elgin sat beside her, staring blankly at the ground with his mouth hanging open. A few moments later he got up and looked in the bucket that Little Mama was eating out of. She grunted at him and moved aside, allowing him to share.

Suddenly something caught Elgin's eye in the water. It was a banana that, somehow, had been tossed onto a patch of floating grass in the canal. The patch of grass was floating close enough to the island that Elgin could wade out and pull it in. The grass had probably detached from one of the other islands where a keeper had left the banana. It was a very large patch, several meters long. The banana was at the end farthest away from Elgin. He leapt off the feeder platform and wandered into the water up to his waist. The floating grass was still too far out for him to reach. However, it was still floating toward the island. For about ten minutes, Elgin patiently watched. Finally, the grass seemed to be close enough. Chirping happily and stretching out his arm as far

---

* "Biscuits" are a manufactured staple diet for primates. They are hard, fairly unappetizing wafers that ensure that the primates are getting all of their nutritional needs.

as he could, he was able to grab hold of one blade of grass. His cheerful vocalizations became louder. The grass broke off in his hands. Elgin gave a frustrated grunt and stretched out his arm again. This time, he was able to grab hold of a bigger clump of grass. His chirps turned into yelps as he excitedly began pulling the grass toward him. Even for someone as strong as a chimpanzee, pulling a patch of floating grass onto land is a difficult task. Elgin used all of his strength as he climbed out of the water, onto the shore, and began to reel it in.

As Elgin was busy pulling up the grass, I noticed that the other chimps had been alerted by Elgin's chirps and yelps. In particular, Nana had climbed off the shelter and was now standing behind Elgin, watching the entire thing. Elgin triumphantly pulled the grass close enough to reach the banana on the other end. When he grabbed hold of the banana, he began screaming with delight. Without a moment's hesitation, Nana ran up behind him, jumped in the air, kicked him with both feet in the back of the head, and stole the banana out of his hands. Elgin sat down on the ground. Once again, he stared at the ground with his mouth hanging open. Nana, on the other hand, was now eating the banana at a safe distance.

From the top of the shelter came a thundering call. Most of the chimps scattered. Elgin climbed under the feeder platform. Nana, who was far from a shelter, crouched down low to the ground. Higgy appeared, standing at the top of the shelter. He called out again. This time, when he called, he jumped from the top of the shelter to the ground. Landing on the ground he charged at Nana, who began screaming. Higgy ran with one arm raised into the air. When he reached Nana, he slapped her across the back. The sound the slap made echoed through the preserve. Higgy calmly returned to the shelter and climbed back up to the top. Nana sat, hugging herself and screaming.

As the day became early evening, the sounds of cicadas and crickets filled the air. I waited for my coworkers to arrive and pick me up.

I watched the chimps wander around the island collecting branches and hay to make their nests. Little Mama made her nest early. She was already sitting in it, watching the other chimpanzees and occasionally glancing over toward me. I noticed how she made her nest. She had neatly woven a bunch of hay and branches together in a perfect circle. She lined the inside of the circle with her burlap sack, then sat in the middle of the nest, her head resting on the back portion. It looked very comfortable.

Inside one of the shelters, I noticed something that I had not expected. Hank, Cashew, Kathy, Nana, and the two infants, Kipper and Chuckie, were all sitting together. Nana was grooming Hank. Remembering what had occurred earlier, I was intrigued. The grooming that was occurring after their fight was establishing an alliance. Though they had violently fought earlier, they were now in the process of reconciling, which would strengthen the bond between the three of them. The fact that Nana was grooming Hank had additional ramifications. Hank had shown himself to be dominant. It was up to Nana to do the reconciling. Hank had confirmed his place with her. The fact that Cashew and Kathy were also sitting with them was a sign that they had all reconciled. I wondered if they would also begin to groom Hank. I looked over at the other end of the island. Cindy was watching the same thing I was watching. I began to wonder if this was her intention all along.

A boat, carrying my coworkers, came from around the island to pick me up. When they arrived, I walked over to my boots, and with great force, pulled them from the mud. With boots in hand, I stepped into the boat and was carried away from Higgy's group. I was already looking forward to arriving there the next day.

Over the course of the next several weeks, I learned my routine. It was fairly simple. I would propel my boat over to an empty island with big buckets of food. In order to move the boat, I would use a large gondola pole (this gave me more control over the boat than an oar). Once I reached the empty island, I would spend the next hour picking up chimpanzee feces and raking up old hay. I would then scatter some food around the island and leave the rest in buckets on the feeder platform. After spreading hay and branches around, I would get back in my boat and leave the island. I would then connect two islands by swinging open the drawbridge and let a group of chimps onto the newly cleaned island. This drawbridge portion of the routine was not as easy as it sounds.

In order to open the drawbridge, I had to pole the boat over to the bridge pulley crank, which was in the middle of the water. The crank was attached by cables to the bridge. Because chimpanzees are really good at walking across things like cables, the crank can be a dangerous place to be. As soon as I opened the bridge, I was exposed to them. For this reason, my boat was attached to a rope that a coworker could hold on the shore. If any of the chimps decided to come charging down the cable, my coworker could pull me and the boat backward, very quickly, away from the crank.

The first time I opened the bridge, I had been warned about this. I was instructed to pay special attention to Gin, who frequently tried to attack zookeepers by running down the cable. I kept this in mind as I climbed into the boat and threw the coil of rope to my coworker. I poled closer to the crank with Higgy's group watching me. When I reached the crank, I looked over at the group waiting to cross. Gin was moving her head up and down wildly. Cindy sat in front. I was obviously taking too long for Cindy because she clapped very loudly at me. Slowly, I turned the crank and connected the two islands with the bridge. Before it was completely in place, Nana jumped on it. This startled me but I kept turning the crank to put the bridge into place.

The group was actually very uniform, at first, in crossing the bridge. With the exception of Nana, who was already on the other island eating, they crossed in a single-file line. Higgy waited to cross until most everyone was safely on the bridge. The only exception to this was Elgin, who was too far behind for Higgy to wait for. In fact, Elgin appeared to not even notice that the bridge had been extended. I watched as Gin crossed the bridge. She stopped right in the middle of the bridge, where the pulley cables were connected. I braced myself. She extended her arm toward me and shouted. I got ready to push myself away from the controls. She lowered her arm and crossed over to the other island. I breathed a sigh of relief. Soon, everyone except Elgin was on the other island. I called to Elgin. He was sitting in the middle of the island, looking away. I clapped loudly. This alerted him and he slowly got up. I looked over at the other chimps on the other island. Everyone was wandering around the island and eating. I turned back to Elgin. He was slowly coming closer to the bridge. I called and clapped to try to get him to move faster, but it was of no use.

Just then, my coworker shouted at me. I had taken my eyes off the other island and the other side of the bridge for too long. I turned away from Elgin and looked at the bridge to find Nana running down the cable at me. Gulping, I felt my coworker pull the boat back. Unfortunately, I was still gripping the crank. The boat slid out from under my feet, leaving me hanging on the crank, suspended over the water. There was absolutely nothing good about my predicament.

"Let go!" my coworker shouted.

Nana was now face-to-face with me. Her mouth was open and she was screaming. I let go of the crank and sank into the water. When I came up for air, Nana was sitting on the crank, turning it, and making the bridge go back and forth. Elgin, who had finally made it over to the bridge, wanted to join in the fun. He grabbed his end of the bridge and began lifting it up and down. I wondered if the bridge was strong enough to endure all of this. Pretty soon, there was a whole group of chimps jumping and playing on the bridge. Many of them took turns shouting at me in the water.

I swam over to my boat (which was now all the way back at the mainland). I climbed in the boat and took a look at the mess I had created. I had no idea how I was going to get all of the chimps off the bridge and over to the correct island *and* get Nana off the crank. As I was trying to figure out my next move, I heard Higgy's now-familiar loud call. Almost instantaneously he came running across the bridge. Within moments, Nana was off the crank and, along with the rest of the chimps (even Elgin), on the correct island. I quickly poled over to the crank and shut the bridge. Higgy had helped me out.

2002
Loxahatchee, Florida

My first couple of years at the animal park were spent getting to know the chimps. I spent more time with chimpanzees than I did with any human. I learned their personalities, their likes and dislikes, and what made each one unique. There were some that I really liked and some I really didn't. The one thing that remained constant in my view of these chimpanzees was my sheer amazement at Higgy's dominance. There was a call that Higgy produced that would demonstrate his dominance at any given moment. He would begin with a slow and quiet introduction which would lead into a louder buildup. The climax of the call would entail loud screams and amazing visual displays of him swinging branches or pounding his hands and feet on the ground. At this point in the call, all of the other chimps in his group would join in a chorus of hoots. Everyone participated, even the very young. The call and response almost reminded me of a sea shanty, with Higgy as the captain.

I would also marvel at how much time Higgy would spend with younger chimps. Hank followed Higgy around like a shadow. When Prime could get away from his mother, he too would follow Higgy. I would oftentimes see Higgy, Hank, and Prime sitting together far off from the rest of the group. I would wonder about what they were communicating together.

At twelve years old, Hank was also impressive. One of Hank's unique characteristics was his dedication to his mother. Anytime that Cindy called out, Hank would leave whatever he was doing and run to his mother. It was strange to see Hank so attached to his mother because he was so enormous.

As the years progressed, I noticed that Hank and Cindy were spending more time with Nana, Cashew, and Kathy. They would all sleep in the same shelter, eat together, and frequently groom each other. Prime would also sometimes join the group. It appeared that Prime looked to Hank the same way that Hank looked to Higgy.

Neither Prime's mother, Tonic, nor Nana's mother, Gin, wanted anything to do with this new social group. Gin only wanted to spend time with Higgy. She rarely socialized with any other chimp. Tonic also spent most of her time with Higgy. Even though Prime was young, he was free to spend time with Hank, Cindy, Nana, Kathy, and Cashew because Cindy would act as a sort of babysitter.

The solidarity of this social group was really displayed the first time we let Higgy's group in the new indoor chimpanzee facility. None of us was quite sure how the group would react to being inside together. Higgy's group was the second group allowed inside. The first group was Nolan's group of ex-lab chimps. We felt that Nolan's group, because of its size, age, and less volatile disposition, would be a better fit for the test group. Nolan's group's visit to the house had gone over extremely smoothly and without incident. The chimps calmly walked into the house, took treats from us, and went back out to their island. Higgy's group, we assumed, would be quite a bit different.

The indoor space was set up in such a way as to allow the chimps as much freedom of movement as possible. If they felt trapped upon entering the house, they would never come back.* There were six rooms they had access to—three on each side. Between the rooms were sliding doors in the access space. This way, if we wanted to confine a chimp to one room, we could shut the sliding doors. To access the other side, the chimps had to crawl up through a tunnel that extended over the hallway that the keepers could occupy. The keepers were caged away in this hallway with chimps on either side and above them. When we prepared the house for Higgy's group, we closed off the overhead tunnels (they would be much more easily handled on one side of us and not over our heads). We kept all of the sliding doors between the three rooms open, allowing the chimps to have access to three rooms.

I was curious to see who would go right into the house without fear. I soon had my answer. As soon as the bridge was extended, Elgin, for the first time ever, was the first to walk across. When he entered the house, a keeper gave him a candy reward. Elgin, as always, made vocalizations in celebration of his treat. This prompted a few others to cross the bridge. Cindy started, followed by Hank, Cashew with Kipper, Kathy with Chuckie, Nana, and Prime. The eight chimpanzees were, like Elgin, greeted by a keeper with treats. Seeing that there was another room they could enter, all of them, except Elgin, followed Hank into the next area. Cindy noticed that there was a sliding door at the access way they had just crawled through. She walked over to it and shut the door. The eight ran around their new room, vocalizing and displaying.

The sounds coming from the house were now more than enough temptation for the rest of the chimps to enter. All of Higgy's group, except for Little Mama, walked across the bridge and entered the

---

* Still, no matter how much freedom there appeared to be in the house, nothing could mask the fact that the chimpanzees were more confined inside than they were outside. Because of this, every effort was made to make the indoor facility seem as friendly as possible. This was accomplished with treats and open doors.

house. I went outside to see where Little Mama was. She was sitting with her back to me on top of the shelter. She apparently had no interest in exploring the house.

When I came back into the house, I saw the bulk of Higgy's group in the first room. In the other room, Cindy sat beside the closed sliding door while the rest chased each other around and played. Higgy noticed that the sliding door was closed and walked over to it. Cindy got up and walked away. Higgy slid the door open and entered the second room. When he was in the room, Hank and the others walked into the third room. Cindy then shut that sliding door behind them, leaving Higgy alone in the second room. Higgy didn't try to follow them. He didn't even vocalize. He walked back into the first room.

After the chimpanzees went back outside, I watched as Hank and the rest of the eight sat at one side of the island away from the group. Later, I heard Higgy giving his loud call. During the climactic portion where everyone would normally join in, Higgy vocalized alone.*

2003
Loxahatchee, Florida

Early one morning, while I was cleaning the island next to Higgy's, I stopped for a while to watch Higgy's group. Tonic had recently had another baby, named Bamboo. The birth of Bamboo caused Tonic to completely wean Prime. This, of course, was not something that Prime wanted. He would approach Tonic and attempt to nurse. Tonic would

---

* Getting the chimpanzees to actually leave the house was a chore unto itself. Far from being afraid of the house, the chimps didn't want to leave. Cindy, in particular, refused to leave. We ended up having to load the outside island full of things that the chimps loved (sports drinks, cheese, frozen orange juice, etc.).

gently push him off and walk away. Prime would then scream and carry on. At times, the screaming was so loud and continuous that Tonic would give in and pick up her four-year-old son and allow him to nurse. As time went on, Tonic would stop giving in and would leave Prime to his tantrums.*

That morning, I noticed a new phenomenon. Prime approached Tonic. Tonic walked away. Prime went through his normal screaming ritual. A few moments later Nana picked him up and calmed him down. She then carried him over to Kathy, Chuckie, Cashew, and Kipper and sat him in the middle of them. Instantly, Prime seemed at peace.

Over the next few weeks, I watched as this occurred every time Prime had a screaming fit. The tantrums were becoming less and less frequent. Soon, Prime stopped approaching Tonic altogether. In fact, he rarely, if ever, left Hank's side. The eight chimpanzees were now a solid alliance. They slept only next to one another. Only in limited instances would they socialize outside of the alliance.

A few weeks later, the alliance was sitting together on one side of the island. Higgy was nearby with Little Mama and Elgin. The rest of the group was on the opposite side of the island. Abruptly, Cindy walked away from the alliance. She wandered over to Higgy who greeted her with a grunt. Cindy stopped and stared at him. She began making low hooting sounds. At this, Higgy stood up, his hair standing on end. The two of them stared at each other for several moments. Suddenly Cindy lunged at Higgy and bit him in the leg. Higgy grabbed Cindy and pinned

---

* There are few things more grating in this world than the temper tantrum of a juvenile chimpanzee. The screams are loud and high pitched, the movements are exaggerated, and they can go on for hours. The weaning process generally involves this type of behavior. Some mothers are tougher than others, letting the juvenile cry for hours. Other mothers give in. However, giving in has its consequences. Some juveniles are not weaned well and depend on their mothers long after they should. If the mother then dies, oftentimes the juvenile will not survive.

her to the ground. Cindy screamed. Hank came running over to her. Upon seeing the situation, Hank froze. He looked at Higgy, then his mother. He looked back at Higgy and charged toward him. Little Mama and Elgin both ran to the other side of the island. Cindy silently slipped away out of sight. Nana, Cashew, and Kathy surrounded Higgy and Hank. The two males fought loudly. Both were covered in blood. Gin came running from the other side of the island. Leaping into the air, she tackled Hank. Nana, Kathy, and Cashew piled on top. Prime stood in the distance performing a display by swinging his arms back and forth in an exaggerated fashion. The fighting continued for a few more minutes. Then, as quickly as it had started, it stopped. Hank's alliance walked to one side of the island. Higgy and Gin went to the other side. Later Higgy received grooming from Gin and Little Mama. Hank was being groomed by Nana and Cindy.

Hank and his alliance had begun an attempt to take power away from Higgy. What had been put into play by Cindy was now being carried out by her son and his coalition. Higgy, the alpha male who had overseen the group since its formation, was about to lose his power. There was no obvious explanation for why Cindy had started this. There was no obvious reason for why an alliance of females rallied around Hank. The only motivation was simply that it was in their nature to overthrow Higgy. It is the nature of chimpanzee groups to change. Hank and his alliances were just as much pawns of nature as Higgy was its victim.

Hank had been groomed by Higgy to be in control since he was very young. Cindy seemingly knew this and used Hank's dedication to her to force him into action. At a certain point, Hank had been directed as much as he could be directed by the alpha male. It was time to revolt against his alpha male, take what he had learned, and shape his own world. Cindy was there to ensure he fulfilled this destiny.

Soon, Hank stopped needing Cindy's prodding. He began to accept the ambition that his mother had forced upon him. He began patrolling the island with his alliance. He would take food from members of Higgy's alliance like Elgin and Little Mama. He would posture and display at Higgy multiple times a day.

Early one morning, I watched as Cindy approached Hank to groom him. Nana was sitting with Hank. As Cindy normally did, she moved in front of Nana to get to her son. This time, something different happened. Nana stood up and postured aggressively at Cindy. Cindy grunted at her. Nana swiped at Cindy. This caused Cindy to scream and reach out to Hank. Just as he had done with Higgy before, Hank looked at Cindy then looked at Nana. He then turned to Cindy and lunged at her. Cindy screamed and ran away. She continued to scream as she sat in the middle of the island. She began jumping up and down. As the minutes wore on, her screams became guttural cries. Finally, Little Mama approached Cindy and put her hand up to her face in an act of reassurance. Cindy touched and held Little Mama's arm. The two of them walked together over to the other side of the island. Later that day, I saw that Higgy had joined them. Higgy, Little Mama, and Cindy spent the rest of the day grooming each other. Cindy had been ousted by her own son from the alliance she had created.

In a very brief period of time, Hank had gone from being a young follower to becoming an ambitious leader. Unfortunately for Cindy, she no longer factored into Hank's success. His new alliance didn't need her. Hank had used all that he could from Cindy. She was a symbol of where Hank had come from, not where he could go. Hank turned his back on his mother. The consequences of Cindy's scheme had turned against her.

And so, finally, I suppose, he would be able to look upon the sun itself and see its true nature, not by reflections in water or phantasms of it in alien setting, but in and by itself in its own place.

—PLATO

9

War

2004
Loxahatchee, Florida

Higgy faced toward a strong wind as he sat at the edge of the water. He stayed very still, watching and waiting. Across the water
was the object he was studying: a zookeeper's rowboat being rocked
back and forth by the wind. Though a small corner of it remained on
land, most of the boat was floating in the water. Each time a large gust
of wind would blow by, the boat would slide a little bit more off the
land. Strong waves on the water lifted the corner of the boat up off
the land and back down again.

In the distance, on top of their shelter, stood Hank surrounded by
his alliance of Nana, Prime, Kathy, Chuckie, Cashew, and Kipper.
The seven of them, like Higgy, silently watched the boat.

When the boat finally detached itself from the last fragment of land it was holding onto, none of the chimps vocalized. The wind and waves began carrying the boat toward Higgy. In preparation, Higgy stood up. Cindy, Gin, Elgin, and Little Mama gathered around him. Steadily, the boat made its way over to the five chimpanzees on the edge of the island. When the boat was in reach, Higgy stretched out his hand and grabbed the edge of the boat. He held the boat still as Cindy, Gin, Little Mama, and Elgin all calmly stepped in. Just as Higgy was about to step into the boat, a zookeeper appeared at the door of the indoor holding facility. The zookeeper began vocalizing a distress call to another zookeeper, who was still inside.

The other zookeeper appeared, holding a bottle of soda to his mouth. When he looked at Higgy, the other chimps, and the boat, the bottle of soda fell to the ground. Immediately he began yelling at Higgy and gesturing wildly to him. When Higgy saw this, he placed one leg inside the boat and pushed the boat out into the canal with his other leg. Once completely in the boat, Higgy reached down and picked up the gondola pole.

Hank vocalized from the top of the shelter. Higgy turned and called back to him. The rest of the chimps in the boat were relaxed. In front of Higgy, to his right, was Elgin. He was seated, facing forward, with his right arm resting on the side of the boat. To Higgy's left was Little Mama. She was clutching her burlap sack in front of her. Like Elgin, she too faced directly ahead. In front of Elgin and Little Mama, seated in the center of the boat, was Cindy. Gin was in front of everyone, climbing up on the bow of the boat. When Higgy first attempted to propel the boat with the gondola pole, he only managed to rotate the boat in the water. Gin was now facing the island and Higgy's back was now to the zookeepers. Elgin, Little Mama, and Cindy didn't move or change their expressions.

The zookeeper jumped into the water and began swimming toward the boat. At this point, Higgy succeeded in pointing the boat back toward the shore. Using the pole, he propelled the boat forward. The boat was now quickly headed toward the shore. The zookeeper intercepted the boat before it could reach the land and held onto it. He looked up to see that Gin was right above him. She screamed at him and began searching around the boat. Finally, she found a long-handled brush, picked it up, and began hitting the zookeeper on the head with it. The zookeeper sank into the water. When he came up for air, she swung the brush at him again. This time, he was able to duck out of the way.

Swimming away from the boat, he noticed that the end of the safety rope (the one normally used to pull the boat back from the crank in case of emergency) was floating near him. The other end was still attached to the boat. He picked up the rope and swam back toward his coworker. He shouted something at her which made her run inside and grab a fire extinguisher. She threw the fire extinguisher to the zookeeper, who caught it in the water. Slowly, holding the fire extinguisher above his head, he made his way back to the boat.

He arrived at the boat on the opposite side of Gin. Holding the fire extinguisher in one hand and turning the boat with the other, he was able to point the boat back toward the island. He shoved the boat as hard as he could. When it hit the edge of the island, he sprayed the fire extinguisher into the air. The chimps, fearing the fire extinguisher, jumped off the boat and landed back on the island. The zookeeper shouted loudly to his coworker. She pulled the boat. The boat retreated from the island. The zookeeper grabbed it and rode it all the way back to the shore. Higgy stood at the edge of the water and shouted. Gin jumped up and down. Hank began displaying from the top of the shelter. The zookeeper crawled up onto land, looked over at the chimps on the island, and collapsed.

As I lay there, I looked up at the sky and pondered what had just occurred. Higgy had conceded his group to Hank. He was leaving with what was left of his alliance. They were going to a different location, away from Hank, Nana, Prime, Kathy, Chuckie, Cashew, and Kipper. What had truly stunned me was the fact that everything had been accomplished in silence. Yet, somehow all of the chimps knew exactly what they were going to do. Little Mama, Cindy, Gin, and Elgin all knew to join Higgy at the water and to silently climb into the boat. Hank and the rest of his alliance knew not to get in the boat with them. The entire thing had seemingly been planned. I sat up and looked over at the group. Higgy and his alliance had retreated to one side of the island. Hank and his group were still on top of the shelter. This war had just begun.

There were noticeable changes in Higgy now that he was being challenged. For one thing, he had lost much of the swagger in his walk that was so distinctive. His displays had also changed. They were less controlled, more unpredictable than before. This was the first time he had ever been challenged and it was appearing to cause him a great deal of stress.

A few weeks after the boat incident, I arrived at the park one morning and began my rounds. This entailed me looking at every chimpanzee to make sure that none of them had been injured overnight and that everyone was acting healthy and normal. When I arrived at Higgy's island, the first thing I noticed was that Gin had blood dripping down her chin. She was grooming Higgy and chewing on something. I looked for any sort of cut on her face. Instead of finding any sort of gash, I found that the blood was coming from her mouth. Each time she chewed, more blood would dribble out of her lips. I tried to see what she was chewing on, but her mouth was closed tightly. I called to her but she didn't turn around. I threw a banana over to her to see if she would open her mouth so I could see inside.

She didn't pick it up. Little Mama grabbed it instead.* Gin continued to groom Higgy with her mouth closed.

I looked around at the other chimps in the group. That's when I noticed Hank. He had a strange expression on his face. He was walking around with just one corner of his mouth open extremely wide. His walk was fairly unstable. I, again, looked through the binoculars, this time to get a closer look at Hank's mouth. Hank wasn't opening one side of his mouth. What I was actually seeing was that Hank's right cheek was missing. His teeth and gums on that side were completely exposed. There was blood all over his right ear and shoulder. I looked back over to Gin. She now had her mouth open and was spitting something into her hand. She looked at it for a few seconds then put it back in her mouth and resumed chewing. I could only assume that it was Hank's missing cheek.

Hank wobbled over to Nana. She pulled his head close to her and started grooming his cheek. For the next few weeks, Hank and his alliance were quiet. There were no fights or big displays. For the time being, it appeared that Higgy, thanks to Gin, had regained control of his group.

Hank's cheek healed surprisingly quickly. Within a month, it was hard to tell that anything major had happened to him. During this time, he became increasingly more contentious. Frequently he could be seen perching himself on the roof of a shelter and stamping his foot very powerfully against it. Then he would add loud vocalizations. This would climax with him throwing a large object (usually a rock or a bucket) off the top of the shelter and screaming. Higgy would watch the displays from a distance. His only reactions would be quiet grunts.

Higgy began countering Hank's displays with his own shows of

---

* Little Mama taking anything from Gin was cause for great concern. This *never* happened! Something was very out of the ordinary with Gin.

strength. These were louder and more powerful than Hank's, and they usually concluded with Higgy charging at whatever chimp happened to be closest to him (usually Elgin).* Showing his power, he would hit the chimp with his open hand as he screamed. Like Higgy, Hank would watch from a distance. As the weeks went on, the displays grew more intense.

Despite the displays, everything else seemed to be back to normal. Higgy was spending more time with Hank's alliance. At one point, Higgy, Nana, and Cashew were grooming each other in the shelter. Higgy began acting like an undisputed alpha male again. It was, perhaps, this sense of false calm that led Higgy to let his guard down, a mistake that Hank's alliance would seize as an opportunity.

I had just set up an empty island for Higgy's group. New branches and fresh hay covered the ground. Fruits, vegetables, and popcorn were scattered around. The island was ready and I was prepared to open the bridge. I threw the rope to my coworker and poled the boat over to the crank. The group waited patiently, as they always did. Nana and Prime were in front of the rest of the group. Sitting calmly behind them was Cindy. Hank was a few chimpanzees behind her. Higgy was sitting outside of the line, surveying the group. When the bridge opened, Nana and Prime jumped on and ran to the other island. Once there, they immediately started to eat. The rest of the group followed. Higgy, as usual, stayed where he was and watched everyone pass. Elgin was surprisingly quick going over the bridge and was in front of Little Mama, who was holding the burlap under her arm as she sauntered over the bridge. Once everyone was safely on the other island, Higgy began to cross the bridge.

---

* You may wonder why Higgy would attack a member of his own alliance. Here, Higgy is displaying his power, not actually attempting to hurt another chimp. Though the charging looked violent, the chimp he ran at was never hurt—usually just shaken and startled.

I looked over at the chimps on the island. I noticed that Elgin, Little Mama, and Cindy were all sitting where most of the food was. I found this strange because, normally, Nana and Hank would occupy those areas. I wondered why Elgin, Little Mama, and Cindy were being allowed to eat whatever they wanted. I looked around the island. I realized that I didn't see Hank or Nana.

I turned back to Higgy, who was now in the middle of the bridge. Just as he reached the exact center, Nana ran onto the bridge. The hair on Higgy's back and shoulders stood straight up. Nana was now face-to-face with him in the middle of the bridge. I looked over to see Hank and Prime at the edge of the bridge, staring at Higgy. Vocalizing, Higgy began trying to walk past Nana to get to Hank. Nana reached between Higgy's legs, grabbed his testicles, and yanked down as hard as she could. Higgy made a horrible sound. The howls were long and distorted and didn't seem like anything I had ever heard from a chimp.* He continued howling as he lay down on his back in the middle of the bridge, holding his scrotum. Nana ran off the bridge and grunted to Hank. With Prime following, they walked from the bridge to the feeder platform and began eating the newly set-out food. Higgy remained at the center of the bridge, wailing.

I found it strange that none of the chimps had come to Higgy's defense. He remained on his back, crying, for several minutes. Yet no one, not even his alliance, came to his aid. Finally he got up. He looked over at me for a bit, turned around, and walked back to the old and now empty island. No one followed him. He had the entire island to himself. He climbed up one of the shelters and refused to cross over the bridge. Higgy spent the night alone.†

---

* See Masudi's vocalizations in chapter 5.
† Occasionally Higgy would choose to spend an evening alone. Once he made this decision, it was impossible to get him to change his mind. It was always a major inconvenience

The next morning, Higgy appeared ready to join his group. He was pensively waiting by the bridge. I examined Higgy's group. All of them appeared to be acting normally. Nana and Hank were down by the water. Gin was with Tonic and Tonic's baby, Bamboo. On the ground, Little Mama was grooming Elgin. She seemed especially interested in Elgin's left foot. I looked through the binoculars to find that it was completely covered in blood. From what I could see, there was a large hole that pierced his foot. Elgin noticed me looking at him and made a move to get up. He wasn't putting any weight on his right leg at all. After a few hobbling steps, he fell over. Little Mama ran over to him and started grooming his foot again. Elgin, left without Higgy, had clearly been attacked in the night. I now understood why Higgy was so eager to rejoin his group.

I now had a dilemma. Once Higgy rejoined the group, he was, no doubt, going to take immediate vengeance for Elgin's foot. The other chimps in Higgy's group began to assemble across from Higgy. Gin screamed and reached out toward Higgy, then reached out toward me. I began to fear that someone might try to jump across the canal to Higgy. There was nothing I could do. I had to open the bridge. I looked over at Elgin. He and Little Mama were sitting at the far end of the island. Hopefully, I thought to myself, they would remain there and stay out of the impending conflict.*

I put the boat in the water, grabbed the gondola pole, and got in. Making my way over to the bridge, I feared the tense situation in front

---

because he would take up the one empty island, making it impossible to move any of the other groups of chimps. Oftentimes, Elgin would see that Higgy was on the old island by himself and run back to him. I'm not sure why Elgin was so excited to spend an evening with Higgy on a dirty island without any food. Higgy never seemed to pay him any attention when this would happen.

* Little Mama was always highly adept at avoiding conflict. During group fights, she would quietly sneak away to a hiding spot and wait there until the battle ended. Because she was so low ranking in the group, she had little to gain by participating in such squabbles.

of me. Higgy was standing perfectly still and perfectly silent, looking directly ahead at the group across from him. The group, meanwhile, was lined up, side by side, on the other end of the bridge. Nana was rocking back and forth. Gin was screeching. Hank was swaying from side to side. Cindy was calmly sitting behind Nana.

Finally, I arrived at the crank. I looked over at Higgy.

"Please be calm," I whispered, and opened the bridge.

Higgy leapt into the air and rocketed toward his group. Nana lunged forward to meet him halfway across the bridge. Yet, something stopped Nana. I looked over to see that Cindy was holding onto one of her feet. Nana screamed and tried to hit and bite Cindy. Calmly, Cindy stood up without letting go of Nana's foot and flung her through the air away from Higgy. Nana landed and got up. Higgy was already across the island and was coming straight for her. Nana covered her head with her hands. Higgy's blow landed across her back. The sound of the hit echoed across the water. Higgy then turned to Cashew. He charged toward her, and slapped her as hard as he had slapped Nana. Hank then charged at Higgy. Higgy turned and charged back at Hank. The two met in midair and tackled each other to the ground. The fight continued and they rolled into the water. Once they hit the canal, both stood up on two legs, waist deep in the water. I could see that Higgy had a massive cut on his arm. Hank had a gash across his face.

Little Mama and Elgin had now gone to the center of the island, from where they watched. They were soon joined by Gin and Cindy. Next, Nana came and sat beside them. Prime showed up behind Nana. Pretty soon, all of the chimps were sitting around Little Mama and Elgin watching Hank and Higgy fight. For a brief moment, they appeared unified. I remained at the crank, also watching. Finally, Higgy and Hank separated. Once they separated, the group split in two. Hank's alliance retreated over to Hank on one side of the island, while Higgy's alliance gathered on the other side.

Every day, the fighting continued. Every morning I would find a new injury on another chimp. It was beginning to seem obvious that this war was going to continue for quite some time and it wasn't going to end well.

One night, I had returned to the animal park very late after taking one of the chimps, Peter, to the dentist.* That late, the park was completely silent and dark. Luckily, that evening, there was a full moon so I had a nice view of the chimp section. I set Peter up in the chimp house and closed it up. I decided to check on Higgy's group. I drove my truck over to their island. Just as I had imagined, the two camps were sleeping separately. Just then I noticed that Higgy was away and sitting on top of the feeder platform. The moon shone down on him, like a spotlight. He was rocking back and forth and looking down below him. Just then, I noticed what he was looking at: Hank was sitting down beside the feeder platform gesturing up to Higgy. What was this late-night meeting about? Why was it occurring in silence? How did it begin? Neither Higgy nor Hank paid any attention to the fact that I was in front of the island. They were deeply entrenched in whatever it was that they were communicating between them. I stood and watched them for a while before I got back in the truck and left.

The next day I was cleaning and setting up an island for White

---

* There was only one veterinarian we knew of that was willing to perform dental work on chimpanzees. The only stipulation was that he wanted to use his own office and his own equipment. Because of this we would have to bring the chimps to him, which was at a standard dog-and-cat type of veterinary clinic. He would work on the chimp after his office closed. At the end of the day, we would wheel a carrier, containing a sedated chimpanzee, into his waiting room. Usually, there were still customers in the waiting room so we would cover the carrier with a sheet so that they couldn't tell that there was a chimp inside. However, it never failed that the chimp would wake up and make some sort of vocalization. The responses from the people in the waiting room were varied. Most of the time, people would want to see the chimp. On at least one occasion, the vocalization sent an elderly woman running out of the office.

Ass's group. From out of the corner of my eye, I could see something occurring on Higgy's island. Something was being repeatedly thrown high into the air. I couldn't tell what it was. It could have been a blanket or a stuffed animal. Still, I couldn't be sure. I dropped what I was doing and climbed into my boat to investigate.

I made my way over to Higgy's island. I still couldn't make out what was being thrown into the air. When I got in front of the island, it became clear. Bamboo was sitting by himself in front of a shelter. From behind the shelter, Prime came running. He ran up to his infant brother, picked him up by one leg, and flung him far into the sky. He watched as Bamboo sailed way up high and then crashed back down into the island. Bamboo, who was remarkably durable, got up looking disoriented. As soon as he was up, Prime would circle around again and repeat the action.

Tonic, apparently, wasn't aware of what was occurring. She was sitting with Gin and not paying any attention to Prime and Bamboo.* I grabbed the fire extinguisher and sprayed it into the air. I yelled at Prime. Tonic sat up immediately and looked around for Bamboo. She saw him sitting alone and ran over to him, vocalizing the entire time. Higgy also looked over and saw. He went charging at Prime. Prime attempted to retreat to his mother. However, Tonic moved away leaving him exposed to Higgy. Nana jumped in front of Prime. Higgy switched the object of his aggression to Nana. When he reached her, Nana jumped up and bit him in the face. This brought Gin down to the scene. She tore into Nana, biting her on the side. Within moments, the entire group was involved in another large fight.

The incident with Bamboo underscored the major problems that the group would suffer if Higgy ever lost his alpha male status. The

---

* This was not as irresponsible of Tonic as it sounds. Chimpanzee mothers will frequently allow older siblings to take care of offspring in their later infancy for periods of time. I would imagine that Tonic trusted Prime not to throw Bamboo in the air.

chimps that he had done so well protecting would no longer receive his guardianship. The challenges to his status had tremendous ramifications for the entire group. Higgy had shown that he was an incredibly confident leader. This leadership protected a large and diverse group that contained a complex female-dominance hierarchy. The group also contained three adult males. With the grand exception of the current war, this complicated group had run extremely smoothly. Higgy was also in charge of chimps with ages ranging from one-year-old Bamboo to sixty-eight-year-old Little Mama. Both Bamboo and Little Mama were protected from any less-than-gentle chimpanzees in the group. Add to this mix Elgin, who was completely reliant on Higgy for survival.

It was not believed that Hank would be able to govern as well as Higgy. He had not shown himself to protect the weaker individuals. There was no evidence of Hank caring for chimpanzees like Bamboo, Little Mama, or Elgin. If Hank became alpha male, these chimps would, almost certainly, be negatively affected and might not even survive.*

It was clear that Higgy and his alliance were not winning the war. Yet there were no signs of Higgy abdicating his status to Hank. All signs pointed to Higgy fighting on endlessly. The war could continue for years. Chimps could be severely injured or killed. For this reason, it was decided that the animal park would step in and end the war. This would be accomplished by rounding up Hank and his alliance and sending them away to another zoo. One zoo, at the time, was in need of a chimpanzee group to fill its new exhibit: the Lincoln Park Zoo in Chicago.

---

* This is not to say that Hank wouldn't have been a good alpha male in another circumstance. He had certainly learned from the best. However, he was still very young and Higgy's group was so diverse and complex that only the best alpha male had any chance of controlling that population. Because the philosophy of the animal park was to let the chimps naturally govern themselves, we relied heavily on our alpha male chimpanzees.

The Lincoln Park Zoo had just completed work on a multimillion-dollar chimpanzee exhibit. The exhibit was very different from the islands of the animal park. It featured both an indoor and outdoor portion. While in the indoor portion, the public could be up close to the chimps, separated by a thick window. The highly interactive exhibit had such features as caves (where human children and apes could both enter and be separated by glass), touch screens where guests could learn about the chimps, and a naturalistic-looking environment. The outdoor portion of the exhibit contained large trees, streams, and climbing structures. It was determined that this would be a perfect place to send Hank and his alliance. The Lincoln Park Zoo readied their exhibit for the entrance of Hank, Nana, Prime, Kathy, Chuckie, Cashew, and Kipper.

Meanwhile, the war carried on. It was obvious that the sooner Hank left the island, the better it would be for everyone. Little Mama, in particular, was having a terrible time during the war. Her role as the babysitter of the group had diminished. Prime, who at one point was with Little Mama quite a bit, no longer had anything to do with her. Chuckie and Kipper were no longer seen with her at all. Nana, who used to play with Little Mama, never acknowledged her. Occasionally, she would be seen holding Bamboo, but since the throwing incident, Tonic didn't let him out of her sight for long and would take him back from Little Mama after only a few brief moments. Little Mama spent most of her day sleeping alone in the shelter. Occasionally, Cindy would sleep next to her, but for the most part, Little Mama was alone.

On a summer morning in 2004, Higgy's group was brought into the chimp house. Hank's alliance was transferred into a separate room. When the sliding door closed, Higgy saw Hank for the last time. With the rest of his group, but without Hank's alliance, Higgy left the house and returned outside to their island. Just like that, the war was over. Higgy climbed to the top of a shelter. He looked down at his group. He looked around to the other chimpanzee groups. He tilted his head to the sky and gave an amazingly loud vocalization. At the climax of the vocalization, the rest of his group joined in.

Hank's group had been moved into individual travel carriers. Hank, Nana, and Prime each got their own carrier. Kathy shared one with Chuckie. Cashew shared one with Kipper. They were loaded into the back of a van, and the next day they were all on a cargo plane bound for Chicago. They would enter into a completely different world. They would go from the hot and humid environment of south Florida to the cold and windy climate of Chicago. Instead of being surrounded by the Florida Everglades, they would now be surrounded by the traffic of Lakeshore Drive. They would now have exponentially more human interaction than what they had at the animal park. The public would be much closer to them, being face-to-face with them rather than inside a car. The keepers would work one-on-one with them on a daily basis. Nothing would be the same for these seven chimpanzees ever again.

That evening, I remained at the animal park. I sat in front of Higgy's island, monitoring the group. There was no evident sense of loss being exhibited in their behavior. They had just lost seven members of their group and it didn't seem to affect them at all. Still, I noticed a few changes. Higgy had his old walk back. He was patrolling the boundary of the island with Elgin following dutifully behind him. I also noticed that Little Mama had been holding Bamboo for over an hour. When she had taken Bamboo, she had walked right up in front of Tonic and picked up the baby as if it was all planned. Tonic didn't resist and Little Mama carried Bamboo over to the other shelter. This caused me to once again obsess about how these chimps were communicating. Did Tonic somehow communicate to Little Mama that it was now all right for her to hold Bamboo for an extended period of time?

The evening lost all traces of sunlight while I sat on the muddy ground. I thought back to a few years prior when Koko's Internet chat had so profoundly disappointed me. I reflected on how much more amazing everything was that I had experienced with the chimpanzees in front of me than any "talking ape." Even if, during that Internet chat, Koko had spoken eloquently and in fluent human language, it would have paled in comparison to watching these chimps naturally communicate with each other on their own terms. It would have never fascinated me as much as watching a group of chimpanzees scheme and fight through their social system, culminating in a war. It seemed to me that every moment we spend trying to turn chimpanzees (and other apes) into lesser versions of humans are moments we miss watching how amazing these animals are on their own terms.

I began to think of the research I had been studying in the classroom. I thought of the chimpanzees in the Mahale Mountains who were using their own set of vocalizations and the implications, therein, for vocal learning. I thought of the research that had occurred, almost a decade ago, at the animal park which showed the same thing, but with the chimps in front of me. I began to wonder if they were using these learned vocalizations to communicate the complex processes involved with Hank's uprising and rebellion. I wondered if these vocalizations were responsible for Higgy's planned boat escape from the island with his alliance. I thought, again, about the vocalizing between Higgy and Hank while Higgy was in the boat. What was being communicated? I began to wonder if Hank would carry the vocalizations that he learned from his old group into his new group. Would he begin to add his own vocalizations? I knew that, in humans, groups that become isolated begin to form their own dialects. I knew that different environments, different periods of stress, and a different social hierarchy cause dialects to evolve on different paths. Hank's group was going to experience a completely different environment. They were also going to go through the stressful experiences of being split from their group and placed in an unknown situation. On top of this, without the rest of the group, the social hierarchy would change. If chimpanzee vocalizations were truly a chimpanzee language, then all of these factors should cause Hank's group to begin to form their own dialect.

I began to plan out a project which would look at everything I had been wondering about. If chimpanzees learned their own vocalizations, like human language, then it stands to reason that these vocalizations would evolve (like human languages do). The evolution would begin as a slightly different dialect then, eventually, become its own system of vocalizations—a separate chimpanzee language. I could record the calls from both Higgy's and Hank's groups and compare them. I could see if they were growing apart. If Hank's vocalizations were beginning to diverge from Higgy's, a new dialect would be forming within Hank's group. Hank's dialect would continue to evolve until, eventually, the calls of Hank's group would be unintelligible to the chimps in Higgy's group.

I would begin by recording every vocalization that I heard from Higgy's group and identifying it with a corresponding behavior. I would arrive at a number of individual vocal phrases (chimp "words," if you will) used by Higgy's group. I would then go to Hank's group in Chicago and identify the same chimp words. After a couple of years, I could compare the two groups to see if the individual words were changing (or completely disappearing) in Hank's group.

Over the next few months I would formulate, in great detail, the specifics of my project. It would take years, but I was determined to both record the entire lexicon of Higgy's group and see if, in years, that lexicon was changing in Hank's group.

This project would be one more step in my quest and mission to understand the apes on my own terms. As with my previous experiences with the chimpanzees, I could see the hidden mechanisms of nature at work. I could watch the unseen hand of creation mold, form, and operate something as critical as communication. Like lifting the face off of a mechanical watch, I could view, if not understand, what makes a group of chimpanzees function together. By watching how these invisible instruments control and operate chimpanzee communication, I could better understand how they affect other aspects of nature, including the human species.

That first evening without Hank, with the new project spinning through my head, I got up off the mud to head home. I looked back at the island to see Cindy sitting alone. She blew a raspberry to me and clapped. I reached into my truck, grabbed a banana, and threw it to her. I wondered if she felt betrayed or alone. After eating the banana she retreated to a shelter where Little Mama was laying in a nest. She gave soft grunts to Little Mama, who sat up. Cindy began making a nest next to her.

> We had seen God in his splendors, heard the text that nature renders. We had reached the naked soul of man.
>
> —ERNEST SHACKLETON

10

Nebula

There are places and times that belong in the realm of the truly magnificent. The animal park at night is one such example. Because of its seclusion, the sky is free from any light spilling over from a city and there is an indescribable darkness. Everything that can be seen is being illuminated by objects in space. With the barrier of the blue sky removed, one's fragment of the world is free to take its place in the universe.

When the moon is not out, the darkness is especially profound. During these nights, it is difficult to see anything at all. One is provided with a glimpse of the night sky that is, usually, never seen. The constellations glow with a stunning brilliance. Within the constellations, deep space objects shine down upon the earth, their light traveling for thousands, sometimes millions, of years.

In the years that followed Hank's departure, the image of the park on the night that Higgy and Hank had their midnight confrontation was etched in my everyday memory. I had been awestruck by the night and how dark, calm, and silent everything was. I began to look for any excuse to observe the chimps after the sun went down.

One night, when I was attempting to get a glimpse of the chimps through the darkness, I decided to aim my binoculars up at the night sky. I wanted to get a closer view of what, in space, was lighting my world on Earth. Through the binoculars, the points of light became more defined. In some cases, colors and shapes became apparent. The most amazing object I found was the Crab Nebula. At first it appeared as nothing more than a smudge in the sky. As I continued to stare at it, whether by imagination or perception, I was able to make out the colorful clouds of gases that comprised it.

The Crab Nebula was once a super-massive star. About seventy-five hundred years ago, the star exploded, creating a supernova. The light from the explosion did not reach the Earth until about a thousand years ago, when it was recorded by astrologers of the day. Today all that can be seen of the once-great star are its remnants: a stellar cloud of gas shaped like a crab. Within the cloud, the gases are coalescing together into clumps. Eventually these clumps will become new stars and new star systems. So when one views the Crab Nebula, one is not just observing the remains of a dead star, but also the beginning of new stars being born out of its remnants.

Sixty-five hundred light years away, the light of the nebula was hitting my binoculars. After a while, I put the binoculars down and looked over to the remnants of Higgy's group. I could barely make out the unmistakable shape of Little Mama, sitting up, on top of a shelter. When my eyes focused and adjusted, Little Mama's features became more apparent. The light from every object in space had filtered into the animal park, allowing me to see. The principles and mechanisms that operated what was in the sky were also operating what was surrounding me. Higgy's group had collapsed. What remained of the group was in the process of forming new groups. The lexicon of calls from Higgy's group was now having to take different forms—a form which would work for Hank and his new group, and a form which would work for the new version of Higgy's group.

The calls of Higgy's group had come from the fragments of other groups. Little Mama had brought the original lexicon over from the wild. Her doomed group, in Africa, had passed it on to her. She had spread it to Cindy, Higgy, Gin, and Elgin. They, in turn, had passed it throughout the group; each of them interjecting their own features, dictated by their own histories. This built the language of Higgy's group. That language was now spread out like the gasses of a nebula cloud—forging the basis of Hank's new communication system.

As I sat in the mud, Little Mama, who was sitting in the dim glow of the stars, lay down in the nest she had made at the top of the shelter. What Little Mama, her communication system, and the chimps that were using this communication system represented to me was not just a look into how chimpanzees communicate; rather, it was a look inside the inner workings of the universe, a glimpse of how things change and how change is accommodated.

The desire to see this change occur drove my determination to study and compare the calls of Higgy's group and Hank's group. What I wanted for this study was to be able to visualize what was going on vocally. If Hank's calls were changing, I wanted to be able to actually see it and document it. In this, I would get a glimpse at the process which allows for a group of chimpanzees to live together and, in a broader sense, get a glimpse at how any social animal operates via certain laws; these laws being one small aspect of the hidden machine that operates the universe.

I felt something touch my back. I looked behind me to see a giraffe, silhouetted against the stars, towering over me. This giraffe, who frequently attempted to steal chimp food out of the back of my truck, had bent over and nudged me. I imagine he was looking for a late-night piece of fruit. I got up to walk over to the truck (one never wants to be stepped on or kicked by a giraffe). When I stood up, he backed away. I looked over at Little Mama, who now seemed to be sleeping, then back at the giraffe. The night sky shone down on the three of us; three different species occupying the same infinitesimal portion of the universe. Each of us three surviving this universe, whether we were conscious of it or not, by the same physical properties—the properties that operate biology on Earth, the physics of the universe, and the stars in the sky.

I began recording the vocalizations from Higgy's group soon after Hank's departure. My goal was to record and isolate phrases that were being repeated at different times within the same behavioral contexts. In this way, I hoped to discover not only the calls but also a bit about the meaning of the calls that they were using. This was going to be a difficult task. The most important part of this was to distinguish between the calls and to define the parameters which made each one unique. I could then attach a correlating behavior to the call and make my best guess as to the information it was trying to convey. At the end, I hoped to have a collection of vocal phrases that Higgy's group was using and a corresponding meaning attached to each. In a sense, I was going to create a Rosetta stone for the group's vocalizations. Once I did this, I would take recordings from Hank's group and see if they were using the same phrases and if those phrases had changed at all due to the split. If, in fact, they had changed, I could make the case that Hank's group was developing their own dialect.

The microphone I used looked like a large satellite dish. This microphone (called a parabolic microphone) was capable of picking up even the slightest whisper from far away. It was plugged into a laptop computer. I was able to listen to all of the sounds that the microphone was gathering through noise-canceling headphones (which were plugged into the laptop). I merely had to point the microphone in the general direction that the sound was coming from and the sound waves would enter into the large dish. They would then be transmitted into the computer, processed and recorded with sound-analysis software, and finally transmitted up through my headphones. I would then number the vocalization, list the individual producing it and the individual(s) receiving it, and jot down the behavioral context that was occurring when the call was made. Fortunately, Higgy's group was very vocal. One needed to merely point the microphone toward any gathering of two or more chimps. The result would be an amazing recording of chimpanzees vocalizing back and forth. Even when the encounter seemed silent (I was standing away from them, across the canal), the parabolic microphone would reveal a myriad of soft calls. The effect was similar to pointing binoculars up to a seemingly empty portion of the night sky, only to find a host of stars through the lens.

After years of recording the chimps, I had to analyze them. I did so by creating spectrograms out of each vocalization. Remember that a spectrogram is a visual depiction of a sound, providing such data as the duration of the entire sound, the amplitude (or energy/volume) of the sound, the structure of the sound,* the frequency of the sound waves (or pitch), and how much amplitude each sound wave is being given. For example, a traditional chimpanzee loud call, structured with an introduction, buildup, climax, and descent looks on a spectrogram like a series of smudges. The first smudges (the introduction) look like evenly spaced blobs of the same shade. The next series

---

* The structure refers to the different elements within a sound and the breaks within these sounds. For example a "hoo hoo hoo" phrase would appear as a three-element vocalization on a spectrogram (appearing as three blobs next to one another).

of smudges (the buildup) look, again, like evenly spaced blobs; only this time, they get progressively darker (representing a buildup of amplitude, or volume) and progressively higher on the graph (representing an increase in frequency, or pitch). The climax appears like a massive dark blob (representing a loud sound that incorporates many different frequencies). The descent looks like a reverse of the buildup, with the smudges getting lighter and lower. The resulting spectrogram is a complete description of a sound represented by one picture.

When I had all of the calls converted to spectrograms, I printed them out, laid them on the floor, and looked for patterns. Then, without looking at anything else, I grouped the spectrograms together that looked alike. Some of them didn't look like any of the others, so those were set aside. When I was done, I had my first initial grouping of the calls. This, however, was not enough for me to be able to identify each grouping as a chimp "phrase" or "word."

Next, I had to look at the behaviors associated with the calls. With some of the groupings, all (or most) of the calls had the same general behavioral contexts occurring. These groupings were able to remain in consideration. Other categories had several different behaviors. These groupings were taken away. I was left with fewer categories, but more defined groupings. However, this still wasn't enough for me to make the determination that what I was looking at were truly chimp phrases.

Next, I needed mathematical justification. This would be the hardest criteria for each category to pass. If the categories didn't have any statistical cohesion, then they would be discounted. To do this, I took the numeric data from each phrase. This included the duration of the call, the duration of each call element, the three loudest frequencies (or pitches) of each element, the mean frequency of the entire call, and the amount of time it took for each element to reach its peak amplitude (or loudest point). Since I was comparing different units of measurement (seconds of time and hertz of frequency), I had to standardize the data with a formula that converted each measurement into a geometric distance. I was then able to statistically cluster the data together. I was surprised to see that, more often than not, the categories that I had created visually and behaviorally held together mathematically as well. Though I had to put aside hundreds of vocalizations, I was able to *definitively* arrive at twenty-five vocal phrases that Higgy's group was reliably using. I then set out to define each phrase by the corresponding behaviors, the relationship between the sender and receiver(s), the contexts in which the call was produced, and the intensity of the vocalization. I used this to compile a "phrase book" for Higgy's group.

So here, without further wait, are the behaviorally, spectrally, and statistically defined vocal phrases that Higgy's group was using:*

"Hallelujah!": This call was produced by almost every chimp in the group during times of positive excitement. This included seeing zookeepers bring treats and watching an impressive (and nonaggressive) solo display by another chimp. The call itself was a series of equally spaced barks occurring at the same pitch.

"I need help.": This occurred when a lower-ranking individual appealed to a higher-ranking individual for some sort of assistance (dealing with another chimp's aggression, help with bringing hay and branches up to the top of a shelter, etc.). The call was a short series of low-pitched yelps.

"Come here!": This call, most likely, had its origins with Cindy and was acquired by Higgy at an early age. It is a raspberry sound. It always occurred when a dominant individual was aggressively trying to summon another individual. Both Cindy and Higgy used this vocalization almost exclusively. Frequently it was used toward the zookeepers.

---

* The "translations" here are based on the behavioral context common to the individual phrases.

"I am in control and there is no need to worry.": This was mostly a Higgy call, but was also occasionally used by Gin and Cindy. The call would occur after a tense situation (aggression, a chimp being hurt, etc.). The call would be directed at no one in particular. It is the only phrase which contains all the elements: an introduction, a buildup, a climax, and a descent.

"Look at me.": This call would be heard when one individual was attempting to get the attention of another individual (or group of individuals). The call would always be accompanied by exaggerated gestures, such as slapping the ground or an object. The vocalization started with an introduction, followed by a buildup and a climax with no descent.

"Everything is going to get better.": This was given during times of reassurance. This call was most often seen given by mothers, directed at their juveniles. Occasionally it was uttered when food was arriving on the island—again, given by a mother to her offspring. The call featured a long quiet buildup with a very short climax that stopped abruptly.

"Prepare yourselves!": This call was produced in anticipation of something profound (a big fight brewing, food arriving, the veterinarian arriving, etc.). It was always produced during highly excitable times and would draw responses from most everyone else in the group. This call began with a short buildup and concluded with a loud, long, and high-pitched climax.

"Please stop.": This was a defensive call given when an individual was being attacked by another. The associated behaviors indicated that this call functioned as a plea rather than a defensive threat. It began with a screaming climax and ended with a descent.

"Let's fight!": This call always anticipated a physical confrontation. The call was very long in duration and contained a buildup, a climax, and a descent. It usually occurred as two individuals circled each other.

"I found food!": This was most often heard when a chimp found a

hidden treat somewhere on the island. When it was uttered, all of the other chimps would come running to investigate. It would also be used when the zookeepers were spotted in the distance. It was a high-pitched-sounding buildup with a mild climax and a short descent.

"I am so sick of you attacking me.": This tantrumlike call was wild and violent, given by low-ranking individuals who were constantly being attacked by higher-ranking individuals. Contextually, the buildup, climax, and descent call appeared to be both an expression of frustration and a quick act of surrender.

"Mom!": This was used by juveniles calling out for their mothers. Anytime this call was heard, the mothers would respond quickly. The entirety of the buildup, climax, and descent were very loud and very high pitched.

"You have disobeyed me.": When this call was given (almost always by Higgy), the receiver would cower. The buildup, climax, and descent were always accompanied by aggressive gesturing (stomping and hitting the ground). However, it was never followed by a physical altercation.

"We're about to eat!": This was always yelled when food was being placed around the island. It contained only a quick buildup.

"Mom, come back!": This highly intense call was always used by juveniles when their mothers would walk away from them. It was frequently heard from Bamboo when Tonic would leave him. He would follow a very long buildup with an extremely violent and long climax.

"Mom, I'm hungry.": This call was uttered by juveniles to their mothers when they would either want to nurse or eat something that the mother was holding. It was a soft vocalization which contained both a buildup and a climax. There was a variation (which I counted as another vocal type) which was the exact same vocalization, but in reverse (a climax, then a descent). The frequencies, durations, and contexts were the same.

"Stop it!": This call was just a loud short climax and occurred when an individual was being hassled by another individual (usually a juvenile responding to another juvenile).

"I need to be groomed.": This was a plea to be groomed. Most of the time it was followed by a grooming session. On a few occasions, Elgin would use this to ask one of the females to groom him. However, he was usually rejected. It was a very low-pitched vocalization which contained a buildup, a climax, and a descent.

"I'm happy with you.": Used exclusively by Higgy, this call was given to other individuals when he would offer them reassurances (grooming, touching, etc.). He would produce a calm buildup, with a mild climax, then follow it with a very quiet descent.

In addition to these phrases, there were also two distinct "mating vocalizations" (given by females when they mated with Higgy) and three distinct "display vocalizations" (given during wild solo displays and not directed at anyone in particular). One of the display vocalizations was exclusively done by low-ranking individuals like Elgin.

All twenty-five phrases were noticeably distinct in sound and the associated specifics of behavior. After identifying them, I would be able to pick them out in Higgy's group. It became fascinating to listen for them and try to almost discern a conversation.

2006
Chicago, Illinois

Prime sat alone on a tree branch, dangling his feet. The only other members of his group that were outside with him were Kathy and Chuckie. However, they were on the other side of the exhibit. After a few minutes, they got up and walked inside to sit with Hank and Nana. In the two years since leaving the animal park, Prime had become a bit of an outcast from the rest of the group. Hank seemed to have little time for him, Nana didn't seem to like him, and the other four stayed to themselves. This left him without an ally or playmate.

Inside, the rest of the group sat together. Kathy and Kipper had plopped themselves beside Cashew and Chuckie, who were napping. Nana was silently grooming Hank, who was leaning against a Plexiglas wall. Behind the wall, guests of the Lincoln Park Zoo were watching, pointing, and tapping on the glass. Behind the guests were information stands, complete with interactive video screens and a giant twenty-foot photograph of Higgy's face. The picture of Higgy was placed directly in front of Hank's enclosure. A photographer from Chicago had taken the picture back when it was initially decided that Hank was going to be moved there. He had come to take pictures of the incoming group, but couldn't resist a picture of the magnificent-looking alpha male. The picture turned out so well that it became the centerpiece of the new ape house. There were few places within the exhibit that Hank or any of the other chimps could go to avoid Higgy's stare.

I stood in front of Prime with my microphone. I was in an outdoor observing area of the ape house. I was frustrated. None of the chimps were making any calls at all. I had been there for two days and had only recorded one half of a distorted call. The reason I only got half of the call is that I had begun to doze off. The start of the call shook me awake and I quickly hit record on the computer. As soon as I began recording the call stopped. I didn't even have enough time to see which chimp had produced it.

Surrounding me were zoo guests who were paying more attention to the giant microphone than the chimps. From my vantage point, in addition to Prime, I could see the chimps inside and, beyond them, the giant Higgy head. The reason I stationed myself outside, in this area, was to keep the acoustics in the recording as similar as possible. Any sort of echo or reverberation could have an effect on the data I was collecting.* Therefore, I measured out a certain location outside, away from the chimps, which would mirror the distance of where I stood when I was recording Higgy's group. For this reason, I found myself in the middle of the puzzled-looking crowd, pointing a parabolic microphone at a group of completely silent chimpanzees.

The tediousness of waiting for the chimps to vocalize was becoming more unbearable by the minute. I passed the time looking around me and observing the zoo guests. I was tempted to point the parabolic microphone toward different groups of people and eavesdrop on their conversations, but the fear of missing another vocalization kept me from doing this. Just as I was about to doze off again, I heard a raspberry sound. I turned around, expecting to see Hank. Surprisingly, I saw that it came from Prime, who was still sitting on his tree branch. The raspberry sound, or *"Come here!"* (as I have it in my phrase book), was only used by Higgy and Cindy at the animal park. Because it was a dominant call, it would make sense for Hank to use it. Also, the call had originated with his mother. The fact that a low-ranking individual was using such a call immediately represented a change in its usage.

I began recording and tried to discover the context in which Prime was using this call. The call, it seemed, was being directed toward Nana, who had just walked outside and was directly under Prime. This call, which broke the silence, began an entire series of calls. Having compiled my phrase book, I began to listen for anything familiar. What I witnessed was an incredible exchange.

Prime continued to vocalize this raspberry sound to Nana. *"Come here!"* was the message he was sending.

---

* In order to account for any sort of environmental variation of the acoustics, I did a number of tests. This involved me standing at a predetermined distance away from the microphone, in both locations, and reciting the names of the presidents. I would then analyze my own vocals to see if they read exactly the same in both areas. Any difference in the acoustic environment had no affect on the spectral data.

Nana completely ignored Prime. She continued to walk, keeping her eyes forward. She found a piece of lettuce on the ground and began to eat it.

Prime began acting incensed. He began slapping the tree branch with his hand and calling out a distinctive introduction, followed by a buildup and climax.

"Look at me," he expressed to Nana.

Nana looked up and began posturing at Prime by standing up on two legs and swaying her arms back and forth.

"Let's fight!" she conveyed with a call.

At this, Prime leapt off the tree branch, landing on Nana. The two chimpanzees rolled around and produced garbled and unintelligible vocalizations. Finally, Nana pinned Prime and bit him in the leg.

"Please stop," he transmitted to Nana through a screaming climax and descent call.

Nana let him go and the two chimps separated. Nana returned inside and Prime climbed back up to his branch.

I looked over at Hank. The alpha male had stood up and was monitoring the situation. His behavior was noticeably different from how he had acted at the animal park. He appeared calmer and more in control. He didn't feel the need to charge Prime and Nana. He allowed them to work it out on their own, but was at the ready in case it got out of control. It instantly reminded me of Higgy. From behind Hank, the gigantic poster of his old alpha male's stare was a looming presence. It made me think that, in some way, Higgy was being channeled through Hank and was still in charge of this group.

Finally, I had recorded actual vocalizations from Hank's group. The rest of my recording sessions in Chicago went much more smoothly. Similar exchanges continued to happen. In addition, the Lincoln Park staff would record and document the calls after I left. Because of this, I was able to collect a full survey of vocalizations.

2006
Boca Raton, Florida

The halls of Florida Atlantic University's anthropology department were covered with spectrogram printouts. On the floor were twenty-five piles, each one representing the phrases used in Higgy's group. Across from these piles, laid out in a straight line, were all of the spectrograms from Hank's group. I began the tedious process of visually, behaviorally, and mathematically sorting through them. Each one could be placed into one of Higgy's twenty-five categories, be put into a new category, or thrown out altogether.

The process was almost identical to the way I had originally classified Higgy's calls, except, this time, I already had twenty-five predetermined phrases. In order for the call to officially belong to any one phrase, it had to meet the same standards: it had to be visually structured the same way, it had to be within a similar behavioral context, and it had to statistically cluster together with the others. The sorting revealed that Hank's group was recorded using fifteen of the twenty-five phrases that Higgy's group was using:

"Hallelujah!"

"I need help."

"Come here!"

"I am in control and all is well."

"Look at me."

"Prepare yourselves!"

"Please stop."

"Let's fight!"

"I found food!"

"I am so sick of you attacking me."

"Mom!"
"You have disobeyed me."
"We're about to eat!"

The recordings also revealed them to be using two of the three solo display calls (one of which was the low-ranking display).

Ten of Higgy's phrases were never recorded in Hank's group. That is not to say that these never occurred, just that they were never witnessed. These were:

"Everything is going to get better."
"Mom, come back!"
"Mom, I want to eat." (variations 1 and 2)
"Stop it!"
"I need to be groomed."
"I'm happy with you."

Hank's group was also never recorded using two of the solo display calls. In addition, none of the females ever used either of the mating calls.

Hank's group also added some new phrases (or, at least, phrases that were never recorded in Higgy's group). These calls seemed to be completely vocally distinctive, so it would be unlikely that they were variations on other calls. In all, there were five phrases that were unique to Hank's group:

"Calm down.": This occurred when one individual was reacting to another's aggression. The call, which had a buildup and descent but no climax, was a bit out of the ordinary from any of the others.

"A special treat!": This call was only given when in close proximity of a zookeeper. It always occurred when a zookeeper was up close giving a special treat to the individual. The call consisted of only a quiet descent.

"Please give me.": This call was also only seen in close proximity of a

zookeeper. It occurred when a zookeeper held something that the chimp wanted. It contained a buildup, climax, and descent.

There were also two solo display calls which were repeated often and were completely distinct from the display calls of Higgy's group.*

I sat back and looked at the data that I had so far. Seeing which phrases were being repeated versus the phrases that were not being used was beginning to make clear how these vocalizations functioned. What was especially interesting were the offspring-to-mother phrases that had not been witnessed within Hank's group. I began to think about this in relation to the change in environment. Higgy's group lived on a series of large islands, surrounded by other groups of chimpanzees. Hank's group now lived in a more tightly secure area without any competing chimp groups in sight. It would stand to reason that the juvenile chimpanzees would feel far safer being apart from their mothers in the Lincoln Park exhibit, rather than in the open expanse of the animal park. For this reason, I hypothesized that there wouldn't be the immediate need for a phrase as *"Mom, come back!"* This setting also explains why reassuring phrases such as *"Everything is going to get better"* and *"I'm happy with you"* wouldn't be used as much. The increased sense of security and the lessening need for reassurances may also account for the disappearance of *"I need to be groomed."* The smaller group, and the more control that zookeepers had on food distribution at the Lincoln Park Zoo, could have accounted for *"Mom, I'm hungry"* to vanish. Finally, the social dynamics of the juveniles had changed considerably since they were at the animal park. There were now two quiet cousins, an outcast juvenile male, and an adolescent female. Before, there had been a wild array of juveniles at the animal park. This change would

---

* Displays are such an important aspect of showing one's identity as both a group and an individual that it is not at all surprising that Hank's group would have developed different vocal phrases for these.

lead to less bickering and, thus, would be the reason *"Stop it!"* would have been lost.

I began to think of this in terms of human language and human dialect. So much of what we say is a product of its functionality in relation to our environment. Different social environments require different words and phrases. A different abundance of resources demands different ways to ask for our basic needs. When these things change, so do our dialects. In the same way, we add phrases when we encounter new situations and new environments. Hank's group had added two phrases specifically geared toward the new situation of having increased interaction with human zookeepers (*"A special treat!"* and *"Please give me"*). The new social dynamics of Hank's group demanded a new form of an all-important vocalization (*"Calm down"*).

Now it was time to concentrate on the fifteen phrases from Higgy's group that Hank's group was using regularly. In order to accomplish this, I used the same numeric data that I had used to group the vocalizations (the duration of the call, the duration of each call element, the three loudest frequencies of each element, the mean frequency of the entire call, and the amount of time it took for each element to reach its peak amplitude). For each comparison, I would statistically determine if Hank's group was vocalizing differently than Higgy's group.* So, for example, when I compared *"You have disobeyed me,"* I first compared the duration of the entire call. I found that there was no significant difference. I then compared the mean frequency of the entire call. Again, I found no significant difference. After this, I took each element of the vocalization (the buildup, climax, and descent) and compared the top frequencies, the time it took for each element to reach its peak amplitude, and the

---

* I used a logistic regression to determine if the slope naturally divided the vocalizations of Higgy's group from the vocalizations of Hank's group. If it did, the comparison was determined to be statistically different.

general duration of the element. In all cases, *"You have disobeyed me"* was found to be statistically identical. I then came to the conclusion, for this phrase, that Hank's group was vocalizing identically to Higgy's group.

When I had finally compared all of the vocalizations within all fifteen phrases, the results were remarkable. Seven of the fifteen phrases had shown a statistical difference in at least one comparison. The other eight phrases were being produced by Hank's group identically to how Higgy's group was producing them. The differences were slight and usually in just one area. However, this was enough to show that the calls of Hank's group and the calls of Higgy's group were beginning to diverge from each other. Both groups were now on their own separate evolutionary paths. Both groups were adjusting their calls to fit their situations. The phrases that were showing differences were:

"I need help.": The duration of the call with Hank's group was significantly longer. Everything else remained identical.

"I am in control and all is well.": Hank's group had a longer buildup element to this call.

"Prepare yourselves!": Again, the buildup of this call was longer when anyone in Hank's group was producing it.

"Let's fight!": This phrase had the most dramatic change. The entire pitch of this phrase was much lower with Hank's group. Also, like the others, the buildup was longer.

"I found food!": The buildup element was considerably longer with Hank's group.

"Mom!": All elements, except the buildup, were shortened with Hank's group.

Lastly, the low-ranking solo display in Hank's group had a shorter buildup but longer climax.*

---

* I find it fascinating that the general rule in the evolution of dialect in Hank's group is that the buildup gets longer. I also find it fascinating that the only example of this not being the

I looked at my data and thought about the reason each change had occurred. In humans, a change in social leadership affects the dialect because, phonetically, everyone begins subconsciously mimicking the leader, with the individual idiosyncrasies of the leader's speech becoming common to everyone within the group. I went back to the piece of evidence for this occurring within Hank's group—the raspberry phrase, *"Come here!"* I am guessing that Hank picked the phrase up from his mother. The fact that everyone in the group was now using it regularly, while the phrase in Higgy's group was relegated to Cindy and Higgy, may have meant that Hank had influenced the others into using the phrase. Other changes may have been due to Hank's individual phonetics that the others were now copying.

The stress of the separation and move may have led to such changes. As we know from human phonetic studies, anxiety affects speech. If the affect goes on long enough, the change will remain within the group. Such an affect could have occurred within Hank's group.

Whatever the reason, Hank's group was beginning to sound different from Higgy's group. This fact had, all at once, shown that chimpanzees develop dialects. Successive generations of Higgy's group and Hank's group would continue to build and change their dialects. In time, the two groups would be unintelligible to each other. This fact, to me, defines chimpanzee vocal communication as a language.

So there it was. After years of recording, weeks of analysis, and nights of sorting through spectrograms, I had my answer. Chimpanzees have vocal phrases which are unique from group to group. These phrases evolve through the development of dialects. These dialects are based upon the ecological situations that a group finds itself in. Phrases get added, dropped, and changed based on their social and ecological functionality.

---

case is the low-ranking solo display, where it is the opposite. I can only imagine it has something to do with the change in social dynamics.

At some point, the dialect of Higgy's group had begun its own evolutionary journey. Each of the individuals had influenced that dialect over the years. However, where had that original dialect started? Did it begin with Higgy's group, or did it have its origins before that? How far back had it gone? I began to think about the individuals making up Higgy's group. Who brought to the group this unique and highly complex system of calls that they were using? Did it have a connection to a dialect being used in the wild? I began to wonder where that original seed had come from; what had been the *foundation* of the dialect they were using? I jumped in my car and drove out to the animal park. I needed to see Little Mama.

2006
Loxahatchee, Florida

It was almost as if Little Mama was waiting for me; as if she knew I had just found out the answer to a great riddle that she had authored decades before. She sat at the edge of the canal, looking like a sage with her familiar burlap sack around her head. I stepped out of my car, sinking my feet into the muddy ground. Little Mama stood up and held up her hand. She opened her mouth and grunted happily. I threw her a banana. Before she could get to it Gin ran down and snatched it away. She sat down beside Little Mama and ate it. Seeing that food was being thrown, Cindy approached the other two. She sat down, clapped her hands, and stared at me. Higgy walked over from the other side of the island. Behind him, shaking as he walked, was Elgin. The two male chimps gathered around the other three. All five stared at me.

What I had seen in my phrase book, and in the spectrograms, were images of something that had taken over seventy years and traveled halfway around the world for me to see. It began its journey when a little chimpanzee was captured in Africa, thrown into a burlap sack, and brought to the United States. Over the last seventy years it had been changed and distorted by the gravity of big events: other chimpanzees, new places, and civil wars. It existed in a stable form for many years. Finally, it fragmented and split; a new group now using its remnants as the seeds of its own system.

I imagined Little Mama's group in Africa. I pictured them using the phrases I had come to know by heart. I thought of her group being destroyed at the hands of humans. Yet, the group lived on. They were heard within the calls of Higgy's group. They were echoed throughout the ape house of the Lincoln Park Zoo. No poacher or animal broker could ever stop the sort of perpetuity that is dictated by nature, biology, and the physical laws of the universe. It exists despite us. It is the great earthly eternal and it is more magnificent than any trick we can teach an animal to perform.

Twelve hundred miles away from Little Mama, Hank's group was huddled together. They would communicate in order to build new alliances, create new strategies, comfort each other, reprimand each other, and enjoy each other. This would all be based on a system of communication, a chimpanzee language, that had come from across the ocean, half a century before any of them were born. Little Mama's father, the old alpha male from the Jong River, lived again within Hank's calls to Nana. Little Mama's mother, the young female, lived again when Cashew called to Chuckie.

Going back even further, Little Mama's mother and old alpha male were echoing previous generations of chimpanzees. Within their phrases they were channeling an unthinkably long lineage of chimp calls that have evolved with each successive age. Each generation etched their own imprint within the language; an imprint recalling their own history, their own periods of stress, their own periods of happiness, their own periods of peace, their own periods of war, their own periods of tragedy, and their own social hierarchies. The lexicon of calls that were being made by Little Mama, and propagated by Higgy and Hank, was a complete phonetic record, hidden from view but there all the same, of a large and vast story of an ancient legacy of chimpanzees.

Seeing that I had no more food, the other chimpanzees walked away. Little Mama remained in front of me. I watched her as she watched me. After all of the research, it became more apparent to me than ever that Little Mama was the incarnation of overlooked magnificence. She was the nebula that we can't see because of the city lights. She was the carefully constructed ant mound that we run over with the lawn mower. She was the summer rainstorm that we run inside to avoid. She was the talking chimpanzee that we never hear. She was the miracle that we miss while we create the myths.

> That which is below corresponds to that which is above, and that which is above, corresponds to that which is below.
>
> —THE EMERALD TABLET OF HERMES TRIMEGISTUS

CODA

Annulus

In a dimly lit hall, I looked out at the dour faces of those who had come to hear my presentation. It was eight o'clock on a Saturday morning during the seventy-sixth annual meeting of the American Association of Physical Anthropologists. It was also the last day of a very long conference. Those that had made it out of bed looked anything but excited by my title, "Exploring diachronic change in the population-specific vocalizations of chimpanzees (*Pan troglodytes*)."

As I stammered through descriptions of chimpanzee call structure, vocal analysis, and phonetic change, I couldn't help but think that I wasn't doing a good job conveying what I had witnessed. I flipped through slides of spectrograms, regression charts, and pictures of nebulas. I looked over to see my coworker, who had helped me with my research, roll her eyes at the nebula slide. I looked back down to find that I had lost my place in my notes.

This was the second presentation I had given on my research in two weeks. The first had been at a conference in Chicago. There, I was able to have everything nicely laid out on a poster. I was supposed to station myself in front of the poster and give my presentation to anyone interested.

When I got there, I found that I was beside a researcher who had apparently trained several lab chimps to perform an extremely hard puzzle that he had constructed. This seemed to amaze the conference guests. In fact, his crowd spilled over in front of my poster. While he was talking, I suppose that he got too hot because he took off his coat and hung it over my poster. My results, along with a picture of Little Mama, were completely concealed. This was too much. While he waxed on about his chimpanzees' amazing cognitive skills, I looked at my poster, looked at him telling a joke to the crowd, and looked at the crowd laughing at his joke. Just as I was about to throw his coat at him, I looked over and saw the open bar. Perhaps, I thought, that was a better idea. I slipped away, completely unnoticed, and ordered an Irish whiskey and club soda.

As I stood there, I felt someone tap me on the shoulder. When I turned around, I saw that it was a primatologist who, for three decades, had been instrumental in several of the language-trained ape projects. The now elderly man asked me if I was the one who had analyzed the chimp dialect.

I nodded.

He then said something to the effect of, if he had only realized that he could have just listened to what the animals were saying, he wouldn't have spent so much time and money trying to teach them to talk. He slapped me on the back, laughed, and walked away.

I smiled and took a sip of my drink. I looked over at my poster. The researcher's coat had fallen off my poster and was now on the floor. The coat was being stepped on by several people. Little Mama's picture was now visible again. I raised my glass and thought to myself, *Cheers, Little Mama!*

2007
Loxahatchee, Florida

Echoing across the islands, the cries of a newborn chimpanzee broke the still of the night. The sound alerted all of the chimpanzees in Higgy's group to the top of the shelter where Gin had just given birth. By the time the group reached the shelter, Gin was cleaning her new offspring by the light of the stars in the sky. Higgy sat beside Gin and the new baby.

The group, now numbering eleven, were all able to fit on top of the shelter. They all crowded around Gin, attempting to get a glimpse of the newest member of their group. Gin picked up the infant female and put her to her breast. The infant immediately began nursing. Higgy cocked his head to the sky and produced a bellowing call which reverberated across the sky.

Bamboo, now four, cut through the crowd and got close to the new baby. Gin didn't seem to notice so Bamboo stretched out his arm and touched the infant's leg. Gin gave an abrupt, climactic yelp. Bamboo immediately ran away. Higgy ran after Bamboo. When he reached him, Bamboo reached out toward him and gave a low-pitched buildup, a quiet climax, and a low-pitched descent.

"I need to be groomed," he vocalized.

Higgy responded with a calm buildup, climax, and descent of his own, *"I'm happy with you."* Then he began to groom Bamboo.

After a while, the crowd of chimpanzees had dispersed. The only one left beside Gin and the new baby was Little Mama. She sat on her burlap with her hand resting on Gin's arm. The baby was now sleeping on Gin's chest, her eyes closed tightly. Little Mama bent over and put her head right next to the sleeping baby. Beneath the starry sky, Little Mama grunted softly. The baby opened her eyes and looked over at the elderly chimpanzee. At this, Little Mama adjusted the burlap over her head, crawled down to her nest, and went to sleep.

What we cannot speak about we must pass over in silence.

—LUDWIG WITTGENSTEIN

PHOTO CAPTIONS

CHAPTER 1

Little Mama immediately after her arrival at the animal park in 1967. (Courtesy of Terry Wolf.)

CHAPTER 2

Cindy as a pet in the early 1970s. (Courtesy of Terry Wolf.)

CHAPTER 3

Higgy, the alpha male. (Courtesy of Terry Wolf.)

CHAPTER 4

Gin in her 30s. (Courtesy of Terry Wolf.)

CHAPTER 5

Elgin at 27. (Courtesy of Terry Wolf.)

CHAPTER 6

Cindy at the edge of the island. (Courtesy of Terry Wolf.)

CHAPTER 7

Higgy's group enjoying a peaceful moment before the war which would eventually divide them permanently. (Author's collection.)

CHAPTER 8

Higgy, hair standing on end, in a tense moment with Gin behind him. (Courtesy of Terry Wolf.)

CHAPTER 9

Hank's alliance. From left to right: Hank, Kathy with Chuckie on her back, Cashew with Kipper hanging on, Prime, and Nana. (Author's collection.)

CHAPTER 10

Higgy and Cindy looking on. (Courtesy of Christina Cloutier.)

BIBLIOGRAPHY

America Online. 1998. Internet chat with Koko the gorilla.

Bauer, H., & Philip, M. 1983. "Facial and vocal individual recognition in the common chimpanzee." *The Psychological Record* 33:2: 161–170.

Boesch, C. 2002. "Cooperative hunting roles among Tai chimpanzees." *Human Nature* 13:1: 27–46.

Cartmill, M. 1974. "Rethinking primate origins." *Science* 184: 436–443.

Chomsky, N. 1968. *Language and Mind.* New York: Harcourt, Brace & World, Inc.

Clark, A. P., & Wrangham, R. W. 1993. "Acoustic analysis of wild chimpanzee pant hoots: Do Kibale forest chimpanzees have an acoustically distinct food arrival pant hoot?" *Am. J. Primatol.* 31: 99–109.

Clark Arcadi, A. 1996. "Phrase structure of wild chimpanzee pant hoots: Patterns of production and interpopulation variability." *Am. J. Primatol.* 29: 159–178.

Cohn, J. F., & Tronick, E. Z. 1988. "Mother-infant face-to-face interaction: Influence is bidirectional and unrelated to periodic cycles in either partner's behavior." *Developmental Psychology* 24:3: 386–392.

Cowie, R., Douglas, F., Cowie, E., & Romano, A. 1999. "Chan wash emotional true in dialogue and its prosodic correlates." Proceedings of the ESLA International Workshop on Dialogue and Prosody.

Fernandez, R., & Picard, R. 2000. "Modeling drivers' speech under stress." M.I.T. Media laboratory perceptual computing section technical report no. 528.

Furness, W. H. 1916. "Observations on the mentality of chimpanzees and orangutans." *Proceedings of the American Philosophical Society* 55: 281–290.

Gallup, G. G., Jr. 1970. "Chimpanzees: Self-recognition." *Science* 167: 86–87.

Gallup, G. G., Jr. 1987. "Self-awareness." In *Comparative Primate Biology, Behavior, Cognition, and Motivation (Vol. 2B)*, edited by J. R. E. G. Mitchell (pp. 3–16). New York: Liss.

Gallup, G. G., Jr. 1982. "Self-awareness and the emergence of mind in primates." *Am. J. Primatol.* 2: 237–248.

Gardner, R. A., & Gardner, B. T. 1969. "Teaching sign language to a chimpanzee." *Science* 165: 664–672.

Hayaki, H. 1985. "Social play of juvenile and adolescent chimpanzees in the Mahale Mountains National Park, Tanzania." *Primates* 26:4: 343–360.

Hearst, E., & Capshew, J. H. (eds.). 1988. *Psychology at Indiana University: A Centennial Review and Compendium.* Bloomington: Indiana University Department of Psychology.

Hiraiwa-Hasegawa, M., & Hasegawa, T. 1988. "A case of offspring desertion by a female chimpanzee and the behavioral changes of the abandoned spring." *Primates* 29:3: 319–330.

Jakendoff, R. 1977. *X-bar Syntax: A Study of Phrase Structure.* Cambridge: MIT Press.

Kellogg, W. N., & Kellog, L. A. 1933. *The Ape and the Child: A Comparative Study of the Environmental Influence upon Early Behavior.* New York: Hafner Publishing.

Kellogg, W., & Pomeroy, W. 1936. "Maze learning in snakes." *Journal of Comparative Psychology* 21:3: 275–295.

Kienast, M., & Sendlmeier, W. 2000. "Acoustical analysis of spectral and temporal changes in emotional speech." Proceedings of the ISCA Workshop on Emotion and Speech.

Koebner, L. 1981. *From Cage to Freedom.* New York: Penguin.

Kormos, R., Boesch, C., Bakarr, M. I., & Butynski, T. M. (eds.). 2003. *West African Chimpanzees.* IUCN/SSC Primate Specialist Group. Gland, Switzerland, and Cambridge, UK: IUCN.

Labov, W. 1994. *Principles of Linguistic Change, Internal Factors.* New York: Wiley-Blackwell.

Labov, W. 2004. *Principles of Linguistic Change, Social Factors.* New York: Wiley-Blackwell.

Marshall, A. J., Wrangham, R. W., & Arcadi, A. C. 1999. "Does learning affect the structure of vocalizations in chimpanzees?" *Anim. Behav.* 58: 825–830.

Matsuzawa, T., Tomonaga, M., & Tanaka, M. (eds.). 2006. *Cognitive Development in Chimpanzees.* Tokyo: Springer-Verlag Tokyo.

McGrew, W. C. 2004. *The Cultured Chimpanzee: Reflections on Cultural Primatology.* Cambridge: Cambridge University Press.

McGrew, W. C., & Tutin, C. E. G. 1978. "Evidence for a social custom in wild chimpanzees?" *Man* 13: 234–51.

Mitani, J., & Nishida, T. 1993. "Contexts and social correlates of long distance calling by male chimpanzees." *Anim. Behav.* 45: 735–746.

Mitani, J., Hasegawa, T., Gros-Louis, J., Marler, P., & Byrne, R. 1992. "Dialects in wild chimpanzees?" *Am. J. Primatol.* 27: 233–243.

Mitani, J. C., Hunley, K. L., & Murdoch M. E. 1999. "Geographic variation in the calls of wild chimpanzees: A reassessment." *Am. J. Primatol.* 47: 133–151.

Morgan, L. H. 1868. *The American Beaver.* Toronto: Dover.

Muroyama, Y. 1991. "Chimpanzees' choices of prey between two sympatric species of Macrotermes in the Campo Animal Reserve, Cameroon." *Human Evolution* 6:2: 143–151.

Nakamura, M. 2000. "Is human conversation more efficient than chimpanzee grooming? Comparison of clique sizes." *Human Nature* 11:3: 281–297.

Nishida, T. 1983. "Alpha status and agonistic alliance in wild chimpanzees (*Pan troglodytes schweinfurthi*)." *Primates* 24: 318–336.

Nishida, T. (ed.). 1990. *The Chimpanzees of the Mahale Mountains: Sexual and Life History Strategies.* Tokyo: The University of Tokyo Press.

Nishida, T. 1994. "Review of recent findings on Mahale chimpanzees: Implications and future research directions." In *Chimpanzee Cultures,* edited by R. W. Wrangham, W. C. McGrew, F. B. M. DeWaal, & P. G. Heltne. (pp. 373–396). Cambridge, Massachusetts: Harvard University Press.

Nishida, T., Hosaka, K., Nakamura, M., & Hamai, M. 1995. "A within-group gang attack on a young adult male chimpanzee: Ostracism of an ill-mannered member?" *Primates* 36:2: 207–211.

Patterson, F. Dec. 4, 1980. Response to "Monkey Business" by Martin Gardner. *New York Review of Books.*

Patterson, F., & Linden, E. 1985. *The Education of Koko.* New York: Holt, Rinehart and Winston.

Patterson, F. G., & Cohn, R. H. 1994. "Self-recognition and self-awareness in lowland gorillas." In *Self-awareness in Animals and Humans: Developmental Perspectives*, edited by S. T. Parker, R. W. Mitchell, & M. L. Boccia. (pp. 273–290). Cambridge, UK: Cambridge University Press.

Rymer, R. 1994. *Genie: A Scientific Tragedy.* New York: Harper.

Sebeok, T. A., & Umiker-Sebeok, D. J. 1980. *Speaking of Apes.* New York: Springer.

Slobodchikoff, C. N., Kiriazis, J., Fischer, C., & Creef, E. 1991. "Semantic information distinguishing individual predators in the alarm calls of Gunnison's prairie dogs." *Animal Behavior* 42: 713–719.

Stanford, C. B. 1998. *Chimpanzee and Red Colobus: The Ecology of Predator and Prey.* Cambridge: Harvard University Press.

Suarez, S., & Gallup, G. G., Jr. 1981. "Self-recognition in chimpanzees and orangutans, but not gorillas." *Journal of Human Evolution* 10: 157–188.

Susskind, L. 2008. *The Black Hole War.* New York: Little Brown & Company.

Takahata, H., & Takahata, Y. 1989. "Inter-unit group transfer of an immature male of the chimpanzee and his social interactions in the non-natal group." *African Study Monographs* 9:4: 209–220.

Takahata, Y. 1985. "Adult male chimpanzees kill and eat a male newborn infant: Newly observed intragroup infanticide and cannibalism in Mahale National Park, Tanzania." *Folia Primatol.* 44: 161–170.

Terrace, H. S. 1979. *Nim: A Chimpanzee Who Learned Sign Language.* New York: Knopf.

Terrace, H. S., Petitto, L. A., Sanders, R. J., & Bever, T. G. 1979. "Can an ape create a sentence?" *Science* 206: 891–902.

Uehara, S., Nishida, T., Takasaki, H., Kitopeni, R., & Kasagula, M. B. 1994. "A lone male chimpanzee in the wild: The survivor of a disintegrated unit-group." *Primates* 35: 275–81.

Velicer, G. J. 2003. "Social strife in the microbial world." *Trends in Microbiology* 11:7: 330–337.

Wade, N. 1980. "Does man alone have language? Apes reply in riddles, and a horse says neigh." *Science* 208: 1349–1351.

Wichmann, A. 2001. "The attitudinal effects of prosody and how they relate to emotion." Proceedings of the ISCA Workshop on Emotion and Speech.

Wrangham, R., & Peterson, D. 1996. *Demonic Males: Apes and the Origins of Human Violence.* Boston: Houghton Mifflin.

Wrangham, R., Wilson, M., & Muller, M. 2006. "Comparative rates of violence in chimpanzees and humans." *Primates* 47: 14–26.

Yerkes, R. M. 1924. *Almost Human.* New York: The Century Company.

Yerkes, R. M., & Learned, B. W. 1925. *Chimpanzee Intelligence and Its Vocal Expressions.* Baltimore: Williams & Wilkins.

INDEX